COMPUTER
BOOK SERIES
FROM IDG

Small Business Comp...
For Dummies®

Helpful Hints

- ✔ Don't turn off your computer until Windows says it's okay. Click the Start button, and then choose Shut Down from the menu. When Windows asks whether you really want to shut down, click Yes. Wait until you see the message that it's okay to turn off your computer.

- ✔ To close a window or dialog box, click the X icon in the upper-right corner.

- ✔ If you need some help, try pressing the F1 key.

- ✔ If you're a neatness freak, right-click your desktop and choose Arrange Icons⇨Auto Arrange.

- ✔ To find out what the icons (or tools) do, hold your mouse pointer over the button for a few seconds. In most programs, you'll see a little box that pops up and gives you a brief description.

- ✔ Move to a specific letter in a list of entries by pressing the letter you want (in many programs).

- ✔ Move to the beginning of a text box by pressing the Home key.

- ✔ Move to the end of a text box by pressing the End key.

- ✔ Move to the beginning of a document by holding down the Ctrl key while you press the Home key.

- ✔ Move to the end of a document by holding down the Ctrl key while you press the End key.

- ✔ Copy a highlighted entry to the Windows Clipboard by holding down the Ctrl key while you press the Insert key.

- ✔ Cut a highlighted entry to the Windows Clipboard by holding down the Shift key while you press the Delete key.

- ✔ Paste whatever is on the Clipboard into your document by holding down the Shift key while you press the Insert key.

- ✔ Copy the screen to the Clipboard by pressing the PrintScreen key.

Handling Files

Note: In the following list, an instruction to press Alt, F, N means you should press Alt, then press F, and then press N. Do not press all three keys at the same time.

To Do This . . .	Do This . . .
Create a new file	Press Alt, F, N
Open an existing file	Press Alt, F, O
Save a file	Press Alt, F, S
Save a file with a new name	Press Alt, F, A
Print a file	Press Alt, F, P
Copy a file to a different folder	Hold down Ctrl while you drag the file to the new folder
Move a file to a different folder	Drag the file to the new folder
Delete a file	Drag the file to the Recycle bin
Undelete a file	Right-click the file in the Recycle bin and choose Restore
Open a file	Double-click the file
Select several files	Hold down Ctrl and click each file
Select a range of files	Click the first file, hold down Shift, and click the last file

IDG
BOOKS
WORLDWIDE™

Cheat Sheet $2.95 value. Item 0287-5.

For more information about IDG Books, call 1-800-762-2974.

...For Dummies: #1 Computer Book Series for Beginners

Small Business Computing For Dummies®

Cheat Sheet

Organizing Programs

To Do This . . .	Do This . . .
Move from one open program to another	Hold down Alt and press Tab until the program name appears
Move back to the first program	Hold down Alt and press Tab once
Move between programs with the mouse	Click the program button on the taskbar
Close a program	Press Alt, F, X
Toggle a DOS program between a window and full-screen	Hold down Alt and press Enter
Close a program that has stopped responding	Press Ctrl+Alt+Del, select the program from the list, and click End Task

Changing System Settings

The Control Panel provides access to many important system options. Choose Settings⇨Control Panel to open the Control Panel.

To Do This . . .	Click This Icon . . .
Add new hardware	Add New Hardware
Add, remove, or change settings for game controllers	Game Controllers
Add, remove, or change settings for printers	Printers
Change date, time, and time zone information	Date/Time
Change display settings	Display
Change how numbers, currencies, dates, and times are displayed	Regional Settings
Change passwords and set security options	Passwords
Change Power Management settings	Power Management
Change settings for multimedia devices	Multimedia
Change settings for your keyboard	Keyboard
Change settings for your mouse	Mouse
Change system and program sounds	Sounds
Change your Internet settings	Internet
Configure Microsoft Outlook Profiles	Mail
Configure network hardware and software	Network
Configure telephony drivers and dialing properties	Telephony
Install a modem or change modem properties	Modems
Maintain 32-bit ODBC data sources and drivers	32bit ODBC
Set up and manage multiple users	Users
Set up programs	Add/Remove Programs
Use Plus! themes to personalize your desktop	Desktop Themes
View system information and change advanced settings	System
View, add, or remove fonts on your computer	Fonts

...For Dummies: #1 Computer Book Series for Beginners

SMALL BUSINESS
COMPUTING
FOR
DUMMIES®

SMALL BUSINESS COMPUTING FOR DUMMIES®

by Brian Underdahl

IDG Books Worldwide, Inc.
An International Data Group Company

Foster City, CA ♦ Chicago, IL ♦ Indianapolis, IN ♦ Southlake, TX

Small Business Computing For Dummies®

Published by
IDG Books Worldwide, Inc.
An International Data Group Company
919 E. Hillsdale Blvd.
Suite 400
Foster City, CA 94404
www.idgbooks.com (IDG Books Worldwide Web site)
www.dummies.com (Dummies Press Web site)

Library of Congress Catalog Card No.: 98-70179

ISBN: 0-7645-0287-5

Printed in the United States of America

10 9 8 7 6 5 4 3 2 1

1O/RQ/QS/ZY/IN

Distributed in the United States by IDG Books Worldwide, Inc.

Distributed by Macmillan Canada for Canada; by Transworld Publishers Limited in the United Kingdom; by IDG Norge Books for Norway; by IDG Sweden Books for Sweden; by Woodslane Pty. Ltd. for Australia; by Woodslane Enterprises Ltd. for New Zealand; by Longman Singapore Publishers Ltd. for Singapore, Malaysia, Thailand, and Indonesia; by Simron Pty. Ltd. for South Africa; by Toppan Company Ltd. for Japan; by Distribuidora Cuspide for Argentina; by Livraria Cultura for Brazil; by Ediciencia S.A. for Ecuador; by Addison-Wesley Publishing Company for Korea; by Ediciones ZETA S.C.R. Ltda. for Peru; by WS Computer Publishing Corporation, Inc., for the Philippines; by Unalis Corporation for Taiwan; by Contemporanea de Ediciones for Venezuela; by Computer Book & Magazine Store for Puerto Rico; by Express Computer Distributors for the Caribbean and West Indies. Authorized Sales Agent: Anthony Rudkin Associates for the Middle East and North Africa.

For general information on IDG Books Worldwide's books in the U.S., please call our Consumer Customer Service department at 800-762-2974. For reseller information, including discounts and premium sales, please call our Reseller Customer Service department at 800-434-3422.

For information on where to purchase IDG Books Worldwide's books outside the U.S., please contact our International Sales department at 650-655-3200 or fax 650-655-3295.

For information on foreign language translations, please contact our Foreign & Subsidiary Rights department at 650-655-3021 or fax 650-655-3281.

For sales inquiries and special prices for bulk quantities, please contact our Sales department at 650-655-3200 or write to the address above.

For information on using IDG Books Worldwide's books in the classroom or for ordering examination copies, please contact our Educational Sales department at 800-434-2086 or fax 817-251-8174.

For press review copies, author interviews, or other publicity information, please contact our Public Relations department at 650-655-3000 or fax 650-655-3299.

For authorization to photocopy items for corporate, personal, or educational use, please contact Copyright Clearance Center, 222 Rosewood Drive, Danvers, MA 01923, or fax 978-750-4470.

is a trademark under exclusive license to IDG Books Worldwide, Inc., from International Data Group, Inc.

About the Author

Brian Underdahl has been a small business owner and author for ten years. He's written or contributed to more than 40 computer-related books, written about computers for a number of magazines, taught numerous computer classes, and spoken to several professional organizations about small business computing. Brian has seen a lot of changes in the 30+ years he's been involved with computers. He knows that good business practices are fundamental no matter what the size of your business.

ABOUT IDG BOOKS WORLDWIDE

Welcome to the world of IDG Books Worldwide.

IDG Books Worldwide, Inc., is a subsidiary of International Data Group, the world's largest publisher of computer-related information and the leading global provider of information services on information technology. IDG was founded more than 25 years ago and now employs more than 8,500 people worldwide. IDG publishes more than 275 computer publications in over 75 countries (see listing below). More than 60 million people read one or more IDG publications each month.

Launched in 1990, IDG Books Worldwide is today the #1 publisher of best-selling computer books in the United States. We are proud to have received eight awards from the Computer Press Association in recognition of editorial excellence and three from *Computer Currents'* First Annual Readers' Choice Awards. Our best-selling *...For Dummies®* series has more than 30 million copies in print with translations in 30 languages. IDG Books Worldwide, through a joint venture with IDG's Hi-Tech Beijing, became the first U.S. publisher to publish a computer book in the People's Republic of China. In record time, IDG Books Worldwide has become the first choice for millions of readers around the world who want to learn how to better manage their businesses.

Our mission is simple: Every one of our books is designed to bring extra value and skill-building instructions to the reader. Our books are written by experts who understand and care about our readers. The knowledge base of our editorial staff comes from years of experience in publishing, education, and journalism — experience we use to produce books for the '90s. In short, we care about books, so we attract the best people. We devote special attention to details such as audience, interior design, use of icons, and illustrations. And because we use an efficient process of authoring, editing, and desktop publishing our books electronically, we can spend more time ensuring superior content and spend less time on the technicalities of making books.

You can count on our commitment to deliver high-quality books at competitive prices on topics you want to read about. At IDG Books Worldwide, we continue in the IDG tradition of delivering quality for more than 25 years. You'll find no better book on a subject than one from IDG Books Worldwide.

John Kilcullen
CEO
IDG Books Worldwide, Inc.

Steven Berkowitz
President and Publisher
IDG Books Worldwide, Inc.

**Eighth Annual
Computer Press
Awards ≥1992**

**Ninth Annual
Computer Press
Awards ≥1993**

**Tenth Annual
Computer Press
Awards ≥1994**

**Eleventh Annual
Computer Press
Awards ≥1995**

IDG Books Worldwide, Inc., is a subsidiary of International Data Group, the world's largest publisher of computer-related information and the leading global provider of information services on information technology. International Data Group publishes over 275 computer publications in over 75 countries. Sixty million people read one or more International Data Group publications each month. International Data Group's publications include: **ARGENTINA:** Buyer's Guide, Computerworld Argentina, PC World Argentina; **AUSTRALIA:** Australian Macworld, Australian PC World, Australian Reseller News, Computerworld, IT Casebook, Network World, Publish, Webmaster; **AUSTRIA:** Computerwelt Osterreich, Networks Austria, PC Tip Austria; **BANGLADESH:** PC World Bangladesh; **BELARUS:** PC World Belarus; **BELGIUM:** Data News, **BRAZIL:** Annuário de Informática, Computerworld, Connections, Macworld, PC Player, PC World, Publish, Reseller News, Supergamepower; **BULGARIA:** Computerworld Bulgaria, Network World Bulgaria, PC & MacWorld Bulgaria; **CANADA:** CIO Canada, Client/Server World, ComputerWorld Canada, InfoWorld Canada, NetworkWorld Canada, WebWorld; **CHILE:** Computerworld Chile, PC World Chile; **COLOMBIA:** Computerworld Colombia, PC World Colombia; **COSTA RICA:** PC World Centro America; **THE CZECH AND SLOVAK REPUBLICS:** Computerworld Czechoslovakia, Macworld Czech Republic, PC World Czechoslovakia; **DENMARK:** Communications World Danmark, Computerworld Danmark, Macworld Danmark, PC World Danmark, Techworld Denmark, **DOMINICAN REPUBLIC:** PC World Republica Dominicana; **ECUADOR:** PC World Ecuador; **EGYPT:** Computerworld Middle East, PC World Middle East; **EL SALVADOR:** PC World Centro America; **FINLAND:** MikroPC, Tietoverkko, Tietoviikko; **FRANCE:** Distributique, Hebdo, Info PC, Le Monde Informatique, Macworld, Reseaux & Telecoms, WebMaster France; **GERMANY:** Computer Partner, Computerwoche, Computerwoche Extra, Computerwoche FOCUS, Global Online, Macwelt, PC Welt; **GREECE:** Amiga Computing, GamePro Greece, Multimedia World; **GUATEMALA:** PC World Centro America; **HONDURAS:** PC World Centro America; **HONG KONG:** Computerworld Hong Kong, PC World Hong Kong, Publish in Asia; **HUNGARY:** ABCD CD-ROM, Computerworld Szamitastechnika, Internetto online Magazine, PC World Hungary, PC-X Magazin Hungary; **ICELAND:** Tolvuheimur PC World Island; **INDIA:** Information Communications World, Information Systems Computerworld, PC World India, Publish in Asia; **INDONESIA:** InfoKomputer PC World, Komputek Computerworld, Publish in Asia; **IRELAND:** ComputerScope, PC Live!; **ISRAEL:** Macworld Israel, People & Computers/Computerworld; **ITALY:** Computerworld Italia, Macworld Italia, Networking Italia, PC World Italia; **JAPAN:** DTP World, Macworld Japan, Nikkei Personal Computing, OS/2 World Japan, SunWorld Japan, Windows NT World, Windows World Japan; **KENYA:** PC World East African; **KOREA:** Hi-Tech Information, Macworld Korea, PC World Korea; **MACEDONIA:** PC World Macedonia; **MALAYSIA:** Computerworld Malaysia, PC World Malaysia, Publish in Asia; **MALTA:** PC World Malta; **MEXICO:** Computerworld Mexico, PC World Mexico; **MYANMAR:** PC World Myanmar; **NETHERLANDS:** Computer! Totaal, LAN Internetworking Magazine, LAN World Buyers Guide, Macworld Netherlands, Net, WebWereld; **NEW ZEALAND:** Absolute Beginners Guide and Plain & Simple Series, Computer Buyer, Computer Industry Directory, Computerworld New Zealand, MTB, Network World, PC World New Zealand; **NICARAGUA:** PC World Centro America; **NORWAY:** Computerworld Norge, CW Rapport, Datamagasinet, Financial Rapport, Kursguide Norge, Macworld Norge, Multimediaworld Norge, PC World Ekspress Norge, PC World Nettverk, PC World Norge, PC World ProduktGuide Norge; **PAKISTAN:** Computerworld Pakistan; **PANAMA:** PC World Panama; **PEOPLE'S REPUBLIC OF CHINA:** China Computer Users, China Computerworld, China InfoWorld, China Telecom World Weekly, Computer & Communication, Electronic Design China, Electronics Today, Electronics Weekly, Game Software, PC World China, Popular Computer Week, Software Weekly, Software World, Telecom World; **PERU:** Computerworld Peru, PC World Profesional Peru, PC World SoHo Peru; **PHILIPPINES:** Click!, Computerworld Philippines, PC World Philippines, Publish in Asia; **POLAND:** Computerworld Poland, Computerworld Special Report Poland, Cyber, Macworld Poland, Networld Poland, PC World Komputer; **PORTUGAL:** Cerebro/PC World, Computerworld/Correio Informático, Dealer World Portugal, Mac*In/PC*In Portugal, Multimedia World; **PUERTO RICO:** PC World Puerto Rico; **ROMANIA:** Computerworld Romania, PC World Romania, Telecom Romania; **RUSSIA:** Computerworld Russia, Mir PK, Publish, Seti; **SINGAPORE:** Computerworld Singapore, PC World Singapore, Publish in Asia; **SLOVENIA:** Monitor; **SOUTH AFRICA:** Computing SA, Network World SA, Software World SA; **SPAIN:** Communicaciones World España, Computerworld España, Dealer World España, Macworld España, PC World España, Computer Sweden, Corporate Computing Sweden, Internetworld Sweden, it.branschen, Macworld Sweden, MaxiData Sweden, MikroDatorn, Nätverk & Kommunikation, PC World Sweden, PCaktiv, Windows World Sweden; **SWITZERLAND:** Computerworld Schweiz, Macworld Schweiz, PCtip; **TAIWAN:** Computerworld Taiwan, Macworld Taiwan, NEW ViSiON/Publish, PC World Taiwan, Windows World Taiwan; **THAILAND:** Publish in Asia, Thai Computerworld; **TURKEY:** Computerworld Turkiye, Macworld Turkiye, Network World Turkiye, PC World Turkiye; **UKRAINE:** Computerworld Kiev, Multimedia World Ukraine, PC World Ukraine; **UNITED KINGDOM:** Acorn User UK, Amiga Action UK, Amiga Computing UK, Apple Talk UK, Computing, Macworld, Parents and Computers UK, PC Advisor, PC Home, PSX Pro, The WEB; **UNITED STATES:** Cable in the Classroom, CIO Magazine, Computerworld, DOS World, Federal Computer Week, GamePro Magazine, InfoWorld, I-Way, Macworld, Network World, PC Games, PC World, Publish, Video Event, THE WEB Magazine, and WebMaster; online webzines: JavaWorld, NetscapeWorld, and SunWorld Online; **URUGUAY:** InfoWorld Uruguay; **VENEZUELA:** Computerworld Venezuela, PC World Venezuela; and **VIETNAM:** PC World Vietnam.   3/24/97

Dedication

To anyone who ever dreamed there was something more to life than working for someone else — go out and give it a try.

To everyone who ever thought of living wherever they wanted — go do it!

To those who know life is for living, not for wishing — you're right.

Author's Acknowledgments

Many thanks to all those wonderful people who contributed to making this book possible: Ellen Camm, Joyce Pepple, Heather Dismore, Joell Smith, Susan Pink, Allen Wyatt, John Preisach, Adam Kowal, Val Stack, Kristine Estensen, Deirdre Straughan, Jeff Larson, and probably quite a few more I've inadvertently forgotten.

Publisher's Acknowledgments

We're proud of this book; please register your comments through our IDG Books Worldwide Online Registration Form located at http://my2cents.dummies.com.

Some of the people who helped bring this book to market include the following:

Acquisitions, Development, and Editorial

Project Editor: Susan Pink

Acquisitions Editor: Ellen Camm

Media Development Manager: Joyce Pepple

Permissions Editor: Heather H. Dismore

Technical Editor: Allen Wyatt, Discovery Computing, Inc.

Editorial Manager: Mary C. Corder

Editorial Assistant: Donna Love

Production

Project Coordinator: Sherry Gomoll

Layout and Graphics: Lou Boudreau, Valery Bourke, Linda M. Boyer, J. Tyler Connor, Derek Gregory, Angela F. Hunckler, Todd Klemme, Heather Pearson, Brent Savage, Janet Seib, M. Anne Sipahimalani, Deirdre Smith, Kate Snell

Proofreaders: Kelli Botta, Vickie Broyles, Michelle Croninger, Sarah Fraser, Janet M. Withers

Indexer: Ty Koontz

Special Help

Suzanne Thomas, Associate Editor; Joell Smith, Media Development Assistant; Access Technology

General and Administrative

IDG Books Worldwide, Inc.: John Kilcullen, CEO; Steven Berkowitz, President and Publisher

IDG Books Technology Publishing: Brenda McLaughlin, Senior Vice President and Group Publisher

Dummies Technology Press and Dummies Editorial: Diane Graves Steele, Vice President and Associate Publisher; Mary Bednarek, Acquisitions and Product Development Director; Kristin A. Cocks, Editorial Director

Dummies Trade Press: Kathleen A. Welton, Vice President and Publisher; Kevin Thornton, Acquisitions Manager; Maureen F. Kelly, Editorial Coordinator

IDG Books Production for Dummies Press: Beth Jenkins Roberts, Production Director; Cindy L. Phipps, Manager of Project Coordination, Production Proofreading, and Indexing; Kathie S. Schutte, Supervisor of Page Layout; Shelley Lea, Supervisor of Graphics and Design; Debbie J. Gates, Production Systems Specialist; Robert Springer, Supervisor of Proofreading; Debbie Stailey, Special Projects Coordinator; Tony Augsburger, Supervisor of Reprints and Bluelines; Leslie Popplewell, Media Archive Coordinator

Dummies Packaging and Book Design: Patti Crane, Packaging Specialist; Kavish + Kavish, Cover Design

◆

The publisher would like to give special thanks to Patrick J. McGovern, without whom this book would not have been possible.

◆

Contents at a Glance

Cartoons at a Glance

By Rich Tennant

"THERE! THERE! I TELL YOU IT JUST *MOVED AGAIN!*"

page 33

"OH YEAH, AND TRY NOT TO ENTER THE WRONG PASSWORD."

page 119

"I'LL GET TO THAT! I'LL GET TO THAT! JUST AS SOON AS I FINISH TRYING ALL MY REPLACEMENT BOARDS FIRST!"

page 7

Y'KNOW, I DON'T MIND LIVING IN A COMPUTERIZED 'SMART HOUSE,' BUT I DO MIND BEING CALLED AN IDIOT BY THE TOASTER.

page 273

YEAH, BUT YOU SHOULD SEE HOW NICELY IT CENTERED EVERYTHING.

page 165

SETTING UP AN INTRANET HAS REALLY HELPED OUR BUSINESS.

page 295

Fax: 978-546-7747 • E-mail: the5wave@tiac.net

Table of Contents

Introduction

I'm really glad you picked up this copy of *Small Business Computing For Dummies*! I'm glad because it gives me a chance to tell you why this book can help you and your small business.

Many people have too much time on their hands, but not you! It takes a great deal of work to start and run a small business. You don't have the time to waste on discovering all the details that computer nerds seem to love. You want the bottom-line facts. You want to know how to do a job without wasting what little time you do have.

That's why this book comes in handy. It doesn't try to turn you into a computer expert, but it does show you a no-nonsense approach to getting the most out of your computer. Instead of becoming a computer wizard, you find out what you need to know to make your computer work for your small business.

How to Use This Book

Computers can be baffling. When something about computerizing your small business has you stumped, such as how to buy the right stuff or what you need to know about upgrades, use this book as a reference. Look through the table of contents or the index to find what you need. This isn't a book you have to sit down and read all the way through. Who has time for that? Instead, turn to the page with the information you want, get what you need, and go on to something more interesting — such as running your business and making some money!

Sometimes you may want to read a bit more. If you have a few spare minutes, go ahead and keep reading. You may find something that solves another problem you didn't even know you had. You may even discover another way to accomplish something a little faster and with a bit less work. At least you'll want to make sure to catch all the cartoons!

Conventions in This Book

If you're going to use a computer, you can't avoid typing sometimes. When you need to type something, I show you what you need to type in bold print like this:

Type **this**

Typing things into the computer can be confusing, so I also give you a description of what you need to type. That way, you know exactly what you need to type and aren't left wondering whether you did it just right.

Other times, you have to select choices from menus when you need to tell your computer to do something. Usually, you choose a menu, such as the File menu, and then choose a command from that menu, such as Open. To make this process clearer, I show the command like this:

File⇨Open

The ⇨ tells you to continue making menu selections until the entire command is entered.

Sometimes I tell you where to find additional information by visiting a Web site on the Internet. I show you a *URL,* which is simply the address you need to type in your browser's address box. URLs usually look something like this:

```
http://www.idgbooks.com/
```

Sometimes, however, URLs are a bit more complicated, as in the following example:

```
http://www.idgbooks.com/cgi-bin/
        gatekeeper.pl?uidg740:%2Fdownloadable%2F
```

I know that looks confusing, but here's a secret: If you have trouble reaching a Web site, you may want to try removing chunks from the end of the URL so you can go to the home page of the Web site. Then you find a button or a link you can click on the home page to get where you really want to be. But how do you know what's safe to remove from the URL? The secret is simple: Each part of the URL that's between a set of slashes (/) has to stay together. In other words, you can drop `gatekeeper.pl?uidg740:%2Fdownloadable%2F` or even `cgi-bin/gatekeeper.pl?uidg740:%2Fdownloadable%2F` from the URL and give that a try. Sometimes you need to drop more than one piece to get to the Web site.

Speaking of Web sites, be sure to visit the ...*For Dummies* home page at `http://www.dummies.com` and click the Really Useful Extras link in the Contents at a Glance column. The Really Useful Extras page contains links to all the Web sites mentioned in the book, so you won't even have to type them yourself. You'll want to add the ...*For Dummies* Web site to your list of favorite sites!

About the CD-ROM

You've probably noticed the CD-ROM that's included at the back of the book. The *Small Business Computing For Dummies* CD-ROM contains plenty of great small business software, including a trial version of QuickBooks. You'll want to have a look at the "About the CD" appendix to find out more about the neat CD-ROM we put together for you.

How This Book Is Organized

This book is broken down into six parts, and each part has several chapters related to the part's theme. Each chapter is divided into short sections so that you can quickly find just what you need. Sometimes you'll just want to go straight to one of those sections, read what you need, and put the book down. Other times, you may want to read a whole chapter. It's up to you and what you need to accomplish.

Part I: Getting Ready for Computers

Part I starts out with the basics. If you aren't even sure whether you need a computer for your small business, this part shows you some of the ways computers can make your business easier to run. It also shows you tons of things you may not even know you can do with a computer. In addition, you find out how to decide what you really need so that you don't have to feel intimidated when you go to buy a computer.

Part II: Choosing Your Hardware

The worst thing about buying computers is trying to sort through all the misleading and downright confusing information. When you head down to your local computer store, do you feel like they have a big "sucker" sign that lights up when you walk in the door? In Part II, you discover how you can get the upper hand, be more confident, and get the computer you really need without paying a fortune.

Part III: Putting It All Together

If you thought buying a computer was hard, wait until you see all the bits, pieces, wires, and cables that appear when you open the boxes. But that doesn't mean you can't put it together without setting off the smoke alarms! You really can get your system hooked together and running. You may even be able to take it a step further and hook two or more computers together.

Part IV: Choosing Your Software

Admit it — you knew all along that computers were pretty dumb, didn't you? Without the right software, computers aren't much smarter than your average brick. If you want your computer to do anything besides take up all that space on your desk, you have to feed it the right software. In Part IV, you find out how to choose the software you need and how to put that software to work.

This part also has a bonus. You know that shiny CD-ROM at the back of the book? It has plenty of great software you can try out, as you discover in Part IV.

Part V: Correcting Problems

Nobody likes computer problems. But problems do happen, and they're never convenient. Your computer will probably figure out the absolute worst time for problems and choose that time to get stubborn. With a little help from Part V, though, you find out how to solve most problems quickly, and how to get someone else to help when you can't do it yourself.

Part VI: The Part of Tens

Who doesn't love lists? In Part VI, you find some great lists that can help you get more from your computer, make certain you're ready for the future, and show you the greatest places on the Web for small businesses. Want to know some fancy tricks to get more out of your computer? Want to find the best prices for that new piece of hardware? Want to get tons of free stuff? Look no further — this part has it all!

The rest

Eventually, you have to get to the end of any book. At the back of *Small Business Computing For Dummies* you find a glossary of important small-business-related computer terms. The glossary takes away the mystery of some of those strange terms that computer geeks use to confuse the rest of us. You also find an appendix that tells you all about the *Small Business Computing For Dummies* CD-ROM.

Icons Used in This Book

If you've thumbed through the book, you've probably noticed some *icons* — those funny little pictures along the edges of some of the pages. The icons tell you something special about the text:

 Computers are full of goofy technical details that normal people can live without. You know, those fussy facts that only computer nerds care about. I label those things with the Technical Stuff icon. You can safely avoid anything with this icon.

 This icon alerts you to handy bits of information that may save you some time or cure your bald spot. Well, maybe the tips won't help the bald spot — after all, I wrote the tips and my bald spot isn't any smaller!

 This is something you should try to remember. You've probably heard this one before, but it bears repeating.

 Watch out for this one! When you see this icon, you can cause problems if you're not careful.

 This icon lets you know about an interesting Web site on the Internet that you may want to visit.

 If you don't like making all those trips down to the computer store, this icon should make your day. It tells you about a program you can find on the *Small Business Computing For Dummies* CD-ROM.

Where to Go from Here

Enough of this introduction stuff — you're ready to roll. Flip through the pages and stop here and there. This is *your* book, so feel free to dog-ear pages, highlight important stuff, and put mustaches on the cartoons. Go ahead and make notes in the margins — you aren't going to be taking any tests, and you may as well have your notes where they'll do you some good!

Part I
Getting Ready for Computers

"I'LL GET TO THAT! I'LL GET TO THAT! JUST AS SOON AS I FINISH TRYING ALL MY REPLACEMENT BOARDS FIRST!"

In this part . . .

When you're starting and running a small business, you have a lot to do. You need all the help you can get! And a computer might be just the right tool to help.

If you're thinking about getting a computer, you're probably wondering what it will do for your business. Part I tells you about the many ways a computer can help. You discover, for example, how a computer can help make your small business look a lot bigger, and how a computer can help your business get a lot bigger, too.

After you decide that you need a computer, how can you figure out exactly what you need? Well, Part I also shows you how to get ready for computers by helping you figure out what computer stuff you really need.

Chapter 1

Why Your Business Needs a Computer

*R*unning a small business is a lot of work. Running a small business, making some money, and keeping your sanity may seem like a miracle. Doing it all without some computer help is just about impossible in today's crazy world. This chapter explains some of the neat things computers can do so that you'll have more time for business or for nonessentials such as eating and sleeping.

What's the Plan?

You probably don't go on a trip without making some plans. You figure out what cities to visit, what sites to see, and when you'll be where. If you go someplace popular, you call ahead to make reservations, too — unless you *like* driving around all night looking for a Vacancy sign. Well, your business needs a plan, too.

Just what the heck is a business plan, anyway? It's a realistic look at your status and your future business possibilities. You need a business plan if you want to borrow money to help get your business started. A business plan lets your banker or other investors know whether you have a chance of repaying their investments.

The *Small Business Computing For Dummies* CD-ROM

The CD-ROM that accompanies this book has lots of useful items. Some things on the CD-ROM are *trial* versions — you can try out the software several times to see whether it's for you. The software on the CD-ROM isn't free, but because you already have the disc, it's a convenient way to get your hands on some good programs.

Even if you don't intend to borrow money for your business, it's still a good idea to create a business plan, if for no better reason than to figure out whether you have a chance of making money. "Gee, I lost a little bit on each one, but I figured I'd make it up by selling a lot."

Fortunately, your computer can help with the creation of a business plan. All you need is the right software, some facts and figures, and you'll be off to the races (or at least to the bank). Chapter 12 shows you how one piece of software, Jian BizPlanBuilder Interactive, can make creating a business plan almost fun. You can check out Jian at `http://www.jianusa.com`.

You can find Jian BizPlanBuilder Interactive on the *Small Business Computing For Dummies* CD-ROM. See, you've already saved another trip to the computer store!

Are You on the Right Track?

Quick, do you know where your money is? Tracking cash is one of the hardest tasks most small businesses face, although getting the cash in the first place isn't so easy, either!

Tracking your money is called *accounting*. "A counting we will go, a counting we will go . . .." You've probably run into a few accountants — they talk in a strange tongue that includes terms such as "double-entry bookkeeping," "accounts payable," and "depreciation." What's really strange about accountants is that they not only understand those terms, they also have fun using them. Here are a few terms from the secret accountant's dictionary:

- ✔ **Accounts payable** is the stack of bills you owe.
- ✔ **Accounts receivable** is the money other people owe you.

- ✔ **Double-entry** pretty much means each number appears twice: once in a *debit* list and once in a *credit* list. Accountants say double-entry bookkeeping keeps things balanced; I think it helps accountants stay in business.

- ✔ **Debits** are things that shrink your bottom line.

- ✔ **Credits** are things that increase your bottom line — money in the bank, you might say.

The tax collector has no sense of humor and probably won't appreciate an accounting system based on sticky notes in a shoebox. You can save yourself a lot of grief by keeping your business records well organized. You're also much less likely to make a major mistake if you maintain some order.

Fortunately, accounting is another one of those boring but necessary small business tasks that's perfect for computers. Accounting software makes keeping your books bearable. You still have to keep all those receipts, pay the bills, and try to collect the money your brother-in-law owes you, but you won't need to pay your accountant quite so much. Chapter 13 shows you how to use Intuit's QuickBooks to do your own small business accounting. You can check out Intuit at `http://www.intuit.com/quickbooks/`.

You can find an excellent small business accounting program, QuickBooks & QuickBooks Pro Trial Version, on the *Small Business Computing For Dummies* CD-ROM. Boy, with all the time you're saving by not having to go buy software, you'll be able to take a day off!

Processing Your Words

Word processing sounds like throwing a dictionary in a blender, doesn't it? Throw that sucker in there, hit the switch, and see what flies out. "Oh look, isn't that Shakespeare?"

Being able to write effective letters is important, especially to you, the small business owner, because you probably don't have a secretary. Your computer can come to your rescue for writing letters, too. With the right word-processing software, you can hunt-and-peck your way with the best of them.

Here are some reasons why you'll be glad to have word-processing software:

- ✔ Word-processing software helps you write business proposals, collection letters, advertising copy, and more.

- ✔ If you're a lousy speller, word processors can check for spelling errors. If you're just a lousy typist, you can tell your word processor to correct your typing mistakes without even asking. It's pretty weird watching words change right before your eyes!

✔ Word processors can even check on your grammar ("she's down in the cellar making jelly"). Don't expect miracles, though. Grammar checking is more art than science. (Making jelly is more art than science, as well.)

✔ Some people try to use word processors to produce newsletters. If you're tempted to try this, go sit in a corner and repeat one hundred times "I have better things to do with my time." If you want to do a newsletter, get software made for the job. Don't waste your time trying to do it with a word processor.

✔ Word processors change your expensive computer into a really fancy typewriter. Luckily, though, the change isn't permanent — you can still use your computer for other more important things, such as playing Solitaire.

Figure 1-1 shows one example of how a small business may use word processing to promote a new product.

You can save a lot of time by reusing the same basic letter and adjusting the details. After all, Mary at Jones Plumbing Supply probably doesn't know (or care) whether you sent a similar letter to Bob at Towne Fish Market. The fancy term for a basic letter you reuse is a *template,* but you can just call it a standard letter if you like.

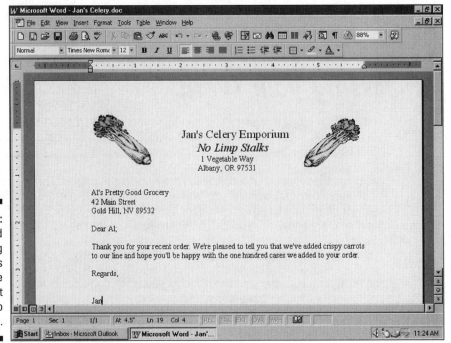

Figure 1-1:
Word
processing
enables
even the
smallest
business to
look big.

You can find out more about word processing on the Web. You may want to visit Corel at `http://www.corel.com/products/wordperfect/cwps8/index.htm` or Microsoft at `http://www.microsoft.com/smallbiz/`.

Crunching Numbers

Computers love numbers. If your computer could have its way, it would spend all day just thinking about numbers. That's pretty lucky for you because a lot of what you do with a computer is crunch numbers.

As if math weren't complicated enough, accountants figured out a way to make it more complicated by creating *ledgers* — large, lined tablets where math problems could go sideways across the page in addition to down the page. Ledgers made it possible for math to be confusing in two dimensions! Ledgers also made it possible to do *cross-tabulations* and other types of fancy accounting calculations.

Eventually, someone figured out a way to make electronic ledgers (otherwise known as spreadsheets) so that computer users could be confused, too. As it turned out, though, spreadsheets aren't too confusing, and they make math much easier. Figure 1-2 shows one way you can use spreadsheets.

Here are some of the ways you'll find spreadsheets useful:

- If you're really into numbers, you'll love the way spreadsheets let you create fancy formulas that no one else can understand. To help out, spreadsheet designers now include four to five hundred *functions,* or built-in formulas. No real person ever uses more than a dozen or so spreadsheet functions, but it's fun to say "My spreadsheet has more functions than yours."

- Spreadsheets are handy when you want to play games with your numbers. "Let's see what would happen if I eliminated the furniture budget and we all worked standing up."

- One problem with spreadsheets is that you have to put in your own numbers and formulas if you want any results. You can borrow someone else's spreadsheet, though.

- Okay, I didn't tell you the whole story about spreadsheets. In the past few years, engineers figured out how to make spreadsheets even more complicated by making them three-dimensional. Now you can be confused in 3-D.

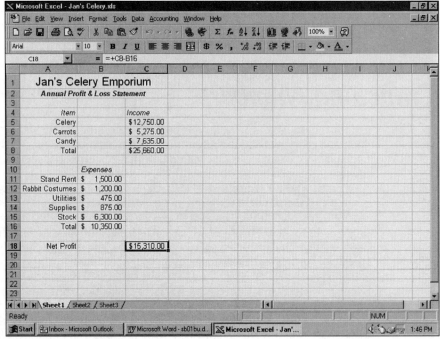

Figure 1-2:
Spreadsheets
make the
computer
do the math
so that you
don't have
to do it.

If you thought you could save a lot of time with a word processor and templates, wait until you see what you can do with a spreadsheet. Most spreadsheets now include a bunch of prebuilt templates; all you have to do is fill in a few numbers. You don't have to be a math whiz to use spreadsheets anymore. You'll find templates for tasks such as calculating loan payments and interest and for setting up a budget.

Want to know more about spreadsheets? Visit these Web sites: `http://www.microsoft.com/msexcelsupport/default.htm`, `http://www.corel.com/products/wordperfect/cqp8/index.htm`, and `http://www2.lotus.com/123.nsf`.

Tracking Your Information

If numbers were the only type of information you had to deal with, you'd probably consider yourself lucky. If you want your business to grow and prosper, however, you probably have much more information to keep track of, such as customer lists, inventory records, and past sales. You could use the old sticky note method to keep track of this information, but because you're getting a computer anyway, why not give the computer another job?

Specialized databases

Even though you can use database managers to keep track of information such as inventory and sales, you may find it's even easier to use a program such as QuickBooks (which you'll conveniently find on the CD-ROM) to handle these tasks. It's not that database managers can't do the job — it's just that QuickBooks has a specialized database management function already built in.

A special category of computer programs called *database managers,* or just *databases,* handles lists of related information. If you want to know which customer bought your last batch of lime green and purple widgets, just ask your database. If you want to know *why* the customer bought them, you'll have to ask the customer.

Here are some things you should know about databases:

✔ Databases can hold any type of information, but a little organization helps. You'll want to break down the information into little bits of related information called *fields.*

✔ You can create your own databases, but you may not have to. Other people have already created plenty of specialized databases, such as contact and inventory lists. Why reinvent the wheel?

✔ If someone tries to tell you that you can create a database in a spreadsheet program, run the other way. Trust me — I tried this myself.

Figure 1-3 shows an example of how you can use a database to keep track of information.

Every time you look up a telephone number, you're looking in a database. See, you already know how to use a database, and you didn't even have to go anywhere near a computer!

You can find out more about database managers on the Web. Visit `http://www2.lotus.com/approach.nsf`, `http://www.corel.com/products/wordperfect/paradox8/enterprise/index.htm`, or `http://www.microsoft.com/access/`.

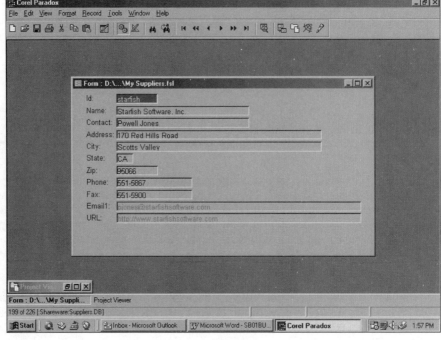

Figure 1-3:
You don't
need a
photographic
memory
when you
use a
database
to keep
track of
information.

It's Not Junk When I Mail It!

If there's one common need in business, it's letting potential customers know you're out there. If you run the only ice cream stand on a busy beach, you need only to put up a sign and hope for a heat wave. Most other small businesses, however, need a different approach.

You could go door-to-door and risk tangling with Fido or Rex, but that lets you talk to only one potential customer at a time. You probably need something that reaches more people in far less time. Junk mail (make that *mass mailings* — it's junk mail only when your competitor sends it) may be the answer. Mailing advertisements you create on your computer can be effective, and you don't have to worry about outrunning the neighborhood dogs, either!

Creating effective mass mailings

After you decide to use the mail to try to attract more customers, you're ready to think about how to make those mailings effective. After all, you don't want potential customers to simply throw your ad in the trash. Here are some of the things you need to consider:

- ✔ Why should a customer be interested in whatever product or service your business offers?

- ✔ Plenty of other people would be happy to get the business, so why should a potential customer consider buying from you?

- ✔ What makes your product or service special? You want the customer to think, "That sounds pretty interesting. I think I'll give it a try."

Remember that business plan I mentioned? Can you see how a good business plan should provide the answers to all these questions? If so, you're on the road to creating effective advertising. Besides using your business plan, you'll find that your computer can give you a lot more help in creating mailings.

Creating your mailing list

After you create your masterpiece of modern advertising, you have to take the next step: getting the right people to read it. Here, too, your computer can be an indispensable tool.

You may decide to mail your advertisements. You can reach a large audience through the mail without spending too much time or money. The key, though, is creating the right mailing list.

Here are some important points about mailing lists:

- ✔ A *mailing list* is just a specialized type of database. Your computer is pretty good at working with databases and can even help you decide whether your mailing list is working.

- ✔ Your current customer list is a good starting point for your mailing list. If you aren't already keeping track of your customers, now is the time to start!

- ✔ To increase your business, you'll probably need a bigger mailing list. You could start at the front of the phone book, but with a computer you have many better options. For example, if your business serves a local area, you can use something like Select Phone from Pro CD, Inc. (`http://www.procd.com/pi/pd/seldlx.htm`) to create a mailing list for your local postal zone. You'll find a discount coupon for Select Phone near the back of the book.

- ✔ If your business serves other businesses, you'll probably want to focus your mailing using the *Standard Industrial Classification* (or SIC) code for the types of businesses you want to reach. That way, you won't be sending ads for your custom bowling ball covers to the local floral shops.

- ✔ After you have a good mailing list, treat it like gold, because that's how your competitors will view it, too. You'll probably spend a lot of time developing your customer and mailing lists — don't be careless and let someone steal them from you!

Chapter 10 provides more information on choosing the right software for managing your mailings using your computer. You'll still need to figure out whether the local florists really may be interested in your bowling ball covers, though.

Here's a place on the Web where you can find out more about mailing lists: http://www.smalloffice.com/services/abii.htm.

Looking Professional

If you want people to take you seriously, you have to look like you mean business. With a little help from your computer, you can make even a small, part-time business you run out of your spare closet, look as professional as the largest corporation. This section offers a few examples of how you can put on your best face.

Creating a letterhead

You need a letterhead for your business. A letterhead tells people your business is real (even if you're just starting out and only hoping to become a real business).

How do you get your own letterhead? Try one of these ideas:

- ✔ If you want to spend a lot of money, go down to your local print shop and have them create a letterhead for you. This is the traditional method, but it limits your flexibility and is often expensive.

- ✔ You can create your own letterhead as a template in your word processor. That way, you print only as many copies of your letterhead as you need. A high-quality printer is necessary to make anything but the most simple letterhead look good, though.

- ✔ Add graphics to spice up your letterhead. Most office software suites include plenty of *clip art,* so you don't have to be much of an artist.

- ✔ If you have a color inkjet printer, throw in a little color, too. You'll probably want to print the body of your letters in black ink, but a touch of color may be just the ticket for getting your letters noticed.

- ✔ Nothing is wrong with a little self-promotion in your letterhead. Go ahead and tell people that your plants have the deepest roots or that your rates are the best in town. (Try to be truthful, too.)

Creating business cards

Business cards sure can be handy, can't they? In one neat little package you can give people your name, your company name, your address, a phone number or two, and even a quick plug for your business.

There's just one problem with business cards: If you move to a new address, get a different phone number, or decide to make any other simple change, your old business cards are useless. Writing your new phone number on the old cards just doesn't look good. But what are you going to do with the 950 leftover business cards? How many bookmarks do you really need?

Once again, your computer is ready to save the day.

Want to make your own business cards? Here's some information to help:

- ✔ Specialty paper companies such as Avery, Paper Direct, and Quill make business card stock so you can print your own business cards using your laser or inkjet printer. You can find Avery at `http://www.avery.com/index_norm.html` and Paper Direct at `http://www.paperdirect.com/`.

- ✔ Laser or inkjet business card stock isn't quite as thick and stiff as the business cards you may have printed commercially, but most people won't notice the difference. However, don't buy the cheapest business card stock — you don't want your business cards to look cheap, do you?

- ✔ If you have an e-mail address, don't forget to include it on your business cards.

- ✔ Although you can buy software for creating business cards, your word processor should work just fine. Begin with a table two columns wide and five rows high that covers the page, and create away.

- ✔ Always use plain paper for your practice sheets — business card stock is too expensive to waste on test prints.

One thing you won't get if you print your own business cards using your computer is that fancy raised lettering on commercially printed business cards. But you won't have to deal with hundreds of out-of-date cards, either.

Creating graphics and signs

Most small businesses need graphics and signs, even if it's only to let people know they're open for business. It looks like you have another hat to wear — you're probably the art department, too. You could draw signs or graphics by hand, but you'd probably prefer that people came into your business instead of turning around and running away. (Well, maybe you can draw better signs than I can.) Why not create your own using your computer?

Figure 4-1 shows a simple sign created on the computer by someone with no artistic talent — that is, me. It looks pretty good, doesn't it?

Here are some things you'll want to know about using graphics:

- ✔ Creating graphics on a computer is *fun*. Don't admit this, however. If anyone asks, just tell them you're working on your big fall ad campaign.

- ✔ A little clip art goes a long way. Don't make your signs so cluttered that no one can read the message.

- ✔ When things go wrong, remember: It's the computer's fault (even if it isn't)!

Okay, so you've seen a quick sampling of some of the ways a computer can help your small business. If you're still not convinced you need a computer, that's okay — the old-time blacksmiths didn't need computers, either!

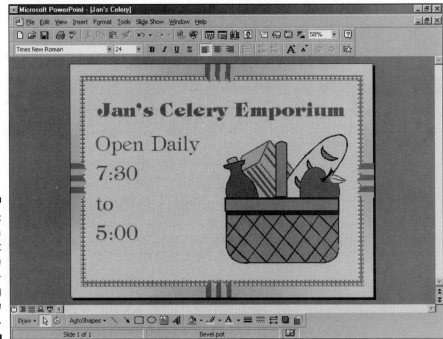

Figure 1-4:
Even a non-artist can create good-looking signs on the computer.

Chapter 2
Buying for Now and Later

. . . .

In This Chapter

▶ Planning for the future

▶ Figuring out what you really need

▶ Avoiding costly dead ends

▶ Finding out about ergonomics

. . . .

*H*ave you ever wondered whether there's a school that turns out salespeople for computers and used cars? Sometimes it seems as if the only difference between the two is that the used car sellers *know* they're lying to you! Computer sales people usually don't know enough about computers to know that they're lying.

Because you're not working for the Pentagon, buying computers (rather than toilet seats) is probably one of the largest investments you'll make for your small business. You don't want to waste your money, so this chapter gives you some guidelines to steer you around the pitfalls that await in the aisles of your favorite mega office supply dealer — including the salesperson who just graduated from the paper clip department.

This chapter is short and general. Right now, it's more important to understand the basics of buying computers for your small business than to worry about all the details.

Don't Be Penny Wise and Pound Foolish!

My father taught me that I could buy a cheap tool over and over or buy a good tool once and have it for a long time. If your focus is on what you have to spend up front, you could end up paying much more in hidden costs. In other words, you can waste a lot of money trying to save a few pennies.

You need the proper balance between a good price and a system that lasts long enough to be worth what you paid. That doesn't mean you have to buy the most expensive computer — leave that for people who aren't spending their own money.

Don't skimp in the important areas

Computers cost a lot. If you're starting out or struggling to make your small business grow, you don't want to waste money buying more computer capability than you need. The bottom line is simple: Get the most for your money.

Your new system has to be good enough to do what you need without draining your bank account. But because you're new to computers, it's difficult to figure out what you need and what you can get along without. Here are some important things to know:

- Computers need plenty of memory to work correctly. Too little memory can make your computer slow, cranky, and downright obstinate. Don't settle for less than 16MB, and get more if you can.

- If you like headaches and eyestrain, get a cheap monitor. Your eye doctor and pharmacist will be happy to take the money you saved. Be especially wary if you see the word *interlaced* anywhere in the monitor's description; that's a sure guarantee it will make your eyes hurt. Make certain your monitor is non-interlaced.

- Headaches and eyestrain, part 2. Cheap monitors can hurt your eyes in another way — they flicker because they don't redraw the screen often enough.

- You can never have too much room on your hard disk. All your programs and anything you save ends up on your hard disk. If your hard disk is too small, you'll eventually run out of space and won't be able to save anything. Want to guess the odds of that happening just when you've spent hours working on a project?

- Do you like the idea of typing in mashed potatoes? If not, you may want to try out keyboards before you buy. Some keyboards make mashed potatoes seem crisp.

- You probably don't *need* a sound card and speakers for most business applications, but you probably won't spend too much for them, either.

Here are some interesting Web sites that can help you find the right computer: `http://www.micronpc.com/default.htm`, `http://www.gateway .com/`, and `http://www.compaq.com/`. Figure 2-1 shows the Micron Web site, where you can use one of the *Small Business Computing For Dummies* coupons to get a bargain on a small business software package.

Figure 2-1:
Use the
Internet to
find your
computer.

Leave yourself an upgrade path

You haven't even bought your computer and already I'm talking about upgrading it? How about a chance to catch your breath first?

Well, you do need to consider upgrades before you spend your money. The computer and software you buy today may serve you well for quite some time, but eventually you'll probably want to do a bit more. If you've planned for upgrades, you can get a little extra service from your equipment and save some money.

SCSI drives and adapters

If you're going to use any SCSI components in your PC, you'll need a SCSI adapter. A few PCs come with built-in SCSI adapters, but in most cases the adapter is an extra cost option. If you do get a SCSI adapter, make sure your hard drives and any other add-ons are SCSI, too, so you'll get the best performance and won't have to worry about compatibility problems.

Unless you can predict the future with complete accuracy, you can't say for certain that you'll be able to get upgrades for your computer when you're ready for them. You can, however, make some good guesses if you start with good information:

- ✔ Most computers have room for the most common upgrade — additional memory. Believe me, you'll need more memory much sooner than you think!

- ✔ Memory comes in several different styles with strange names such as SIMMs, DIMMs, EDO, and SDRAM. When you add more memory, it must be the same type as what's already in your computer. Make certain you write down the type of memory in your system so you'll know what you need when you want to upgrade.

- ✔ You'll probably have room for an extra hard disk, too. If you buy one of those little laptop systems, however, you may have to throw out your original hard disk to make room for a new one.

- ✔ Hard disks come in different flavors, too. Most likely, your new system will have either an IDE (sometimes called EIDE) or a SCSI hard drive. A new hard drive should be the same type as the existing one.

- ✔ SCSI (pronounced *scuzzy*) drives cost more than IDE drives. In the long run, though, SCSI drives can be a better choice because a single SCSI adapter can also connect to many types of devices such as scanners, CD-ROM drives, and tape backups.

- ✔ Although you may be able to upgrade the processor (the "brain") in your computer at some point, it's best to take this with a grain of salt. Processor upgrades can be expensive and hard to get, and don't always produce the expected results.

- ✔ Unless you like having extra beige boxes spread all over your desk, try to find a computer that has one or two unused internal drive bays. Those are the little blank covers about 6 inches wide and $1^1/_2$ inches high that you can replace with a disk drive, a tape drive, a CD-ROM drive, or something else you don't think you need right now.

Sure, you can buy a computer without giving a thought to upgrades. But if you want to make your money work for you, consider the possibility of upgrades before you decide.

Do I Really Need All This?

Computers are a bunch of electronic pieces thrown together so that they'll run *programs,* which are complicated sets of instructions that tell the computer how to do simple tasks, such as add one plus one, or more complex tasks, such as dial your phone and check your e-mail.

But buying a computer isn't fun when you don't know what everything is and does. Is that color doodad and stereo whatsit necessary, or is the salesperson throwing them in to run up the price tag? This section introduces some of those components, so that your next computer shopping trip is at least more understandable, if not more fun.

Assessing your computing needs

Choosing the right parts for your computer is like choosing options when buying a car. You must have wheels, but you don't need the radio unless you want some music. You must have a seat for the driver, but you may need a van if you want to haul around a whole band. You have to assess your needs to determine which vehicle is right for you.

Before you buy a computer for your small business, you should assess your computing needs. Otherwise, you may end up with the single-seater when you really need the van. To help in that assessment, write down answers to the following, so you can go back over your list later:

- ✔ Where will you be using your computer? Do you need to take it with you when you visit customers, or will you use it exclusively in your office?

- ✔ If you'll use your computer primarily in the office but think it may be handy to take it with you sometimes, is the convenience worth paying 50 percent extra for a portable system?

- ✔ How many people will need to use the computer?

- ✔ If more than one person will be using the computer, can he or she share a single computer, or would that disrupt the workflow too much? You may need to consider adding more than one system.

- ✔ If you need more than one computer, will the users need to share information between systems? If so, you may need to connect the systems in a network.

- ✔ Will several users need to share a printer? Would it be better to buy individual printers or a more expensive printer everyone can share?

- ✔ How much printing will you need to do in an average day? If you do a lot of printing, you may need a heavy-duty printer to handle the load.

- ✔ Do you need to print in color? Unless you spend a lot of money, you'll have to decide between printing speed and color.

- ✔ What is the main job you intend to do on your computer? Does this require special software? If so, find out whether the software requires specific hardware.

✔ Do you need any other special hardware or software for any of the jobs you want to do? For example, if you want to work with a lot of graphics, you may need a more powerful computer with lots of memory, plenty of disk space, and special graphics software. Find out whether the software runs only on certain types of computers.

You may have trouble answering some of these questions simply because you don't yet know everything you'll do with your new computer. Most modern computers, however, can handle the majority of your needs. The following sections look at some common small business computing situations so that you can get a better idea about what you may need.

Here are some Web sites you can visit for a bit more help: `http://www.hp.com/Ebusiness/main1.html`, `http://www.epson.com/home.shtml`, **and** `http://www.microsoft.com/smallbiz/default.htm`.

Computers in the single-person office

Most small businesses start out as a single-person office. You do everything: answer the phones, read the mail, sell your products, and take out the trash. You don't have time to waste, and you could use some help.

Buying just the right computer system is probably more important in the single-person office than anywhere else. With so much else to do, you can't afford to have the wrong equipment.

Following are some essentials for a single-person office computer:

✔ A good quality fax modem so that you can send and receive both faxes and e-mail right from your computer. In most cases, you won't need a separate fax machine, so this will save both money and space. You also won't have to deal with all that smelly fax paper. You may want to add an inexpensive scanner, though, so that you can send someone a copy of the latest Dilbert cartoon.

✔ A good printer. You can choose an inkjet if you really need color, but you'll save quite a bit on printing costs if you buy a laser printer instead of an inkjet. Don't even think about a dot-matrix printer, unless you want to look like an amateur.

✔ A good monitor. Because you're the one who'll be sitting at the computer, why not go for a 17-inch monitor instead of that 15-inch one? You'll save the difference by being able to skip a visit or two to your eye doctor.

✔ A comfortable computer desk. I know it's tempting to plop the computer on that old spare table, but soon you'll realize that kitchen tables weren't designed for computers.

✔ A reasonably powerful computer. Yes, that sounds vague, but today's hot system will be old news next month, considering how fast the computer industry is changing. Don't buy the cheapest system you can find, but don't waste your money on the absolutely latest system, either. By buying a step down from the top end, you'll save a lot of money on a computer you can still use two years from now. Don't blow your whole budget on a high-end, expensive graphics workstation if you're going to use your new system only for writing letters. You can always get that 1000 MHz Pentium 6 after you make your first million!

✔ You can't be in your office all the time, so you'll need a good answering machine or the phone company's voice-mail option (if it's available). Some modems claim to do a pretty good job as a small business voice mail system, but few deliver on their promises. You may want to ask for a written, money-back guarantee if you decide to try out a voice modem system.

It's easy to waste time when no one is around to remind you of what needs to be finished. Save yourself the temptation of a major time-waster by not installing games on your office PC. You'd be surprised how much time a few games of Solitaire can waste! If games are already installed when you get your system, you may want to remove them.

Here's an interesting Web site you'll want to visit `http://www.morebusiness.com/`.

Computers when you've added help

Few things are as satisfying as having your business grow to the point where you need extra help. But few things are as frustrating, too, because you can no longer do everything your way. Adding someone to your office complicates your computer buying decisions, as well. Two of you can't type on the same keyboard at the same time, so you may have to learn to share. But if you've hired someone to help out because there's too much work for one person, you've probably noticed there's too much work for one computer, too.

After you start adding people and computers to your office, a strange thing happens. The computers will try to get connected to each other. They'll use subtle little tricks, such as needing a file on another computer or having a printer that someone else has to use. Eventually you'll throw up your hands and give in. Resistance is futile: Your computers are a powerful force that demand connection.

With new people in your office, you must add new considerations to your computer buying decisions:

- If all you need to do is share printers, you might consider a low-cost printer-sharing device. In the long run, though, you'll save yourself a lot of frustration if you network your systems so that you can share files, too.

- The person who uses the computer the hardest should have the best system. Because you've added someone to help you, consider giving him or her the best system. Remember, the more work the new hire can do in a given amount of time, the less the cost to your business.

- You can install several types of networks, but after you choose one, each computer must have the same type of network adapter card and software. Networks use special electronic languages, called *protocols,* to enable the computers to talk to each other. Everyone has to talk the same language. You may want to read *Small Business Networking For Dummies* by Glenn Weadock (published by IDG Books Worldwide, Inc.) before you choose your network.

- You can save some money by skipping some of the extra pieces on the extra computers in your network. If one computer has a large hard drive and a tape backup unit, you can share those with other computers on the network.

- You can save more money by not installing modems in all the networked PCs. You won't need as many phone lines, either. Some networks allow you to share a single modem with the entire network.

It's hard to imagine that anyone working for you may not be totally honest, but you can't afford to find out when it's too late. Be sure that a written record of all company passwords is locked in a safe location, and test those passwords yourself from time to time to make certain no one has changed them without your knowledge.

Here's one of the most useful small business sites on the Web: `http://www.smalloffice.com/`.

Computers when you've grown even more

How big can your business be and still be considered a small business? "If it's jumbo, how can it be a shrimp?"

If your business has grown beyond just you and a few employees, everything you do is on a larger scale. Your office space has to be larger, your telephone system needs several lines, and your computers must fit the needs of a larger organization. You may even need your very own computer wizard (pocket protector optional) to keep your computers running.

Here are some things to consider when your business grows:

✔ If you don't want to spend all your time solving problems, make sure everyone is running the same type of computer (that is, a PC and Windows, or a Mac).

✔ If you want to sleep nights, pay someone else to install and maintain your network. Be sure to get a written agreement on fees before you let him or her in the door.

✔ Don't let anyone bring in "this neat program I got from my brother" — unless you like watching a computer virus kill your hard drive and all your company data. Watch out for sales reps, too. They're famous for bringing in software that can cost you hours in downtime after you discover that your important business software won't run anymore.

✔ If your business needs a piece of software, buy it. Stealing software can be much more expensive than you imagine. If you feel you must "borrow" someone else's copy, don't be surprised when customers and employees start stealing from you, too. If you're not honest enough to buy the software you need, why should anyone be honest in their dealings with you?

✔ Establish a policy that encourages your employees to use their computers during breaks as well as before and after work hours. The more they use the computers, the more they'll learn. If they're learning on their own time, they'll be more productive on your time.

Buying computers for a small business that's grown isn't a whole lot different than buying them for a smaller one, but it is more expensive. Make sure you get your money's worth!

Watch Out for Dead Ends!

Have I got a deal for you! How about this nice old system that was used by a little old lady to play hearts (or Doom) only on Sundays? Buying computers can be a lot like buying a used car. However, you can usually sell an old car. Getting rid of an obsolete computer can be harder — sometimes you can't even give them away!

The personal computer has existed for about 20 years, with a few dead ends along the way. Can you imagine someone trying to run a business using an Apple II, a Lisa, or a CP/M system today? (If you don't remember any of those dead ends, consider yourself lucky!)

Watch out for the high commission push

When you walk into your local office supply or computer store, do you feel like everyone is watching to see who gets to sucker you into buying the albatross no one wants? If not, maybe you need to look around a little more closely.

The reason a salesperson tries to get you to buy a product may have nothing to do with whether that product will fit your needs. Manufacturers often give incentives — extra commissions or other bonuses — to move out dud products.

If a salesperson recommends one product over another, it doesn't mean he or she is trying to cheat you. One product may be a better choice for several reasons. Don't feel as if you have to agree with the salesperson's suggestion, though. It's your money!

If you are offered a bargain price, find out everything you can about the deal. Be sure that you can return the item for a full refund if it doesn't work out for you.

Will the manufacturer be around next year?

Do you know how to build your own computer? Can you write your own programs? If not, you'd better hope that someone will be around to help when things go wrong.

Here are some important considerations:

- ✔ The less you know about fixing your own problems, the more important it is to have someone you can rely on. Joe the computer guy may be happy to sell you a system he built in that rented storage unit, but you probably can't count on him being there next month when your system won't run.

- ✔ Local computer stores may charge higher prices, but you can always go and pound on their doors if your new system doesn't work.

- ✔ Computer manufacturers that sell direct often have a tech support staff you can call at odd hours. If you're planning on running your business during non-traditional business hours, you may want to see when tech support will be available.

- ✔ To a few fanatics, the brand of computer you use is almost like a religion. As a small business person, you can't afford to let someone sell you a computer from a dying computer company. Do you want to bet your business on whether the company who makes your Ralph computer will be around next year?

- ✔ If your new computer uses standard parts, chances are someone will be able to fix it even if the manufacturer goes the way of the Edsel.

In the 20 or so years since personal computers were invented, many computer companies have come and gone. A lot of people ended up with systems they couldn't upgrade, but that didn't stop them from using what they already had. If you choose carefully, you'll get years of service from your new system, too.

Look out for gimmicks

Someone once said that the problem with standards is that there are so many of them. Standards are someone's way of trying to get you to do things their way. If everyone suddenly adopts a new standard calling for diskettes that are twice as thick as a normal diskette, the manufacturer of the new diskettes and drives will make a fortune. If no one changes to the new "standard," the new diskettes will probably disappear as quickly as they appeared.

If you jump on the bandwagon for today's hottest new product, you may be among the first to find out all about a really great technological breakthrough. You may be lucky enough to find something that cuts your workload in half, saves you lots of money, walks your dog, and makes your in-laws think you're okay. Or you may find that you've invested a lot of time and money in a piece of junk.

The computer world is full of people who want to be the next Bill Gates. Most are quite sure that their new 3-D, holographic wizard technology is so wonderful everyone will be willing to take out a second mortgage for the chance to buy one. In a few cases, they're right, but a lot of new, cutting-edge products fade away because the public sees them as gimmicks.

If people who work with computers all the time don't know which products will last and which will fade into oblivion, how can you possibly have a chance? Here are some guidelines:

✔ Never buy the newest thing everyone is wildly hyping. If it's all that good, you'll be able to buy the new, improved version for half as much in six months.

✔ If you need to have some new gadget, buy it with money you were saving for your next vacation. That way, you won't feel so bad when you need to work extra to make up for the time you lost trying to understand how to make the gadget work because you won't be able to afford your vacation anyway!

✔ If the new gadget turns out to be a dud, tell everyone you were doing market research.

✔ If the new gadget turns out to be the best thing since sliced bread, avoid looking at ads for the product. That way you won't see how much the price has dropped.

Does It Feel Right?

Just when you thought it was safe to start thinking about buying a computer, here I go throwing in yet another thing you need to think about. Does your computer feel right?

Ergonomics is a strange-sounding term for a simple idea: Products designed for people should work with, not against, the human body. In other words, your computer shouldn't make you sick.

Ergonomics is an important consideration when you're buying your computers and planning your workspaces. Ignoring the ergonomic aspects can cause all sorts of problems.

Here are some things you need to remember about ergonomics:

- ✔ Ignoring the ergonomic factors can lead to repetitive stress injuries. If you have employees, you can bet they and their lawyers know all about these types of injuries!

- ✔ Ergonomic workstations may help you accomplish more in less time. In addition, you'll feel better if you work in a well-designed environment.

- ✔ Ergonomics is probably more an art than a science. Just don't try to tell that to the ergonomics experts. If you use common sense, you'll be able to save yourself a lot of trouble.

- ✔ As a rough rule, studies have shown that computer desks should be at least 48 inches wide, 30 inches deep, and $25^1/_2$ to $29^1/_2$ inches high. Adjust these measurements to suit your size. If you're like me, you'll need more room to spread out your mess.

- ✔ If possible, your keyboard should be low enough so that your wrists aren't bent upwards. Of course if you want to look like a gorilla sitting at the keyboard, that's up to you. Just don't say I didn't warn you!

- ✔ Visit http://www.eckadams.com/survey.html for some free software that shows you how selecting the right equipment can increase your office productivity.

Don't underestimate the importance of ergonomic factors in setting up your office. Take the time to do it right the first time.

Ergonomics are so important that you'll find lots of Web sites dedicated to the subject. A few of them are http://www.usernomics.com/hf.html, http://www.ergoweb.com/, http://www.airtech.net/, http://www.americanergonomics.com/, http://www.eckadams.com/, and http://www.ergopro.com/.

Part II
Choosing Your Hardware

The 5th Wave   By Rich Tennant

"THERE! THERE! I TELL YOU IT JUST MOVED AGAIN!"

In this part . . .

If you've ever wandered the aisles of a computer store or browsed through the ads in one of those thick computer magazines, you've probably been pretty confused when you were finished. There are just so many choices. Do you choose the sexy portable computer or that system for your desk? Do you want a laser printer, or would that inkjet be a better choice? And what's all this other stuff?

Choosing your computer can be tough. In Part II, I help you figure out what you really need — and what you don't need. You'll also see how you can make certain that you can expand and upgrade your system when it becomes necessary.

Chapter 3

Choosing the Right Small Business Computer

. . . .

In This Chapter

▶ Finding out how to carry your office around with you

▶ Discovering what's inside

▶ My memory fades

▶ Getting enough drive

▶ Figuring out where you should buy your PC

. . . .

*W*hen you're ready to bring out your plastic, it can be scary making the ultimate decision on what to buy. This chapter gets down and dirty — telling you exactly how to choose the equipment best suited to your computing needs.

You may not agree with everything in this chapter — choosing a computer is like that. Your nephew the computer game freak probably won't agree either, but then the best computers for your business needs probably won't be the ultimate game machines. By the way, keep your nephew away from your new computer. Otherwise, he'll probably try some of his "famous" tweaks that will make your system as flaky as he is.

Do You Need a Desktop or a Laptop?

Laptop computers are sexy. If computers were cars, portable systems would be Porsches, and desktop systems would be Ford vans. As you've probably noticed, though, the number of Ford vans on the road far outweighs the number of Porsches. The Porsche may be fun, but the Ford van is a better choice for hauling lumber and fertilizer.

Choosing between desktop and portable computers is a lot like choosing the type of car you drive. If you need something small that you can take with you on a moment's notice, you'll probably choose something different than if you need plenty of extra room. This section discusses some things to consider when deciding which type of system is best for you.

Making your choice

Forget sexy — convenience and comfort is where the real action is. Any computer you buy has to be convenient and easy to use as well as do the job. The last thing you need is a computer that's a good-looking boat anchor.

Does this mean you should skip the laptop and go with the desktop unit? Absolutely maybe. In other words, it depends.

Here are some factors you'll want to consider:

- ✔ If you do most of your work on the go, running from place to place, it would be difficult to argue with the convenience of a portable.

- ✔ If most of your time is spent in the office, you'll get tired of the typical cramped keyboard and smallish screen of a portable unit.

- ✔ You can also have it both ways, as shown in Figure 3-1. Several laptop computer manufacturers produce packages that enable you to have the convenience of a laptop when you're on the go and the full-sized monitor and keyboard you'll want at your desk.

Still undecided and confused? There's more to think about before you decide whether to go with the Ford van or the Porsche.

There goes your free time!

Buying a portable is the perfect way to spend more time at home — you can just take the computer home at the end of the day and put in a few more hours there.

Buying a portable is also the worst way to spend more time at home — rather than have any free time, you'll always have your work right there demanding more of your time. Running a small business takes a lot of time as it is — do you really want to stare at your computer screen all night, too?

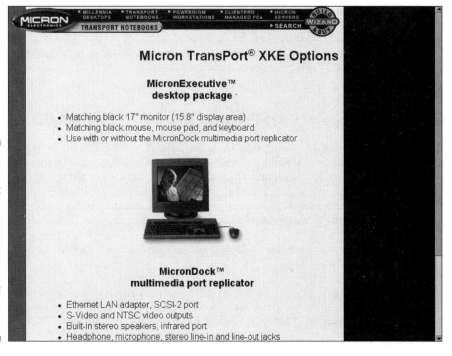

Figure 3-1:
With the right accessories, you can have the convenience of a laptop and the ease of use of a desktop PC.

Do you have money to burn?

One of the easiest ways to compare desktop and portable PCs is to compare their prices. Portables cost much more than desktop computers. How much more? You'd be surprised at the difference. The Ford van and Porsche comparison holds up pretty well in comparing the costs of these two.

Here are some facts you need to consider when choosing between a laptop and a desktop system:

- ✔ If you compare desktop and laptop computers that cost about the same, the desktop unit may be about 50 percent faster. You may have to worry about speed limits on the highway, but not on computers. Faster is better!

- ✔ Desktop and portable PCs that run at the same speed can be hard to find, but the desktop system may cost about two-thirds as much. That's money directly into (or out of) your pocket.

- ✔ If you need the absolute fastest system, only a desktop will do. There's always a lag before the faster processors are adapted to portable use. You'll pay a premium for this kind of performance, but you were probably the kind who peeked at your Christmas presents, too.

✔ Laptops sometimes come with an extra surprise. Some units don't include all the pieces in the list price. "Oh, you wanted *tires* on your car, too?" Be sure you know what's included so that you don't get hit with the added expense of having to buy a diskette drive, extra batteries, a CD-ROM drive, a modem, or cables.

If it was good enough for grandpa . . .

Upgrades are a constant in the computer world. The state-of-the-art system you buy today will be old news in a month. Newer hardware and software versions appear faster than ants at a picnic. Funny thing about those upgrades, though: You can ignore most of them, use what you have, and be perfectly happy. Still, you'll probably decide that some upgrades are so important that you just can't live without them.

Your system choice — laptop or desktop — has an effect on some of your upgrade choices:

✔ Laptop computers generally use proprietary (and expensive) parts. Usually the simplest laptop hardware upgrade is the most expensive method: Throw out the old one and buy a new one.

✔ Desktop systems — with a few notable exceptions — use standard, commonly available parts. If you want to add a faster CD-ROM drive, for example, any off-the-shelf CD-ROM drive could probably replace the one in your existing desktop system.

✔ A few PC manufacturers, such as Compaq and Apple, have tried to limit their customer's choices to proprietary (and expensive) parts. Imagine — desktop systems with all the limited expandability of laptops! Fortunately, most desktop system manufacturers eventually realized that this made their systems a lot more expensive to manufacture, too, so this practice has largely disappeared.

✔ Software upgrades generally aren't affected by the type of system you have. The same version of Microsoft Word, for example, will run on both your laptop and desktop PC.

✔ Software is affected by the operating system on your system. You generally can't run Macintosh software on Windows computers (and vice versa), for example. This pretty much means that you'll be stuck with one type of computer, Mac or Windows, after you choose your first system.

✔ If your computer does everything you need, you don't have to worry about upgrades. Just use your system until it's so old that blue-haired grandmas laugh when they see it. You can laugh all the way to the bank thinking about the money you've saved on unnecessary upgrades.

Laptops are like gold bricks — lots of money in a small package

Would you leave your gold watch or fancy camera sitting on a park bench while you went for a walk around the park? Do you leave the keys in the ignition when you park your car in an airport garage? You'd have to be pretty stupid or careless to do these things, wouldn't you? Why tempt fate by leaving expensive items where they could be easily stolen?

Laptop PCs can be a real security problem. If you're not careful, someone can ruin your whole day (or worse) by making off with your system. Here are some things to think about if you're considering buying a laptop:

✔ Laptop computers are much easier to steal than just about any other office machine. They're expensive, light, easy to conceal, popular, and a snap for thieves to sell.

✔ What's worse than having someone steal your laptop PC? Realizing that whoever took your system now has access to all your data — your address database, your confidential business plans, your checking account files, and even your private letters. Even if you have backups, how much damage could someone do with all this private information?

✔ You can gain some security by using the password feature offered in the setup program on your laptop. This feature is intended to prevent others from starting your PC unless they know the right password. However, no password option provides total security. Someone who really knows computers can probably bypass any password protection without too much trouble.

Laptop computers aren't quite as expensive as gold bricks. Still, if you decide a laptop is just what you need, don't say I didn't warn you not to leave it on a park bench!

Choices, choices

If you decide that a portable unit is what you need, an amazing and somewhat bewildering array of choices awaits. To help decide which unit is best for you, consider the following:

✔ Portable computers come in several different sizes. Generally, the larger units have more features, such as a built-in CD-ROM drive, but the smaller ones are easier to stuff in your pocket. (Okay, so maybe your pockets aren't *that* big, but you get the idea.)

✔ All portables run on batteries. Except for the smallest, simplest pocket organizer types, they all use rechargeable batteries. Some even have a spare battery pack so that you can keep on working when the batteries poop out. Make sure you find out the estimated working time between charges — and then figure you'll be lucky to get about two-thirds that in real life.

✔ *Active matrix* displays are brighter and more colorful than *passive* displays. Active display panels also cost more and run the batteries down more quickly.

✔ Passive display panels often have backlights so that you can use the system when there isn't much light. Active displays don't usually need backlights. Make sure you can turn the backlight off when it's not needed so that you can extend the battery life.

✔ Many systems require you to swap components in and out as you need them. If you need to use a CD-ROM, you may have to swap out the diskette drive. If you're not careful, it's easy to forget to bring all the pieces or to lose a drive you've swapped out.

✔ Try to get all the pieces you'll need when you buy your portable; manufacturers often change models and you may have trouble later getting accessories that fit.

✔ Make certain the processor is designed for portable use; processors designed for desktop systems use more power and will run the batteries down quickly. The newest, most powerful processors usually come out in desktop versions a few months before the laptop version is released.

Want to find out more about portable computers? Visit `http://www.intel.com/mobile/index.htm` and `http://www.zdnet.com/cshopper/`.

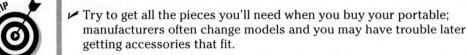

Choosing the Brains in Your PC

Whether you decide on a desktop or a portable PC, you'll be faced with more questions. Which processor should you get? Should you get the "real thing" or a clone? (A *clone* in this case is a processor made by someone other than Intel.) Who shot JR?

Every PC has at least one *processor*. That's the brain in the computer. In the Windows world, the processor may be named 486, Pentium, or Pentium II. In the Mac world, processors have names such as 603 or 604E. The processor is a complicated jumble of millions of transistors packed onto a little piece of silicon (the same stuff as beach sand, but a *whole lot* more expensive).

Selecting the best processor

Choosing the right processor out of the dozens of choices is one of the most difficult decisions you'll face in deciding which PC to buy. Why are there so many choices? How can you make sense out of the whole mess?

Here are some clues to help you sort through the choices:

- If you've decided on a particular software package you just can't live without, find out what kind of computer it requires. If the software runs on only a Mac, for example, you can eliminate computers that run Windows. Most software is available for either Windows or the Mac, however, so this may not be an issue.

- If you want to run software that lists a requirement such as "486 66 MHz" on the package, that's the minimum system you can consider. If it will run on a 486, it will run also on a Pentium (and a *whole lot* faster).

- Processor speed is measured in *megahertz* (MHz) — millions of cycles per second. But because each type of processor works differently, you can't compare processors based on their rated clock speed. For example, a 100 MHz 486 is much slower than a 100 MHz Pentium.

- Some processors use a "performance rating" rather than a speed rating. For example, AMD processors are usually rated "as fast as" a specific Intel processor. But since processor speed isn't the whole story, take these claims with a grain of salt.

- Intel used to name its processors using numbers, but changed that with the Pentium. That's why you'll see names such as Pentium Classic, Pentium with MMX, Pentium Pro, and Pentium II. Even though they all share the Pentium name, they're different.

- Why are there so many choices? Manufacturers can't afford to drop the older, slower processors simply because they've developed something better. It takes a lot of sales to recover the cost of creating a new processor.

- The fastest processor within a given family is always the most expensive. You can usually save a bit by choosing the second fastest rather than the fastest, and you probably won't notice the small difference in performance, either.

Choosing the right class

At the risk of jumping into the middle of a major war, I can't ignore one of the touchier questions new computer users face: Should I buy a Mac or a Windows PC? You have to make a decision, though, so I'll offer some information that I hope is unbiased:

- Mac users always claim that their systems are easier to use than Windows PCs. The truth is, all modern systems work pretty much the same. Oh sure, you'll see small differences that one side or the other will claim are huge, important advantages for their systems, but these are all petty and feeble attempts to make the "other guys" look bad. My take? Ignore these claims.

✔ About ten Windows PCs are in use for every Mac. This doesn't mean the Windows PC is better than the Mac, but it does mean you may find it easier to buy Windows software. Stores tend to carry more programs for Windows systems than for Mac systems simply because they go for the bigger market.

✔ Although the same software titles are generally available for both Macs and Windows PCs, some software, especially some graphics packages, were originally designed for Macs. Although these packages may work a little better on a Mac, the differences between Mac and Windows versions will probably be minor.

✔ Because Apple retains nearly total control over the Mac world, Mac systems are usually said to be a bit easier to set up. Unfortunately, this nearly total control also means that components are a bit more expensive because there isn't the competition there is in the Windows world.

✔ Finally, in recent times, Apple has had some rough going. They've lost quite a bit of market share, and many people are questioning how long Apple may be around. It's pretty unlikely that Apple will fold or that the Mac will disappear, but the prospects do make some people a little worried.

No matter whether you buy a Mac or a Windows system, your new computer will help you run your small business more efficiently. If you can, ignore people who try to push you one way or the other and just choose the system that feels the best to you.

Intel versus the clones

One thing you'll encounter in the Windows PC world that you won't see in the Mac world is a choice of different brands of processors. Oh sure, most Windows PCs have Intel processors, but several companies have built a thriving business in *clones*. When you buy a Windows PC, it doesn't have to have an Intel processor.

In deciding between an Intel processor and a clone, here are some things to consider:

✔ Clone processors aren't true clones (exact copies of the original Intel processors). Various patents and copyright issues prevent that. Instead, the clones are processors that work pretty much like the Intel processors while using different circuits. It's like sending a package across the country. Just because there's an interstate highway doesn't mean everyone has to use it. Some people choose to take a different, scenic route to get from point A to point B. As long as your package gets to its destination, what difference does it make which route was used?

✔ Intel has a copyright on the Pentium name, so clone manufacturers can't use Pentium in naming their processor chips. You can get a rough idea of the level of the chip by looking to see the numbers used in the name. The original Pentium (the "Pentium Classic") is essentially a level 5 chip; the Pentium Pro and Pentium II are essentially level 6 chips.

✔ Some clone processors use a faster *bus speed* to improve performance figures. But because most other chips in the computer were designed to operate at the bus speeds associated with Intel processors, this can cause intermittent computer problems that are difficult to diagnose.

✔ Systems with clone processors are generally cheaper than those with Intel processors. If saving a few hundred dollars is at the top of your list of considerations, be sure to see what's available in clone systems.

✔ No matter which processor is in the system you select, make certain you can return the system if it doesn't do the job.

If you want to find out more about some of the different brands of processors, you can visit the processor manufacturers on the Web. Don't expect unbiased information, though. Here are the sites for Intel, AMD, and Motorola: `http://www.intel.com/businesscomputing/desktop/index.htm`, `http://www.amd.com/products/cpg/cpg.html`, and `http://www.mot.com/SPS/MotorolaPowered/techspot7.html`. Figure 3-2 shows the Intel processor Web site.

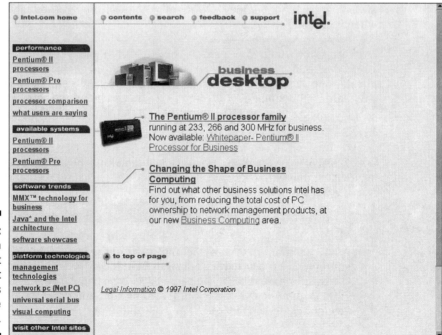

Figure 3-2:
You can find out more about processors on the Internet.

How Much Memory Do You Really Need?

Another choice you'll have to make is how much memory to get in your computer. *Memory* (otherwise known as RAM) is the place in your computer where your programs go to run. If you don't have enough, programs run slowly. If you have too much, everything runs just fine, but you've wasted some money you could be spending on useful things like Flight Simulator.

Because computers were designed by the ultimate nerds — electrical engineers — lots of things about computers don't make sense in the real world. Memory, for example, is measured using strange units called *bytes*. A byte is made up of eight *bits*. A byte is also the smallest amount of memory that can be normally used (if anything in a computer can be considered normal). To make matters worse, bytes are counted using units called *K* or *MB*. One K is 1,024 bytes, and one MB is 1,048,576 bytes — 1K times 1K. The official reason for these strange numbers is that computers do everything by calculating powers of 2. (I think the real reason is to make it harder for normal people to understand.) Make it easy on yourself and just remember that 1K is a little more than a thousand, and 1MB is a little more than a million.

Don't confuse memory and disk space. Both are measured in bytes, but they're used for different things. Your hard disk stores programs and information. To actually use those programs or information, you have to load them from the hard disk into memory. That's why hard disk space is always larger than memory — you need somewhere to store all your junk when you aren't using it.

Here are some things you need to know about memory:

- ✔ You need at least 16MB of memory to run today's software. Don't believe it if someone tells you that you can get along with less — you *can* jump out of an airplane without a parachute, too, but would you want to?

- ✔ If you want to run more than one program at the same time, get at least 32MB of memory. More memory will help your computer run faster and will enable you to save time by having several programs loaded into memory together.

- ✔ If you intend to work with a lot of graphics, get at least 64MB of memory.

- ✔ All the memory in your system must be of the same type. You can sometimes have two different *sizes* of memory modules installed, but the memory must be of the same type. If possible, order your system with as much memory as you'll need so that you don't have to mess around inside your PC later.

✔ Don't lose your computer's owner's manual. If you need to add memory in the future, the manual should describe what type to add and whether you'll need to do anything special to make the system "see" the new memory.

✔ Memory is easily damaged by static electricity. Be careful when handling memory modules, and don't let your cat play with them!

✔ Always get a bit more memory than you think you'll need. The first personal computer I programmed had 256 bytes of memory, and we thought 4K was a lot!

Before you go out and buy memory, you may want to check prices on the Internet. Here's one place you can buy memory from the same people who supply memory to many PC manufacturers: `http://www.micron.com/crucial/`.

Who Are You Calling Scuzzy?

Thought you had made enough decisions? Well, you need to think about a few more items, such as how is your system going to talk to its parts? If you said "pick up the phone and call," go stand in the corner!

For a few minutes, think of your computer as a complex little city. The people or, in this case, the data need to go to lots of different places. Data must move in large groups, so the city has a number of buses to move the data from place to place. When a lot of data must be moved at the same time, the buses can become crowded and everyone has to take his or her turn. If things get really crowded, the whole city slows to a crawl, and your computer takes forever to accomplish anything.

Your computer isn't a city, but it does use *buses* — electrical connections, in this case — to move data between your disk drives and memory, between memory and the processor, between the processor and your video adapter, and so on. There are several different types of buses, but one main bus line — the one connected to the expansion slots. Most data moves across this bus line, and that can be a problem. "What are expansion slots?" you ask. They're connectors inside your PC that enable you to plug in all sorts of expensive new bits and pieces, such as modems and sound cards.

The primary expansion bus on a PC is called an ISA (Industry Standard Architecture) bus. It's called that because it's the same as the original expansion bus slots on the IBM PC AT. Modern PCs usually have a second expansion bus called the PCI (Peripheral Component Interconnect) bus that is a lot faster than the ISA bus. Expansion cards are designed to fit either the ISA or the PCI bus, but not both. Before buying new components to plug into your system, you need to check which types of slots are open.

What a SCSI bus!

A third type of bus was common on the Mac before it became popular on PCs: the SCSI (pronounced *scuzzy*) bus. The SCSI bus has a few big advantages over the other types of buses, and a few things that will drive you crazy, too:

- ✔ On a single SCSI adapter, you can connect up to seven devices, such as a hard disk, a CD-ROM drive, a scanner, or a CD burner (a drive that creates CD-ROMs). This is often the only way you can add this many components to a PC.

- ✔ A SCSI adapter can route a lot of data around the normal expansion buses. It's like adding a subway system to a city. People who want to continue to ride the old-fashioned bus can still do so, and they'll probably find that the buses run a little faster because they're not so crowded.

- ✔ The SCSI bus can be picky about something called *termination*. That just means that both ends of the bus must be terminated with special resistors so that signals don't bounce back and confuse everyone on the SCSI bus. Unfortunately, termination problems can be confusing to figure out, especially because termination may be automatic or manual.

- ✔ SCSI adapters sometimes have three connectors, but you're allowed to use only two at a time. If you want to connect extra devices, you use a *daisy-chain* cable that goes from one device to the next. Then you get to have more fun making sure the termination is correct.

- ✔ SCSI devices usually cost more than other devices. But SCSI devices are usually faster, too (sometimes a lot faster).

- ✔ You may have problems finding SCSI devices at your local mega office supply store. That may be a blessing in disguise, because you shouldn't expect advice on configuring SCSI devices from the paper clip department graduate.

The SCSI versus IDE war

Just when you thought it was safe to cross the street, here comes another bus — the IDE (or EIDE) bus. The IDE (Integrated Drive Electronics) bus was designed for a single purpose: connecting hard disks to the computer.

EIDE is just an expansion of the IDE bus that allows larger disk sizes. Any IDE hard drive you can buy today is really EIDE, so you don't have to worry about it. The original IDE bus had a different purpose than simply being an easy way to connect hard disks to computers. A long time ago, Compaq

Computer wanted to be the only source for expansion components for its computers. That way, Compaq could charge more when people realized that their 20MB hard disk just wasn't big enough. Compaq's plan was pretty good: It designed its computers so that some of the electronics normally on an adapter card were moved to the disk drive itself. This prevented you from going out and buying just any disk drive, because it wouldn't work in your Compaq computer.

Eventually, other computer manufacturers realized that using IDE disk drives would allow them to simplify their systems by eliminating the disk drive adapter. Compaq's grand scheme spawned a whole new type of disk drive, and the IDE bus became a standard.

When you're choosing between SCSI and IDE, consider the following:

- ✔ IDE disk drives are generally cheaper than SCSI drives. But because SCSI drives are always faster, you get what you pay for.
- ✔ Because the IDE bus was designed only for connecting hard disks, IDE isn't nearly as flexible as SCSI. But all modern PCs automatically come with IDE built in, whereas you generally have to pay extra for a SCSI adapter.
- ✔ The IDE bus was expanded to enable you to connect IDE CD-ROM drives in addition to hard disks. You still can't connect things like scanners, though.
- ✔ Most modern PCs have two IDE channels, and each can connect to one or two drives.
- ✔ IDE buses run as fast as their slowest component. Because hard disks are faster than CD-ROM drives, it's best to connect IDE hard disk and IDE CD-ROM drives to different IDE channels. Your system probably won't come this way, though, because the manufacturer would have to spend an extra quarter on an additional cable.

Virtually all PCs you can find in most office supply or computer stores have IDE rather than SCSI disk drives. If you want the higher performance and extra expansion capacity of a SCSI system (and want to be able to say "I have a scuzzy computer system"), you'll probably have to order your computer directly from a manufacturer or a reseller who specializes in better computers.

If you want to learn more about SCSI adapters, visit http://www.adaptec.com/deskpcon/promo/bone3.html.

Is Yours Big Enough?

Is your hard disk big enough, that is? There's an unwritten rule: Data always expands to fill all available space. It's just like your junk drawer — junk is always ready and waiting to fill all the nooks and crannies until there isn't room for anything else.

Believe it or not, the first personal computers didn't even have hard disks. If you wanted to save your work, you pulled out another diskette. Pretty soon, though, the piles of diskettes started filling your junk drawer. There had to be a better way. That better way was the huge capacity of the hard disk. Who could ever run out of room with all that free space?

There's a good reason why we need so much more disk space than in the past. Nearly everything has become loaded with graphics, and graphics take much more room than simple text. Instead of the old plain text command line, computers now have easy-to-use *Graphical User Interfaces* (GUIs) that eat up a lot of disk space. Instead of being satisfied with reading a description of a flower, now everyone wants to see the flower in full color. Just wait until everyone wants to smell the flower, too!

Most people don't give much more thought to the hard disk in a new PC than they do to the gas tank in a new car. It's there, and that's all most people care about. But if you're spending time and money to get the right PC for your small business, why not make sure everything is right for the job?

Choosing your disk size

It's amazing how much data can fit into the small physical space occupied by modern hard disks. A typical hard disk can hold as much as a thousand or more diskettes. Imagine the storage problems you'd have if you had to store everything on diskettes!

Here are some important facts you need to know about hard disks:

✔ The capacity of computer disks is measured in the same unit — bytes — used to measure memory. But hard disks tend to have lots more space than memory does, so hard disk capacity is often listed in *gigabytes* (GB), which are billions of bytes. A gigabyte is 1,073,741,824 bytes (1,024 times 1,024 times 1,024), but you'll be close enough if you simply think of it as one billion bytes.

✔ Unfortunately, disk drive manufacturers often exaggerate by listing the *unformatted capacity* of their drives. That's like a car manufacturer claiming that a new model can carry eight people, but forgetting to mention that after the seats are installed there's room for only five. What you need to know is the *formatted capacity* — the amount of space you'll have after the drive is ready to use.

✔ At a minimum, make sure that any new system you buy has at least 1.2GB in hard disk space. If you plan on doing a lot of graphics work or collecting a bunch of sound files, or if you don't want to upgrade to a larger hard disk in less than a year, get something bigger.

✔ You may want to consider buying a removable cartridge disk drive, such as a Zip or Jaz drive. These drives act as almost unlimited-sized disks because you can always pop in a new cartridge when you fill one up.

✔ If you need to store a lot of information that won't change, you may want to add a CD-R drive (see Chapter 4), too. These types of drives use inexpensive disks that can store up to 650MB and can be read in any standard CD-ROM drive.

✔ Even if you can't see it from the outside, most desktop PCs have room for at least one extra hard disk inside the case. When you run out of room (and you will — much sooner than you think), you can add an additional hard disk to your system. If you have a laptop, well, you can always learn to live with what you have, can't you?

Choosing disk speed

Size isn't the only consideration in choosing hard disks. If you're storing a lot of information, it's only natural that you'll spend quite a bit of time waiting while the data is stored or retrieved. There's no reason to wait too long, though — computers are supposed to save time, remember?

Unless you're building a computer by selecting each component individually, you probably won't have many choices in hard disk speed. However, consider the following few guidelines:

✔ SCSI hard disks are almost always faster than IDE drives. If you want fast, go scuzzy!

✔ Small access time numbers are faster, but you probably won't see much difference between 8ms and 10ms drives.

✔ Faster rotational speeds, such as 7200 rpm rather than 3600 rpm, mean more data can be read or written in a given amount of time. If you have a choice, go with the faster drive.

✔ Any hard disk is many times faster than any other PC storage system, but some removable drives (such as the Jaz drive) are catching up. Still, no matter how slow a drive is, it's a lot faster than retyping your work!

Be ready for problems

No matter how big your hard disk may be, if you store important information on the disk, eventually you'll have a problem that prevents you from using your information. The more important the information and the more inconvenient the problem, the more likely it will happen. If you have a backup copy, your hard disk will probably never fail — simply because the failure wouldn't cause you any big problems.

Store Wars

When it's time to spend money for your new system, lots of people will be happy to take your little plastic card and run it to the max. Your task is to figure out who will be your computer vendor. With so many choices, where should you shop? This section looks at the options.

Mail-order versus local stores

Thousands of places want to sell you a computer, but you can break them down into two basic groups: those who want to sell you a computer that costs too much, and those who want to charge you too much for your computer. No, wait, that doesn't sound quite right. How about this: local stores versus mail order.

It's a bit simplistic to break down your choices into just two categories. After all, both categories include lots of variations. Local stores include everything from shops selling nothing but computers assembled right in their back room to office supply warehouses to giant electronics stores. Mail-order companies range from computer manufacturers selling only their own brand to companies selling many different brands. Even with all these options, though, your choices really do come down to local stores or mail order.

Here are some considerations in choosing between mail-order and local stores:

✔ Some people think they can save money by shopping at mail-order outlets that don't charge sales tax on out-of-state shipments. If you're tempted by this, you'll probably be interested to know that most states have a "use" tax that is the equivalent of their sales tax. If you buy something from an out-of-state vendor who doesn't charge sales tax, you're liable for the use tax and can be fined for not paying the tax.

✔ Mail-order vendors often are more knowledgeable about their products than people in a local store. Your local store may know all about televisions and VCRs, but if Mary the computer expert is off today, you may end up with Joe the refrigerator guy.

✔ It's difficult for local stores to compete with mail-order stores on price, but don't assume that you'll always save money buying mail order. Most mail-order companies charge for shipping, which can eat into any savings.

✔ Brand-name, popular items are often sold at the same price no matter where you shop. If you can buy it for the same price locally and don't have to wait for it to be shipped, why bother with mail order?

✔ See whether your local office supply store has a business mailing list and get on it as soon as you can. These stores often have special sales or offer discount coupons that can save you a bundle.

✔ Watch the local newspaper for specials. If you have competing office supply stores, they'll often offer to match any lower advertised price plus give you a bit extra. If you see a really good advertised price on something you've been considering, take the ad to the competing store and see whether you can get a better price.

✔ Use one of the Internet shopping guides to search for the best pricing. Local stores probably won't try to match prices from Internet vendors, but many mail-order vendors will.

If you're looking for the best deals online, here are a couple of Web sites you won't want to miss: `http://client.netbuyer.com/cgi-bin/nls_ax.dll/p_index.htm` and `http://web1.pc-today.com/launchpad.html`.

Getting the help you need

There's more to buying computers than just the price you pay. If that weren't true, this would be a short discussion and a short book. Part of the price you pay goes into that intangible area called handholding. How much help do you need, and how much can you expect from your computer vendor?

Surprisingly, it's difficult to make a clear choice between local stores and mail-order vendors in regards to who will give you the most help. Both have their share of bozos and gems.

Here are some help-related issues to consider:

- ✔ If you need to return something, local stores offer a big advantage — they're right there. Even if they don't want to take it back, you've got the advantage of being able to go in and argue in person. I don't suggest using the comment I heard one irate customer make, though: "You can take it back over the counter now or through the front window tonight."

- ✔ Local stores may be willing to come out and set up everything in your office, especially if you're buying a complete system from them. If you are offered this option, take it even if you have to wait a day or two to get your equipment running. That way, you won't be responsible for the new equipment until you know it's up and running.

- ✔ If you're starting out your business in your spare time, look for a vendor that offers extended tech support times. Computer manufacturers who sell direct often have tech support 24 hours a day, 7 days a week. Local stores probably won't be able to match this.

- ✔ Local stores that sell a broad range of products aren't likely to have anyone who really knows computers well enough to tackle sticky problems. Joe the refrigerator guy isn't the one to ask about terminating your new SCSI scanner.

- ✔ Any vendor that specializes in computers should be better at answering your computer-related questions, but it may not be good at giving answers you can understand. If the person selling you the computer seems to be talking a different language, can you expect the guy hiding in the back room to be any better?

Finding someone you can trust

You probably don't know the person selling you the computer, you don't know all that much about computers, and you're going to be spending a lot of money. Sounds like a formula for getting cheated, doesn't it?

To stack the chips in your favor, here are some things to consider:

- ✔ Anyone who specializes in computers will probably know more about what will work than someone who sells computers alongside refrigerators, washers, and televisions.

- ✔ Look for a 30-day, no-questions-asked return policy. Most computer manufacturers that sell direct will offer you this option — but be sure to ask whether there's a written policy on returns. Ask to see a copy *before* you buy. You may be surprised to find out there's a hefty restocking fee on nondefective returns.

✔ Use a credit card rather than pay cash or with a check. Most credit card companies will help you out if you end up with junk the vendor won't support. You may still end up with junk, but you'll have more leverage with the credit card company behind you.

✔ Ask to see the FCC certification certificate, especially if you're dealing with a little computer shop that builds its own systems in the back room. It's illegal to sell computers that lack FCC certification, but plenty of little shops do it anyway. Their computers *might* be okay, but how will you know for certain?

✔ While you're looking for the FCC certification label, make certain the computer has class B certification. Believe it or not, class B is more stringent than class A. Computers with class A certification can't legally be used in a home because they emit too much radio interference. This also makes them more susceptible to outside interference, which can cause all sorts of problems for you.

✔ If you have a problem, don't be afraid to speak up. No one will volunteer to solve problems they don't know about.

Getting what you really want

No matter how all the other issues add up, there's one important remaining issue in the local store versus mail-order choice: Can you get what you really want? Can the vendor deliver the perfect solution to fit your needs? How important is it to be able to specify all the little bits and pieces?

Choosing a computer is always a compromise. You may think the 20-inch monitor would be neat, but your budget may dictate something a bit smaller. A color laser printer would probably be just the thing to make your letters get noticed, but a color inkjet will do pretty well, too, and cost a lot less.

Here are some facts to help you decide what you really need:

✔ You probably can't get everything you want unless you build the computer yourself (in which case you may not get a computer at all). The next best thing is to order a computer directly from the manufacturer. Computer manufacturers who sell directly to the end user (that's you) specialize in giving you plenty of choices.

✔ Many local computer stores, especially those that assemble their own systems, do some customizing. You probably won't find top-of-the-line, name-brand components in their computers, however. Off-brand components might be okay, but if the local store disappears, there probably won't be anyone to back up the warranty.

✔ Large stores that sell packaged systems aren't likely to be interested in doing customization. If what they have doesn't fill your needs, it's up to you to dig in and make the changes. This also means that you're on your own solving any problems with your upgrades, too.

✔ If you do buy a computer that needs upgrades to completely fill your needs, don't forget to try it out before you make any changes. That way, you can solve one problem at a time and not have to wonder whether your changes caused the problem. Never ignore an existing problem by thinking it will go away when you do an upgrade. The problem won't go away, and you'll be faced with trying to solve even more complex problems!

Watch That Warranty!

A warranty is like an insurance policy: You hope you'll never need it, but without it you could be in for some expensive trouble. If your small business depends on your computer, a good warranty can mean the difference between a minor annoyance and a major disaster!

Computers are generally reliable. There aren't many moving parts, so if you don't throw it across the room or punch out the screen, mechanical problems aren't likely to be much of a problem. Still, it's almost a sure bet that when a problem does pop up, it will be at the worst possible moment — such as when you have to prepare a quote for the biggest job anyone's ever given you a chance to bid on. At times like that, you won't care how much you paid for your PC, whether your mother-in-law is coming for the week, or even if that obnoxious sales rep is buying lunch next Monday — getting your computer up and running as quickly as possible will be the only thing that matters.

Computer people love to pass the buck. If there's any possible reason to suggest that you caused the problem, that's what everyone will try to do. How could you cause the problem? Well, in the eyes of someone who's trying to pass the buck and get out of trying to solve your problem, just about anything you do could be the "real" cause of your problems. Here are some things I've heard:

✔ "You upgraded your operating system, and we don't support that version on your model." This is pretty tricky. Of course they don't support a new operating system on this model — they changed the model number when they started shipping systems with the operating system upgrade. The solution? If necessary, lie about it and tell them you're still using the original operating system. If the problem is hardware, the operating system isn't the problem, anyway!

✔ "You added a modem (or a scanner, memory, different display adapter, and so on) and that's causing the problem." They may be right, but not if you've been using the new piece for a while after installing it. If new hardware is going to cause a problem, it will happen immediately — not weeks or months later. If necessary, remove the new piece, demonstrate that the problem still exists, and insist on a resolution.

✔ "You added a new version of the software, and we don't support that version on your model." Starting to sound like a broken record here? Well, software can be a problem, but it seldom causes a hardware failure. Save yourself some time, uninstall the new version, see whether the problem still exists, and. . . .

✔ "It doesn't matter if that new software won't run on your system, our policy is not to accept returns on software that's been opened." A variation on this is the old "We don't accept software returns for any reason." If the software is junk, you shouldn't have to pay for it. You did use your credit card, didn't you? Ask to see the manager, and then make lots of noise at the customer service desk. They'll probably give you your money back just to get you to quiet down and leave the store. Just don't try this too often at the same store!

Getting a good warranty

There are warranties and then there are warranties. Some aren't worth the paper they're printed on; others are designed to make you a happy customer who'll come back next time you're in the market for more equipment.

How can you tell whether a warranty is any good? Other than trying it out yourself after you've already bought the system, here are a few guidelines to consider:

✔ Look for a warranty that says you can get a loaner while your equipment is being repaired. That way, you'll be able to keep working and the burden will be on the manufacturer, not you. You'll need to make sure you have backups, though; otherwise, you won't be able to use your software and data on the loaner.

✔ Make certain the warranty says you can return items with no restocking charge during the first 30 days. Most computer manufacturers that sell direct offer this option, and many of the larger stores will do this, too. It's considered bad form to use this option to obtain equipment for short-term projects, though!

✔ The warranty should cover both parts and labor. Otherwise, you'll get stuck for labor charges that are inflated enough to pay for the parts, too.

✔ Look for a warranty that's at least three years on major items. You probably won't be using the computer yourself more than three years, so longer warranties aren't going to do you much good.

✔ Find out who's going to cover the warranty if your vendor goes out of business. Few small computer stores last very long, and when they disappear, your warranty may, too. Try to get a warranty that provides service from a third party — preferably one of the brand-name national service companies. That way, you'll be able to get your equipment serviced when Al the computer guy decides to become Alphonse the waiter.

✔ See whether your credit card company extends the warranty on items you buy with your credit card. Sometimes this can double the length of the warranty at no extra charge to you.

✔ Avoid buying extended warranties or service contracts. Most failures happen soon after you start using your new equipment, and the extended contract simply helps make someone's boat payment — why not let it be yours? Skipping the extended service contract is a gamble, but you'll probably get a better payback buying lottery tickets than investing in extended service contracts.

Considering on-site warranties

Do you relish the idea of dismantling your whole computer system, packing it up, and driving down to the repair shop whenever there's a problem? Does the idea of figuring out where all those cables go when you have to put it all back together sound like a lot of fun? Can you afford all that time away from your business in addition to all the time you'll lose simply because your computer decided to teach you a lesson in frustration?

No? Well, you're going to like the sound of this: If you shop carefully, you can probably get an on-site repair warranty for your new computer system. Just think, someone else will be taking care of your problems for a change. You don't have to be a huge, multinational corporation to get this kind of service.

Computer problems are always inconvenient, but when you're struggling to get in 25 hours of work in a day, taking time off to get your computer fixed makes things a lot worse. On-site warranties can help. Not only do you get your computer repaired without all the normal frustration of doing it yourself, but you get to watch someone else deal with your problems.

So how do you arrange for on-site service warranty? And isn't that going to be expensive? Actually, it's easy to arrange and probably won't cost anything — at least for the first year or so. Computer manufacturers want your business. Most computer makers that sell direct include the first year of on-site service as part of their standard warranty.

If you live in a small town or a rural area, be sure to ask whether the on-site service warranty applies to your area and whether there are any restrictions on the service. In especially remote areas, you may not get quite as fast service as you might in a large metropolitan area, but you can probably get on-site service almost anywhere. If the manufacturer can't provide on-site service in your area, you may want to ask the manufacturer whether it will pay all shipping charges on repairs and returns to compensate for the lower level of warranty service.

You'll probably have to pay extra to extend the on-site service warranty beyond the first year — even if the warranty on parts is much longer. If the cost to extend the on-site service agreement is reasonable — equal to a few hours of your time — you'll probably want to pay the extra to extend the coverage. Unless you feel that your time has no value, it makes more sense to let someone else deal with any problems you may encounter.

You're not completely out of luck if you decide to deal with a local store rather than buy your system directly from the manufacturer. Although you may need to pay a bit extra for an on-site service contract, you may be able to negotiate with the store on this. Don't be afraid to let them know that you have a small but growing business, and service is an important consideration in your buying decisions. Because one of the best reasons to buy locally rather than mail order is to get better service, you may need to point out the type of service you can get buying directly.

Waiting for repairs

How much is your time worth? No, wait, I'm being serious here, so don't start talking about how little you pay yourself. (Just keep telling yourself how much fun you're having running a small business and how the money isn't really all that important.) How much time can you afford to waste?

The business world is too competitive to allow you the luxury of wasting your time, especially if you're trying to run a small business in which you wear a lot of hats. You simply can't afford a lot of downtime when something in your computer breaks.

Here are some important questions you need to ask:

✔ If you're planning on buying a system directly from a computer manufacturer, ask whether they *cross-ship* replacement parts. This means they'll send out a replacement part and you can return the defective item after your computer is fixed. You'll save a lot of time getting your system fixed, although you will have to supply a credit card number to guarantee the return of the defective item.

✔ Ask how quickly you can expect an on-site service call. If possible, guaranteed next business day service is the way to go. Avoid on-site service contracts that don't specify how quickly you'll get your service call — service should be at your convenience, not the service company's convenience ("we'll be out sometime next week when we can make it to your area").

✔ If you're trying to run your small business in your spare time, find out whether service is available during non-traditional business hours.

✔ If you're buying from a local store, find out whether it has replacement or at least loaner components in stock. If not, you may have to wait a long time while the store ships the defective piece back to the manufacturer for repair or replacement. You can bet it won't bother with overnight shipping, either!

✔ If you can't afford any downtime, you may want to arrange for backups of critical components. Buying a spare modem, for example, could be the cheapest insurance you'll ever get, especially if the spare keeps you in business instead of playing the waiting game. You don't have to buy anything fancy, but you may want to keep your old, still-working components around when you upgrade. That way, you'll at least be able to keep working.

Chapter 4

Adding the Peripherals Your Business Needs

*T*hought you were finished after you chose your PC? Think again, because there's much more to buying your system than choosing the right box. You can choose lots of extra pieces to make your system right for your small business needs, and this chapter helps you decide what else you need.

Those extra *peripherals* include not only obvious items such as monitors and printers, but also tools to protect your work from random occurrences (for example, power failures and brain fade) and special items such as scanners to help you get information into your system. You also read about some things you probably never knew existed, such as drives that let you create your own CD-ROM discs.

Here's Looking at You

Most computer displays look like a small television set but cost the same as a big TV. That is, unless you use a laptop system. A laptop screen looks like an Etch-a-Sketch, and you don't *want* to know how much more a laptop screen costs!

A good monitor can be a big investment. Although you could buy the cheapest monitor, you'll soon see why this isn't a good idea.

Pick and choose what you want

Although the person selling you the computer may not want to admit it, you don't have to buy all the extra add-ons when you buy your system. You don't even have to buy them all at the same place. Modern PCs generally use a fairly universal design, so if you want to add an Epson printer to your HP computer, for example, nothing prevents you from making that choice. However, one big advantage to buying everything at one place is that it's much harder for the vendor to weasel out of helping you get your system working properly. If the store also offers a setup service, buying everything from one place means they'll be responsible for making it all work before you ever touch anything. And the fact that you *can* buy some of the pieces elsewhere may help you get a slightly better deal.

Are you wondering why monitors cost so much more than TVs? TVs are designed to be watched at a distance, but you probably sit less than two feet from your monitor. This makes it possible for TVs to have a much lower quality display and still be acceptable. Go and sit two feet from your TV and see how long you can stand it; you'll probably give up soon (unless you're cheating by not turning the set on). TVs are designed also to show a moving picture, whereas your monitor often has to display information that doesn't change much. The TV's moving picture tends to hide the poor image quality, but you'd quickly notice if your monitor had fuzzy, grainy images. If you don't believe it, try this: See how many of the credits you can read next time there's a movie on TV. Your monitor can easily display text one-tenth that size with great clarity.

There's another, nontechnical reason why monitors cost more than TVs. Monitors are a high-profit item compared to computers. Next time you see an ad for computers at what looks like unbelievable prices, look for "monitor sold separately" somewhere in the ad.

Choosing the right monitor

Most people don't put enough thought into choosing the right monitor. By the time you consider all the options inside the computer, you're ready to scream. Throwing in one more decision is almost too much.

Choosing a monitor can be confusing. Here are some guidelines to help make some sense of your options:

- ✔ If you decided on a computer that's some color other than basic beige, you may find that the manufacturer makes a matching monitor. If this isn't the monitor you want, don't worry; the color of the case has nothing to do with how well the monitor works.

- ✔ Some manufacturers mount speakers on the monitor. Generally, the speakers are low quality and shouldn't be a major factor in your decision.

- ✔ Some computers, especially some Macs, require a special connector or cable to connect the monitor to the PC. Make certain the monitor is listed as compatible with the type of system you're buying.

- ✔ Be sure to check on the warranty for whatever monitor you select. Don't assume it's the same as the computer's warranty.

- ✔ If you buy a computer manufacturer's private brand monitor, you'll probably have to depend on the computer manufacturer for any repairs. A name-brand monitor may cost a bit more, but you'll have more options if you need repairs.

- ✔ Look for front panel controls that enable you to adjust vertical and horizontal size, vertical and horizontal position, and *pincushion* (the effect where the sides of the display are bowed in or out). Cheap monitors may lack some of these controls, making it difficult to size the display so that it covers the entire screen.

- ✔ If you intend to do a lot of work with photos, try to find a monitor with color adjustments. These adjustments are either manual or controlled by software.

- ✔ Be sure the front of the screen has a non-glare coating. Otherwise, bright lights in your office or sunlight shining in the window may make the display almost unreadable. You can buy glare filters, but they tend to cut down the brightness and clarity. Why not get a monitor that doesn't need an extra cost add-on?

Choosing the right size

Clothing manufacturers have it easy. They can sell clothes that don't fit anyone very well by using the label "one size fits all." No matter what anyone says, the same shirt that fits a 5-foot tall, 100-pound person just won't work for a 6-foot 5-inch, 200-plus-pound person (I know this from firsthand experience).

The same thing applies in choosing the right monitor size. Many years ago, Apple computer introduced its first Macintosh systems with tiny 9-inch, monochrome, built-in monitors. At that time, most PCs had 14-inch color displays, but some people actually liked that tiny Mac screen! Today, hardly anyone settles for even the 14-inch displays, and your choices range all the way up to 36-inch displays intended for viewing from your sofa across the room.

Here are some things to consider in choosing your monitor size:

✔ Monitor size is measured diagonally, but that doesn't mean everyone measures quite the same way. The stated size is the diagonal measurement of the picture tube inside the monitor — not the area you get to see. Be sure to find out the *viewable area* — the amount of the screen you can see when you're using the monitor. This will probably be 1 to 2 inches less than the picture tube's size.

✔ At the very least, upgrade to a 15-inch monitor rather than a 14-inch one. You won't spend much, if anything, for this upgrade.

✔ Nowadays, 17-inch monitors are more affordable and are an excellent choice, especially if you intend to run more than one program at the same time. With the bigger screen, you can have more than one program window visible and still have room to work.

✔ Screen resolution is measured in *pixels,* which are the smallest picture element. Because monitors use the same 4 x 3 screen ratio used in standard TVs, resolution is always expressed in this ratio, too. That's why you see screen resolutions such as 640 x 480, 800 x 600, 1024 x 768, and so on. The first number is the number of pixels across the screen, and the second is the height of the screen in pixels.

✔ It's generally accepted that 14-inch monitors can't display resolutions above 640 x 480 without making everything on the screen too small to read comfortably.

✔ Fifteen-inch monitors do well at 640 x 480 and can usually display 800 x 600 fairly well, too.

✔ Seventeen-inch monitors display 1024 x 768 without making the display too small. An 800 x 600 resolution is acceptable on a 17-inch monitor, but 640 x 480 would be wasted on this size monitor. If your eyes are good, 1280 x 1024 may be acceptable, but you may also be reaching the edge of eyestrain.

✔ Check to see that the monitor can handle the resolution you want to use without flickering. If possible, get a demonstration. At a minimum, the monitor should support a 75 Hz, non-interlaced display at the desired resolution. Despite what some salespeople may try to tell you, higher vertical refresh rates are important, and some relatively inexpensive displays can support 100 to 120 Hz rates quite well.

Make sure your monitor doesn't give you headaches

Just looking at a low-quality monitor can give you a headache. And that's aside from the fact that computers can seem like a pain in the anatomy, too. The wrong monitor can actually make you sick! That's one more problem your small business doesn't need.

Monitors work by sweeping a beam of electrons in a series of lines across the inside of the picture tube. Televisions work the same way, but with an important difference. The TV screen is redrawn in two steps. The first pass paints all the even-numbered lines, and the second pass paints all the odd-numbered lines. This happens fast enough, 30 times per second, that you don't notice that you're seeing only half the lines on each pass. This *interlaced* display is good enough for TV viewing, but if you tried to use this *refresh rate* on your monitor, the resulting flickering would give you a big headache in no time.

It's much harder to paint the lines on the screen at a higher rate. The electronic circuits have to work much faster, and you need much finer control of the position of each dot of light. In fact, even if you ignore any other considerations, just changing from an interlaced to a non-interlaced display requires twice as much speed. A middle-level computer monitor has to handle information at least ten times as fast as a TV to be acceptable.

Think you can ignore the flickering and get along with a cheap monitor? Think again. Studies have shown that the flickering of a poor quality monitor affects people even if they don't notice the flickering. Irritability, headaches, and loss of productivity are some of the minor problems this may cause. In extreme cases, the flickering may trigger neurological and physical symptoms as severe as seizures. In more practical terms, if you're irritable, you'll probably drive away potential customers, making the money you saved on a cheap monitor a pretty poor investment!

Here are some interesting Web sites where you can find out more about some high-quality monitors: `http://www.hitachi.com/Pfinder/5004.html`, `http://www.nec.com/nectech/monitors/welcome.htm`, and `http://www.maginnovision.com/mag_ware/`.

Choosing the Right Printer

Someone once predicted that we'd all be working in "paperless offices" before too long. If you had invested in paper company stocks when that prediction was made, you wouldn't have to be trying to make a living with a small business today!

It's a pretty safe bet that your small business will need to produce a lot of things on paper, such as invoices, letters, and orders. Which printer will fit your needs?

In the early days of PCs, people didn't have many good choices in printers. Some people even adapted clackity old teletype machines so that they'd have a way to print the output from their computers. They were slow, noisy, and had poor quality print, but at least you could get something on paper.

Next came dot-matrix printers. They used a bunch of pins in a print head to form the letters as they moved back and forth across the page. Dot-matrix printers were still noisy, but they were a little faster and the print quality was better, but still poor enough that everyone knew you were using a computer printer rather than a typewriter. If you wanted a higher quality printer, you used a typewriter or bought a daisy-wheel printer. Both were noisy and slow, but at least they produced quality output.

You're lucky that you're in the market for a printer today. Modern PC printers are faster, cheaper, quieter, and have higher quality print than ever before. See, waiting was a good idea!

Although it's still possible to buy one of those old dot-matrix printers, you have better choices now: laser printers or inkjet printers. Read the following sections to find out more about each before you make your decision.

Almost every component you get with your computer will have all the cables and connectors needed to connect that component — everything except your printer, that is. Before you leave the store or hang up from ordering your system over the phone, make sure the order includes a printer cable. For PCs, you want a 10-foot, IEEE parallel printer cable. (You can get a standard printer cable, but an IEEE cable is higher quality and isn't that much more expensive.)

Laser printers

Laser printers sound like something from *Star Wars,* don't they? Actually, laser printers aren't nearly that exciting, but they *do* use a beam of light to create the image that appears on the paper.

Not all laser printers use lasers. Some use LEDs (light emitting diodes) instead. What does this mean to you? Absolutely nothing! Both laser and LED printers work the same and produce similar results. LED printers don't have quite as cool a name, but no one is going to know the difference if you call them all laser printers.

Here's some useful information about laser printers:

> ✔ Laser printers work almost like photocopiers. Instead of a scanner, though, laser printers have a cable that connects them to your PC. Your PC tells the printer what to print, the laser makes toner stick to a drum, the toner is transferred to the paper, and a heater melts the toner so that it sticks to the paper.

✔ Laser printers produce extremely high-quality output. Most lasers can put as many as 600 dots in an inch — a lot more than you can.

✔ Color laser printers cost several thousand dollars, so color generally isn't a practical option in laser printing. If you need color, buy an inkjet printer.

✔ Printing with a laser printer is economical. Besides the cost of the paper, you need to buy toner (which usually comes in cartridges, or if you really like to make messes, in kits so that you can refill your own cartridges). Toner may seem expensive at first, but it lasts for thousands of pages.

✔ If you need fast printing, it's hard to beat a laser printer. It's easy to get a laser printer that pumps out 10 to 12 pages a minute.

✔ Laser printers use a lot of power while they're printing. If you don't have a separate electrical circuit, at least skip using the toaster while you're printing.

✔ Because laser printers have to fuse the ink to the paper, they tend to get hot inside. When clearing paper jams, be extra careful not to burn yourself.

✔ Speaking of paper jams, buying the cheapest possible paper is a sure way to cause jams in your laser printer. Make sure any paper you buy is labeled for use in laser printers, not just in copiers.

The Web has plenty of sites where you can find out more about small business laser printers, such as `http://www.hp.com/peripherals/printers/main.html` and `http://www.lexmark.com/printers/busprinters.html`. Figure 4-1 shows the Hewlett Packard printers Web site.

Inkjet printers

Inkjet printers have been around for a number of years, but they've become much more popular in the last few years as their quality has improved. An inkjet printer may be right for your small business (and they're a lot more fun than laser printers, too).

Inkjet printers work by spraying ink from tiny little nozzles onto the paper. Color inkjet printers have several different colors of ink, and they spray them together to create a broad range of colors. Different brands of inkjet printers use different methods of spraying the ink, but the effect is similar in all cases.

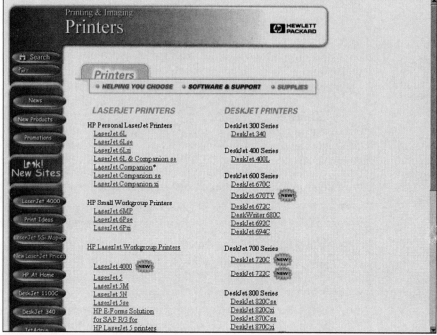

Figure 4-1:
You can get help choosing the right printer for your small business on the Web.

Here's some useful information about inkjet printers:

- Not all inkjet printers can print in color, and some require an extra-cost color kit. Make certain you take this into account when comparing the prices of different inkjet printers.

- Inkjet printers can't keep up with the speed of laser printers. If you need to do a lot of printing, consider buying a laser printer (or maybe both types).

- The rated print speed is usually somewhat overstated, especially for inkjet printers. Not only that, but color printing is usually much slower than black-and-white printing.

- Some inkjet ink isn't waterproof and can smear if it gets wet. Make sure you find out whether the ink will be waterproof when dry, especially if you're going to print mailing labels! The Post Office probably won't refund your postage if your labels smear and your mailings can't be delivered.

- Most inkjet printers need special and expensive paper to print at their highest-rated resolution. Try to get a plain-paper print sample so that you can see what you can expect from regular paper.

- A lot of inkjet printers can handle larger paper sizes than laser printers can. Some inkjet printers can even print on banner paper, so you can make window signs.

✔ Inkjet printers may seem like quite a bargain until you discover how quickly they go through expensive ink cartridges. Full-color pages printed at the highest quality settings can cost a dollar or more per page.

✔ If you need to print a large number of copies of full-color pages, find out how much your local office services store charges for color copies. They may be much cheaper than printing the copies yourself.

Choosing between the speed and low cost per page of a laser printer and the excitement of the splashy color of an inkjet printer may be one of your harder buying decisions. You could just throw the budget out the window and buy both.

Want to know more about inkjet printers? Here are some interesting Web sites you'll want to visit: http://www.epson.com, http://www.hp.com/peripherals/printers/main.html, and http://www.ccsi.canon.com/.

Most PCs are set up to handle only a single printer, so you'll need an extra printer adapter if you want to run two printers from a single PC. A printer adapter is a card that you plug inside your system. Adding an extra printer adapter can cause conflicts with some of the other bits and pieces inside your computer. One inexpensive adapter that can eliminate this type of problem is the TC-020-EP1 from Byte Runner Technologies (http://www.byterunner.com). Their mailing address is 1316 Willow Grove Drive, Knoxville, TN 37932. You can reach them at 800-274-7897 or 423-470-4938.

They Say That Backing Up Is Hard to Do

Backing up your data isn't the same as putting your car in reverse. Backing up on a computer means making a copy of the important information so that disasters such as a hard disk failure or someone pounding your computer into submission won't put you out of business. (You wouldn't get *that* mad at your computer, would you?)

Everyone's heard of Murphy's Law: Whatever can go wrong, will go wrong. You may not know that there's a special Murphy's Law regarding computers and small business: Problems always occur when you can least afford them and always destroy the files that will do maximum damage to your business. If you're way behind and you've just spent the whole weekend typing in the week's orders so that you can send out your billing, guess who'll be knocking at your door?

Many things can corrupt your files and cause your computer to destroy hours or even months of work:

✔ The power may go out just before you click on the Save button or, worse, just after your computer is writing to the disk.

- ✔ Your hard disk may decide it's spun enough times and now is a good time to come screeching to a halt. You'll be forgiven if your screams are louder than the horrible "fingernails on the blackboard" sound a dying disk drive makes to announce that your data is toast.

- ✔ A bug in a program may crash the system and take a bunch of files along with it to the bit bucket. You can probably guess which files will be the first to go.

- ✔ That game your nephew played on your system last week may have had a virus that's been slowly working on your files, just waiting for a chance to thumb its nose at you.

- ✔ You may accidentally press the Del key instead of Enter when you're in a hurry. Of all the things that can happen to your data, operator error is most likely to bite you.

Before you hit the panic button, you'll want to know that there is hope. Just because problems can happen doesn't mean you have to let them take over. You can fight back and protect your small business from Mr. Murphy's mischief. All you need to do is make sure your important data is stored someplace safe so that you can restore your work if a problem does hit.

Backup equipment

The right equipment can take the pain out of backing up your files. Backing up to disks may be okay for someone who's a casual PC user, but your small business needs something better. You need to make backing up easy enough so that you actually make the backups rather than promise yourself you'll do it as soon as you have the time.

The real purpose of backups

No matter what type of equipment you choose for your backups, you can save a lot of hassles, time, and money by putting your brain into gear before you begin. A backup has one purpose: to protect your data in case a problem destroys your files. There's no reason to waste a lot of time backing up things you already have safely stored elsewhere, such as your programs. You can easily reinstall any programs using the original program disks, so you can safely skip the program files when you do a backup. Just make backups of your work, and your backups will go much faster and use far fewer cartridges. Backing up takes a few minutes a day, and you'll be protected. Well, you may still do something dumb now and then, but if you have good backups, you won't have to let anyone know about it.

Tape drives

One of the first backup devices was the *tape drive* — a unit that backs up data onto small cartridges holding several hundred feet of magnetic tape. Although the cartridges look something like an audio cassette, they're made according to much higher standards. Tape drives have several advantages and a number of disadvantages as backup devices:

- ✔ Some tape cartridges hold huge amounts of data, in some cases several gigabytes. You can pop in a tape and back up lots of data without needing to change cartridges.

- ✔ Tape drives work best as unattended backup units. If you're going to be backing up a lot of data, backing up to tape can take a long time, especially if you're adding to an existing backup set.

- ✔ Tape drives generally don't allow random access. If you want to restore a single file from a large tape, the drive will probably have to start reading at the beginning of the tape and continue until your file is found. This can take a *long* time.

- ✔ Different brands and types of tape drives often aren't compatible. If your system goes up in smoke, you may need to find another system with the same type of tape drive to restore your files.

- ✔ No matter what type of backup device you choose, make certain your backup cartridges are stored someplace off-site. The last thing you need is to have both your computer and your backup data destroyed in a single disaster. Take the cartridges home with you, or if your business is in your home, store your backups in a fireproof safe deposit box. Treat your backups like gold — they'll be worth much more than gold if you need to restore your data.

Here are some Web sites where you can find out more about tape drives: `http://www.iomega.com/product/prodguide/ditguide/index.html`, `http://www.hp.com/go/colorado`, and `http://www.tapedisk.com/index.html`.

Zip drives

Zip drives are a new challenger to tape drives as a backup device. Zip drives use a disk cartridge that holds 100MB of data. That may not sound like much compared to some tape cartridges, but Zip drives have a lot to offer:

- ✔ Zip drives offer true random access, so you can access a single file on a Zip drive much faster than on a tape.

- ✔ Zip drives are cheap. You can buy a drive for $100 to $200, depending on the model, and cartridges cost about $15.

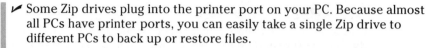
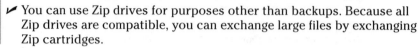

✔ Some Zip drives plug into the printer port on your PC. Because almost all PCs have printer ports, you can easily take a single Zip drive to different PCs to back up or restore files.

✔ You can use Zip drives for purposes other than backups. Because all Zip drives are compatible, you can exchange large files by exchanging Zip cartridges.

Here's the Zip drive Web site: `http://www.iomega.com/product/prodguide/zipguide/index.html`.

Jaz drives

If the 100MB Zip cartridge sounds small, how about jumping up to the 1GB Jaz drive? Jaz drives work just like Zip drives but hold ten times as much on a single cartridge.

Jaz drives have some unique advantages and a few minor disadvantages. Jaz drives aren't primarily intended to be backup devices, but you'll find they do a pretty good job anyway:

✔ Jaz drives cost $300 to $400, depending on whether you want an internal or external unit. If you have an open drive bay (a blank spacer about one and a half inches high and six inches wide) on the front of your PC, get the internal model and save $100.

✔ All Jaz drives use a SCSI connection, so you also need a SCSI adapter if you don't already have one. External Jaz drives have the option of connecting to the printer port using a separate, special adapter.

✔ Jaz drives are quite fast, so you can use one in place of extra hard disks to keep from running out of room on your system. At about $100 for a 1GB cartridge, Jaz drives give you fairly cheap expansion room.

✔ If you install programs on a Jaz cartridge, you have to make certain the cartridge is in place before you can run the program. This means you probably won't be able to run two programs at the same time if they're installed on different cartridges.

✔ No matter which backup device you choose, try to have it installed and tested before you get the system. That way, you won't be the one tearing out your hair trying to make everything work together.

Still haven't been able to decide what type of backup equipment is right for you? Get more information on Jaz drives at `http://www.iomega.com/product/prodguide/jazguide/index.html`.

The rest

People may try to sell you other backup options, but I wouldn't recommend any of them. Some, such as removable-disk hard drives, are a poor bet because they're proprietary and not popular. If your PC were damaged, you'd have your backup cartridge, but where would you go to restore your files? You'd need to find someone with the same removable-disk hard drive.

 A few companies offer backups over the Internet. You pay a set fee and can store your backup data by sending it across the Internet to their computer. Although this gives new meaning to "off-site backups," you'll definitely want to weigh the drawbacks before depending on this method for protecting your valuable business data. The Internet isn't the most secure place for your data, and it takes a long time to send a lot of information over a typical modem connection. Here's one place that offers backups over the Internet: http://backupvault.com/.

No matter how promising some new device sounds, most exotic peripherals don't last long in the PC marketplace. Before you invest in some fancy new backup device that the computer salesperson is trying to push on you, remember that your purpose is to have a backup that will let you restore your data with the least hassle when disaster strikes. Stick with popular, proven technology and let the computer nerds play with the newest toys; that way, your small business will have a better chance of becoming a larger business.

Considering Other Options

Boy, this computer buying is getting expensive. The monitor is extra, and then you need a printer and some way to back up your work. What else could there be?

Don't worry, you don't have to buy everything in the store. But don't stop browsing, because you could miss out on something that makes your computer do a lot more work for you. To get you thinking, this section describes some interesting bits and pieces.

Scanners

Scanners aren't those squawky little radios people use to eavesdrop on police calls and cell phone conversations. Scanners are something you use to get pictures into your computer. If you've ever used a photocopier, you've used a scanner, but in most photocopiers, the scanner is connected to a printer in the same box. Computer scanners send the scanned image into your computer so that you can store the image, print it, or even play around with it. You can scan a photo of your ex-mother-in-law and turn her into the monster you always knew she was inside.

Here's what you need to know about scanners:

✔ Scanners come in many quality levels. Higher *resolution* — more dots per inch (DPI) — costs more. For most small businesses, 300 to 600 DPI is good enough. In most cases, scanners fake higher resolutions electronically, anyway. Their actual, or *optical,* resolution is what counts. The *interpolated* resolution is just the scanner's best guess at what would be there if the optical resolution were higher.

✔ Color scanners don't cost much more than black-and-white scanners. You'll find many more uses for color scanners, so they're worth the extra expense.

✔ Although you can get color scanners at 30- or 36-bit color depth, stick with the much cheaper 24-bit scanners unless you'll be doing professional photo work. You'll save a lot of money, and your scanned images won't hog so much room on your hard disk.

✔ Scanned images can eat up a lot of disk space. Use lower resolutions and fewer colors to cut down on the file size.

✔ If your scanner software gives you options on how to save your scanned images, try saving the same image in several different formats to see which is best. You'll find that some formats result in files that are much smaller than others.

✔ If all you need is the text on a page, use the OCR (Optical Character Recognition) software that probably came with the scanner to convert the image into text. A page of text may be hundreds of times smaller than the same page saved as a graphics image.

✔ Never send out text from OCR software without first checking the accuracy. Modern OCR software is pretty good, but it can still make some embarrassing errors.

✔ If you're going to scan and save a lot of images, you'll need plenty of storage space. Make sure you don't try to cut corners on the size of your hard disk!

If you decide that a scanner sounds good, what kind should you buy? You can find several main types of scanners, but unless you really like Rube Goldberg type machines, ignore those goofy little handheld scanners you drag across the page. A real scanner won't cost any more, and it won't look like a mouse with a thyroid problem, either!

Connecting a scanner

You can connect a scanner to your computer in three ways. A few models use a proprietary adapter board, which may be fine if you have plenty of space in your system, but which may be a major pain if you've already filled up the expansion slots with other goodies. Some scanners connect to the printer port and are supposed to allow your printer to connect to the same port. Although this usually works, it can be quite slow, and you can't use your printer while you're scanning. The third (and best) way to connect a scanner is to use a SCSI adapter. If you already have a SCSI adapter installed, you just plug into the external connector on the adapter. If your system doesn't have a SCSI adapter, you have to use the small SCSI card shipped with the scanner. If your expansion slots are all full, this isn't a good option.

Sheet-fed scanners

Sheet-fed scanners aren't the latest in laundry machines; they're scanners that automatically scan a stack of paper one sheet at a time. You fill up their input bin with the pages you want to scan, and the power feed mechanism pulls each sheet through the scanner in turn.

Most sheet-fed scanners are primarily designed for OCR — turning pages you scan into words in a document. No OCR is perfect, but the latest scanners and OCR software are darn good. If the original you're scanning is clean and aligned correctly in the scanner, scanning a document can be much faster than retyping it. (However, you still need to check the output — especially any numbers.)

Sheet-fed scanners aren't good at scanning bulky items, such as pages in a book or a magazine. Some sheet-fed scanners get around this limitation by having a removable scanning head that you can use as a giant handheld scanner. Scanning this way is awkward, but it does work as a last resort.

Most sheet-fed scanners have a limited resolution range. They're typically optimized for OCR, and this usually means about 300 DPI is good enough.

You'll want a sheet-fed scanner if nearly all your scanning will be loose pages of text you don't want to retype. A sheet-fed scanner is much faster than a flatbed scanner (described next) when you're dealing with multiple pages. Besides, with a sheet-fed scanner, you can drop in a pile of pages and go take a coffee break.

Flatbed scanners

Flatbed scanners look like the top part of a photocopier — mainly because that's what they are, the part of a photocopier that takes a picture of the original. Aside from some internal differences, such as an interface circuit that enables the scanner to send the images to your PC, flatbed scanners are mostly just half of a photocopier.

Flatbed scanners are your best choice for the types of jobs that sheet-fed scanners can't handle well, such as scanning pages in books and magazines. You don't have to rip out the page to scan it with a flatbed scanner — something your local librarian will appreciate!

Although flatbed scanners do a good job with OCR, you do have to scan one page at a time. You'll get tired of this after several dozen pages. You can get a sheet feeder attachment for some flatbed scanners, but it won't be for peanuts! Scanner attachments can cost as much as you paid for the scanner.

Flatbed scanners are far and away your best choice if your scanning is primarily graphics images rather than OCR. One reason for this is that flatbed scanners often have much higher optical resolution settings than sheet-fed scanners. To scan at a higher resolution, the scanner head is simply moved more slowly — something that's hard to do with the paper feed mechanism on a sheet-fed scanner.

You'll need plenty of room for a flatbed scanner. You can figure on the scanner being several inches wider and longer than the largest scan size. And although it may seem logical, using the top of your flatbed scanner as your coffee cup's resting place is a recipe for disaster — remember, Mr. Murphy is always watching!

Transparency scanners

You may want to consider one more type of scanner — a *transparency* scanner. Transparencies (usually 35mm slides or negatives) can't be scanned in normal scanners without an expensive add-on, and even then the results won't be anything to write home about. Transparencies have to be scanned using light transmitted through the transparency, and the scan must be at a very high resolution.

Transparency scanners are expensive compared to sheet-fed or flatbed scanners, but if your small business depends on getting images from 35mm slides or negatives into your computer, there's no other choice. Unfortunately, transparency scanners aren't general-purpose scanners. You can't scan anything but transparencies with this type of scanner.

If you need a transparency scanner, you may be able to recover some of the cost of the scanner by offering a transparency scanning service to other people. A local quick printing business, for example, may be interested in this type of service occasionally, and may also be willing to refer other potential customers your way.

Web sites are a good source of more information on small business scanners. Here are some you'll want to visit: `http://www.epson.com/homeoffice/scanners/`, `http://www.mteklab.com/`, and `http://www.umax.com/graphsite/umaxen/scanners/index.htm`. Figure 4-2 shows one of these sites, the Microtek scanner Web site.

Digital cameras

Scanners aren't the only way to put pictures inside your computer. *Digital cameras* are becoming a popular method of taking pictures, too. Digital cameras replace the film of an ordinary camera with an electronic sensor and then store the image electronically.

Figure 4-2:
Find out about scanners on the Web.

Rather than take a picture, have the film developed, and then scan the image to get it into your PC, the camera stores the image in a form that can be directly transferred from the camera into your computer. You save the film processing time and expense, and no one at the store laughs at your pictures. If you need to get a picture into a computer quickly, it's hard to beat digital cameras.

Digital cameras are perfect for taking pictures you'll be publishing electronically, such as on a Web site. If you have a digital camera and a laptop computer, you can take a picture and instantly transmit it using your modem. If you work in real estate, for example, you can quickly send a potential buyer a picture of a new listing, beating all the other agents to the punch. If you sell products you make or grow, you can instantly show customers exactly what's available at any time.

Reasonably priced digital cameras are no substitute for film-based cameras when you need high resolution, such as for photographic prints. Digital cameras generally have resolutions about equal to what you'll see on a computer monitor. Typically, digital cameras may have resolutions in the 640 x 480 to 1024 x 768 range. This may be fine for images you'll view on a monitor, but it's no match for the virtually unlimited resolution of photographic film. A digital image 640 pixels wide looks pretty grainy blown up to 10 inches wide, for example, because there would be only 64 dots per inch. No one would mistake the image for a high-quality photo.

Digital cameras may seem like a great way to save money — no more film to buy and develop. But this lack of film is also one of the biggest drawbacks of digital cameras. Every picture you take has to be stored in the camera's memory until you transfer it to your computer. Depending on the camera model and the quality of the image, you may be able to store from 10 to 100 images before you run out of room. Some digital cameras have slots for removable memory cards that can hold extra images, but those cards aren't cheap. You probably wouldn't want to use a digital camera to record your trip to Tibet, unless you don't take many pictures along the way.

Here are some interesting digital camera Web sites you should visit: `http://www.kodak.com/daiHome/DCS/DCSGateway.shtml`, `http://www.sony.com/mavica`, and `http://www.casio.com/`.

CD-R drives

Your new computer will almost certainly have a CD-ROM drive. CD-ROMs have become the preferred method of distributing software because they're cheap, they hold as much data as 450 diskettes, and they're difficult for most people to copy. Software on CD-ROMs is much easier to install, too. You throw in that one disc and several hundred megabytes of programs are on your hard disk in a few minutes.

Wouldn't it be great if you could create your own CD-ROM discs? Because virtually all PCs now have CD-ROM drives, you could put out your company's catalog, show pictures of your products, or even record a sales pitch that potential customers could hear on their PC or stereo. Just think of the uses your small business could find for such a universal method of distributing large amounts of information in a small package.

I wouldn't be mentioning all this if it weren't possible with yet another peripheral you can tack onto your PC. (Maybe you should give serious thought to a larger desk so there's room for all these neat bits and pieces.) All you need is a *CD-R* (CD-recordable) drive, the right software, and some recordable discs, and you'll be in business.

Before you buy a CD-R drive, consider these facts:

- ✔ CD-R discs are compatible with *most* CD-ROM drives. A few older CD-ROM drives may have trouble reading CD-R discs, but those drives are ancient in computer terms — three or four years old!

- ✔ CD-R discs hold the same amount of data as normal CD-ROM discs — about 650MB. However, because of the way data is recorded on CD-R discs, you'll probably be able to get only about 625MB on most CD-R discs. Oh well, that's still more than 430 diskettes worth on one disc.

- ✔ Adaptec produces the only software you'll want to consider for recording your own CD-R discs. Easy CD Creator Deluxe is the software for Windows-based PCs, and Toast is the name of the software for Macs. If you buy a CD-R drive, make certain it has one of these programs included with the drive.

- ✔ Although CD-RW sounds a lot like CD-R, the two are not the same. *CD-RW* (CD-rewritable) discs aren't compatible with most CD-ROM drives, and cost about ten times as much as CD-R discs. CD-RW discs can be erased and rewritten, something you can't do with CD-R discs. CD-RW and CD-R drives are not the same, either, so you must choose one or the other.

- ✔ If you want to make copies of your CD-ROM or CD-R discs, it's a good idea to make certain both your CD-R and CD-ROM drives are SCSI rather than IDE. SCSI drives are usually much faster and more reliable. Anything that interrupts a recording can ruin the CD-R disc you're recording. And ruined CD-R discs make pretty but expensive beer coasters.

- ✔ Never touch the shiny side of a CD-R, CD-RW, or CD-ROM disc. Fingerprints, scratches, or dirt on the shiny side of the disc can make it unreadable. Don't let your cat bat your discs around, either!

Here are two Web sites where you can find out more about recordable CDs: `http://www.yamaha.com/imagemaps/comp.map?46,77` and `http://www.adaptec.com/cdrec/`.

Make sure it's legal!

If you add a CD-R drive to your system, be sure you have the right to copy anything you put on a disc. Your small business won't have much chance of survival if you get caught making illegal copies. If you don't want customers stealing from you, don't even think about stealing from someone else!

Protecting your power

Other than your getting so mad you throw your PC out the window, do you know the biggest danger to your computer? It's the electrical outlet you plug the system into behind your desk. Or rather, it's the quality of the power that comes out of the wall and goes into your system.

Your computer is full of sensitive electronic components that operate on small voltages. The power inside a four-cell flashlight is high enough to burn out most of the circuits in your system. Is it any wonder that electrical power that jumps or dips by tens or hundreds of volts can fry the insides of a PC?

The power supply inside a PC does a good job of filtering most of the damaging blips and bleeps that come down the power line. The power supply can't do much if the power fails, however, and sometimes it can't stop the worst of the spikes. That's when your computer does strange things to your data — things you'd rather not know about!

Surge suppressors

You may be surprised at how much junk comes into your electrical wiring every day. When machines such as refrigerators or vacuum cleaners start and stop, they create huge spikes and dips that travel down the power lines like buzz saws. Lightning storms send surges of thousands of volts into the power grid. Even flipping on a fluorescent light momentarily puts all sorts of electrical junk on your wiring.

Surge suppressors are electrical filters that are supposed to stop all this junk from ever reaching your computer. In theory, any spikes that hit the surge suppressor should be nipped in the bud and only nice, clean power should make its way through.

The most common type of surge suppressor uses an electronic component that's designed to fail when large spikes hit. Unfortunately, there's no way you can determine whether your surge suppressor has failed and left your computer unprotected. If you want to be safe, replace surge suppressors at least once a year, or whenever you know there's been an electrical problem such as lightning striking your power line.

Save yourself some grief and unplug your computer if lightning is hitting close to your area — even if you do have a surge suppressor.

Surge suppressors don't give you any protection from power failures. If the power goes off, your computer will go off, too. Any work you haven't saved will be lost, so get in the habit of clicking on the Save button often — especially if your area has a lot of power problems.

Uninterruptible power supplies

Although surge suppressors help protect your computer from garbage on the power line, there's only one way to protect against power outages: Buy an uninterruptible power supply, or UPS. A UPS keeps power flowing to your computer even when no power is coming from the electrical outlet — whether that outage is momentary or lasts for several minutes. It doesn't take much of a power outage to ruin the data in any open files.

A UPS uses batteries that are constantly charged when there's power in the outlet. If the power fails, the UPS switches over to battery power and supplies power to your computer.

Here are some things you'll want to know about buying a UPS:

- ✔ If you have a UPS, you don't need a separate surge suppressor. All UPS devices have surge suppression built in.

- ✔ Don't buy a UPS that's too small. A larger UPS will keep your computer running during longer power outages. A UPS that's too small won't give you enough time to save your work and shut down the PC safely. You need at least a 400 VA UPS for most PCs; a 600 VA unit will give you a greater margin.

- ✔ Don't plug your printer, especially if it's a laser printer, into your UPS. You can always do your printing after the power returns, and plugging the printer into the UPS greatly reduces the UPS run time. Laser printers take much more power than your computer.

- ✔ Most UPS devices can also protect your modem from spikes on the telephone lines. Look for jacks on the UPS where you can plug the telephone line from the wall and to the modem. You'll need an extra phone cable for this.

- ✔ Some UPS devices have a separate circuit that can automatically tell your computer to save any open files and shut down when the power fails. Because a UPS has a limited run time, this can be a lifesaver if the power fails and you can't get to your computer to shut it down yourself.

✔ If the power fails when your computer is on but your monitor is off, you may want to leave the computer alone. Most monitors draw a huge surge of power when they're first turned on, and this can cause the UPS voltage to drop too low to keep your computer running.

Find out more about choosing a UPS at: `http://www.apcc.com/english/prods/`.

In this chapter, you see some of the more useful gadgets you can put into, connect to, or otherwise tie into your new computer system. When you're tempted by the latest and greatest new computer gizmo, try to remember one important thing: You've been getting along without it so far, so there's no need to be the first person to buy the new toy. There's a descriptive term for the newest, relatively untested computer technology: "the bleeding edge." It's called that for a good reason. People who have to be the first to jump in the water often find a lot of broken glass is just under the surface. You may get lucky and avoid the traps and pitfalls, but does your small business have the resources to take that chance? If a new computer peripheral turns out to be as good as its promoters would have you believe, you'll be able to buy the updated and cheaper version in a few months, anyway.

Chapter 5
Modem Mysteries

- -

- -

A modem is your computer's link to the outside world. Whether you want to find information on the Internet, send a fax from your PC, or enable your salespeople to have instant access to important online information, a modem is the connection you'll probably use. This chapter provides the information you need to choose a modem and to make it work.

If you think choosing some of the other options for your new computer is confusing, wait until you try to make a decision about a modem. Hang in there, and you'll soon be cruising the Internet almost as well as a ten year old.

Will You Still Talk to Me in the Morning?

When you want to talk to someone across town, you simply pick up the phone and call. You don't need anything besides your phone and the telephone lines, even if you want to talk to someone on the other side of the planet. Well, maybe looking at the clock first would be a good idea; you won't do too much business at 3:00 a.m. Tokyo time.

Your computer can talk to other computers over wires; that's how computer networks function. But the telephone system was not designed for connecting computers together. People talk using *analog* signals, or sounds, but computers talk to each other using *digital* signals.

The mysteries of modem speeds

Modems are rated using a strange-sounding measurement called *baud* (or baud rate). Baud rates generally translate to around ten times the number of bytes that can be sent in one second if everything is working just right. Most of the time, data transmissions will probably be somewhat slower than the modem's top-rated speed.

For two computers to communicate using the phone lines, they both need a converter that changes the digital signals into analog signals at the sending end and then changes the analog signal back to digital at the receiving end. These converters are called *modems*.

Well, maybe I lied a little. Depending on your location, you may have other alternatives to modems, but not if you want to use a standard telephone line. For now, it's best to assume you'll need a modem.

Choosing the best modem

Because phone lines weren't designed for data transmission, modems often encounter a lot of roadblocks to getting your signal through to the other end without errors. Phone lines can be noisy, the modem's signal can be distorted, or maybe your computer is having a bad day.

Choosing the best modem can be difficult. The modem a friend buys may work well for him or her, but may cause you problems. Your phones may be connected to an old telephone company central office with equipment left over from Alexander Graham Bell's original experiments, or you may be connected through the latest and greatest equipment just installed last week. You can guess which one is more likely — especially if you'll be depending on your modem to handle a lot of your small business needs!

Here are some things to consider when you're looking for a modem:

- ✔ Make certain any modem you're considering is fast enough to do the job. Anything below 28,800 (also called 28.8) baud isn't worth the box it's in.

- ✔ Generally, 33.6 modems don't cost more than 28.8 modems, because they're the same hardware with a few software tweaks. In theory, 33.6 modems should be about 16 percent faster than 28.8 modems, but with typical quality phone lines, you may not see much, if any, difference.

✔ Make certain the modem includes fax capabilities. Virtually all modems do include fax, but it doesn't hurt to check. Sending a fax directly from your PC produces much higher output on the receiving end, regardless of whether you're sending to an actual fax machine or to another PC.

✔ Plan on a separate phone line for your modem. That way you'll be able to talk on one line while your computer is using the other line for a data call. Make certain you don't have call waiting on the computer line because the call waiting beep can disrupt the connection and may corrupt your data.

✔ If you must make a data call on a phone line that has the call waiting feature, disable call waiting until the data call is completed. Your computer may be able to do this automatically, or you can do so before placing the call. Usually, you can disable call waiting by dialing one of the following before a call: *70, 70#, or 1170. Your telephone company can tell you which one works in your area.

✔ Some inexpensive modems, such as the 3Com (formerly U.S. Robotics) Winmodem, make your computer do more of the work normally handled by the modem. These types of modems require a special driver (software supplied by the modem manufacturer) to function. If you ever upgrade to a new operating system version, you may not be able to get an upgraded driver, making your modem useless.

✔ In modems, you often get the service you pay for. For example, 3Com provides a toll-free tech support number for buyers of the more expensive Courier line of modems, but makes Sportster buyers pay for their tech support calls. You may want to check on the tech support options before you choose your modem.

✔ Some computer companies, such as Dell Computers, have in the past made OEM deals with modem manufacturers. Unfortunately for you, this means you need to go through the computer manufacturer, not the modem manufacturer, for any service or upgrades. Make sure you find out who handles the modem warranty and service if your system includes a modem as part of the package.

✔ If you buy a modem from a local store, install and test the modem as soon as possible — definitely before you fill out any warranty cards or throw away the packing material. If the modem turns out to be a dud, you can probably exchange it for a different model that may work better.

If you already have Internet access and want more information on modems, visit some of these Web sites: `http://www.globalvillage.com/`, `http://www.practinet.com/`, or `http://www.3com.com/`.

Internal versus external modems

Modems come in two flavors: *internal* and *external*. That isn't a reference to their personality, but rather to where the modem goes — inside or outside your computer's case. In the early days of personal computers, all modems were external models and modem manufacturers could sell the same modem to lots of different people regardless of their brand of computer.

When IBM introduced the IBM PC, the world of personal computers was changed forever. Not only were you allowed to open the computer's case and look inside, but the design included standardized *expansion slots*. Anyone who bought an IBM PC or a PC clone could use the same expansion cards. Modem manufacturers quickly saw an opportunity. By making modems that plugged into a PC expansion slot, they had a huge potential market. Plus, they could sell internal modems for less than external modems because they wouldn't have to supply a case or a power supply; those were already part of the PC itself. Figure 5-1 shows a typical internal modem. It's not pretty, but engineers would hang it on their walls and call it art.

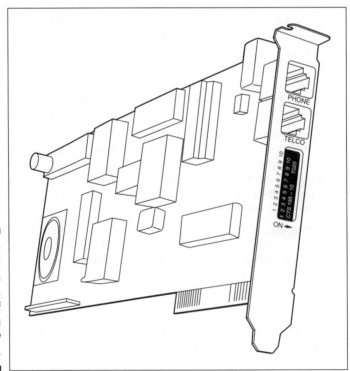

Figure 5-1:
Internal
modems
skip the
fancy stuff
to save you
a few
bucks.

Because internal modems are cheaper but do the same job as external modems, there's no point in discussing the issue: Internal modems are the way to go, right? Well, if a few dollars are all that matters, sure. But you probably have a few more considerations (even if you don't know it yet). Following are some more facts you can throw into the balance to see which type of modem will work best for you:

✔ Virtually all PCs already have two *serial ports* — the type of connection used by most modems. In most cases, both of these ports are unused, and you can easily connect an external modem to one of them.

✔ PCs can generally have up to four serial ports. Internal modems can use any of the four, but you may have to disable one of the existing built-in serial ports to make everything work correctly.

✔ Troubleshooting connection problems is often easier with external modems, especially those with a row of lights to tell you what's happening. Besides, all those blinking lights make it look like your computer is really doing something.

✔ You have to open up the computer's case to install an internal modem. This may not sound like much of a problem, but if you don't know what you're doing inside a computer, do you want to take a chance on screwing something up in the process of installing the modem?

✔ One of the biggest problems with installing new equipment inside your computer is conflicts between the new stuff and the existing equipment. These battles are usually over *interrupts,* or *IRQs.* External modems don't suffer from these problems, but internal ones often do. Interrupt conflicts can bring your computer to its knees, and solving them has been known to make grown computer experts cry.

✔ Internal modems require one of the expansion slots, and these can be in short supply. Before you buy an internal modem, have someone who knows these things open your computer and check to make certain you have the right kind of expansion slot available.

✔ External modems require extra space on your desk, must be connected to your PC and to the phone jack, and usually come with one of those power "bricks" that hog an electrical outlet. Internal modems require only that you plug a telephone cord into the back of your PC.

After your modem is installed and working correctly, both internal and external modems should work just about the same.

If you choose an internal modem, you have to decide how to configure it before you install it. Most internal modems give you the option of selecting the *port,* COM1 through COM4, and the IRQ. Normally you use IRQ 4 for either COM1 or COM3, and IRQ 3 for COM2 or COM4. You may be lucky enough not to have to bother with either one, though, if your operating system supports *Plug and Play*. Windows 95, Windows 98, and Windows NT 5 all support Plug and Play. If you're using one of these operating systems, look to see whether your modem has jumper or switch settings for Plug and Play.

I Want Faster Access

If you end up spending much time online, you'll soon wonder how anyone can be excited about something that moves so slowly. Surfing the Internet using a modem sometimes seems more like crawling than cruising. What you need is a faster way to move data.

Standard modems can't move data fast for one important reason: They have to rely on *POTS* (plain old telephone service), your phone lines. Years ago, long before computer modems existed, most people shared a phone line with a number of their neighbors in a "party line" arrangement. Eventually, though, people decided they didn't want their neighbors eavesdropping on their conversations. The telephone companies were happy to help out because private lines brought in more revenue.

What the phone company forgot to tell people about private lines was that they were the same old lines everyone had been sharing, with a bit more modern technology to keep people from hearing other people's conversations. That is, even with a private line, you're still sharing the circuits with lots of other people. This is accomplished through a number of fancy technological tricks, and it's these same tricks that make phone lines such a poor choice for sending computer data.

Higher speed alternatives

People can get creative when you tell them they can't do something. Computer engineers know you can't send data much faster over standard phone lines, so naturally they try to prove that it's not true. So far, they've been successful — typical PC modems today are more than 300 times faster than the first modems. Still, there are limits, and engineers have again been creative in some of their proposed solutions.

ISDN adapters

ISDN (Integrated Services Digital Network) adapters were one of the first creative solutions to the problem of the speed limitations of phone lines. Unfortunately, the engineers named the solution.

ISDN service uses special phone lines designed for data. It provides either 64K or 128K connections, which is roughly two or four times the speed of a standard modem connection. ISDN adapters aren't modems, but they do the same thing as far as you're concerned, and they're not that much more expensive than a good modem.

Even though you can't plug a standard telephone into an ISDN line, many ISDN adapters include a phone jack so that you can make regular voice calls. You'll want to look for this feature if you decide to go ISDN.

One feature of ISDN lines is designed to make your local phone company happy: In addition to the cost of having an ISDN line, you're also billed by the minute while you're using the line, just like making a long distance call. This can become very expensive, even if the per-minute charge is only a few cents. Make sure you find out how much ISDN is really going to cost before you sign up!

ISDN lines aren't available in all areas because there's a limit to the line distance between the phone company office and your location. Usually, this limit is around 10,000 feet, but it can be hard to determine yourself whether you're within the distance limits. Your telephone company can have an engineer check to see whether ISDN is practical for your location.

Many phone companies limit ISDN lines to business locations. If you're trying to get your small business started by running it from your home, the phone company may not be willing to provide ISDN service. Or it may decide that it can provide the service but that your residential phone line should be reclassified as a business line.

ISDN service may be a good solution if your small business needs fast, reliable data connections, but be aware of the high costs of this type of service. Make sure you get all the facts: the cost of the adapter, the installation charge, the monthly fee, and the usage charges, to see whether ISDN is worthwhile.

If you're really aching for faster Internet access, check out these Web sites to find more information on ISDN: http://www.globalvision.net/ isdninfo.html, http://www.data.com/business_case/ isdn_costs.html, and http://www.dcb.com/isdncode.htm.

The vapor of ADSL

ISDN isn't all that fast compared to modem connections. If you need to send a lot of data, you want something that flies! How does ten times faster (or more) sound? That's the promise of yet another new service the engineers were able to name — *ADSL* (Asymmetrical Digital Subscriber Lines). ADSL is sometimes shortened to DSL, dropping the asymmetrical moniker.

ADSL is supposed to solve the problem of the slow speed of computer data connections by providing a completely digital circuit all the way between two computer systems. The idea is simple: Rather than rely on converting the digital signals in your computer to sounds that can be sent across the phone lines, the digital line allows your computer to transfer data the same way it does on a network.

If ADSL is ever widely available, computer-to-computer communications could be quite different than they are today. You'd be able to send a potential customer a full-color, sound movie clip showing your latest product in action, and you wouldn't spend several minutes getting it there!

Unfortunately, if you call your local phone company to ask about ADSL service, you may find that it's a lot like talking to a blank wall. Actually, talking to a blank wall might be less frustrating, because at least you won't have someone arguing that there is no such thing as ADSL.

Your local phone company may offer ADSL or some variation of ADSL eventually (after it figures out how to get even more money from you by offering this service). For now, you have to be satisfied with something a whole lot slower.

Want to know a lot more about ADSL than your phone company? Then check out this Web site: `http://www.westell.com/westell/adsl.html`.

56K realities

Okay, so ISDN is expensive, and ADSL is still a pipe dream. What about those 56K modems everyone is talking about? Don't they let you blaze across the Internet, as the TV ads claim?

56K modems are yet another innovative solution that computer engineers came up with to solve the problem of transmitting data quickly over phone lines. Unlike ISDN and ADSL, though, 56K modems are designed to work with "normal" phone lines — at least that's what the modem manufacturers would like you to think.

On the surface, you'd expect 56K modems to be about twice as fast as 28.8K and even 33.6K modems, wouldn't you? It seems logical, but that's because you don't know about one of the most important rules in computers. I call it "Underdahl's Rule," and it goes like this:

> What they don't tell you is always more important than what they do tell you.

Modem manufacturers don't want to tell you a number of things about 56K modems:

✔ There are two different types of 56K modems, and they aren't compatible. One is called K56flex, and the other is called X2. Eventually, there will be a single standard and most of the manufacturers have promised to support it. Until then, buying a 56K modem is a gamble because you can't be certain you'll be able to upgrade.

✔ 56K modems are really only 28.8 or 33.6 modems for data you're sending. In theory, data you receive may come in at up to 56K, but the top speed is currently limited to 53K by some government regulations.

✔ You never see any extra speed if you connect to another 56K modem. The higher-speed downloads are possible only if you connect to an online service that has the correct type of server modems. If you call in to your office PC from your laptop, for example, you won't gain any extra speed by using 56K modems.

✔ You get higher speed connections only if your phone line meets certain special technical conditions and you manage to get a noise-free connection. How likely is it that your phone line will be good enough? It's estimated that at least 40 percent of the phone lines in the United States don't meet the technical conditions necessary for a 56K connection.

✔ If you can access the Internet, go to `http://x2.usr.com/connectnow/linetest.html` to find out how you can determine whether your phone line meets the specifications for 56K connections.

Although you may not get any extra benefit from buying a 56K modem rather than a 33.6 modem, you probably won't pay much more, either. If you do have to pay extra for a 56K modem, be sure to see whether the manufacturer will take the modem back if it turns out that 56K doesn't work for you. Many of the better-known modem manufacturers do have this policy.

Here are a couple of Web sites where you can find out more about 56K modems: `http://x2.usr.com/` and `http://www.hayes.com/`.

Why Can't We All Just Get Along?

I bet more bald people work in the tech support departments of modem manufacturers than anywhere else in the computer industry. It's not that modem companies hire a bunch of bald people; it's just that pulling your hair out is the inevitable result of trying to solve the mysteries of why computers so often stop working correctly after you install a modem.

Why should modems be such a problem? After all, they've been around a long time, and millions are in use. Well, do you remember that Murphy guy and his law? He probably has a lot to do with it.

Correcting and avoiding common modem problems

Avoiding problems in the first place is better than trying to correct them after you have them. After all, if it ain't broke, you don't *have to* fix it!

Here are some common modem problems and what you can do to avoid or correct them:

- Conflicts with the existing bits and pieces in your computer are easiest to solve by simply avoiding them — buy an external modem rather than an internal one. External modems avoid most of those conflicts by using one of the existing communications ports.

- You say your external modem won't work? Did you remember to plug it into your power strip and make sure it's turned on? Is your face red?

- Erratic operation of external modems is usually caused by loose cable connections. You did tighten those screws when you plugged in the cables, didn't you? If not, go directly to jail, do not pass Go, and do not collect $200.

- If your modem won't dial, try plugging a phone into the jack labeled "Phone" on your modem and see if you can make a call. If you can't, try plugging the phone into the wall jack that the modem is plugged into and see whether that helps. You may have a bad phone cord between the wall and your modem.

- Make sure the telephone cord from the wall is plugged into the telco (or wall or line) jack on your modem, not the phone jack. Most modems have circuits that cut off the phone jack when the modem tries to make a connection. Until the modem tries to make a connection, it seems as if the two jacks are identical, and you'll go crazy trying to figure out why the modem won't work even though plugging in a phone seems to indicate that everything is okay.

- If your office has a digital phone system, or if you use a laptop when you're traveling, don't ever plug a modem into a phone jack unless you're 100 percent certain the jack is set up for analog phone equipment. Digital phone systems are common in places such as large hotels, and plugging your analog modem into a digital phone jack will create some interesting and expensive fireworks inside your PC.

Port and IRQ conflicts

Installing something in one of the expansion slots inside your PC can be real fun — just like a tax audit is a lot of fun! That's why internal modems are so much more likely than external modems to cause you problems. Internal modems have to be installed in one of the expansion slots, and both port and IRQ conflicts are a possibility.

The problem is simple. When you install an internal modem, the modem must be configured as a *communications port* — a hardware device that connects your computer to the outside world. (Printers are usually connected to your system using another type of port — a parallel port.) Communications ports, or COM ports as they're commonly called, need to be able to tell your computer when they're ready to provide some data. To do so, they interrupt your computer using a special electrical signal called, appropriately, an interrupt.

Your computer is usually busy, and needs a little help to determine just who is trying to get its attention. Imagine the confusion that would occur in the shopping mall if a child yelled "Mom, come to the information booth" over the public address system and no one knew for certain whose child was speaking. There'd be a stampede as every mother in the mall descended on the information booth. Now imagine the difference if someone announced, "Mrs. Horatio Hornblower Jones, please come to the information booth."

In your computer, interrupts are sent on special lines that tell your computer exactly who's trying to get the system's attention. These lines are called IRQs, and they serve the same function as announcing a specific name over the PA system.

A PC has 15 IRQs, but a lot of them are used by the system, and others are grabbed by some of the installed components. In almost every case, anything that uses an IRQ is stingy and won't share its IRQ with anyone else. That's why IRQ conflicts are such a problem: IRQs are scarce and usually can't be shared.

COM ports are a special case. COM ports can usually share IRQs with each other, but only one COM port that's sharing can be active at one time. For example, if you install an internal modem set up as COM3, and your mouse is connected to COM1, you have a problem because COM1 and COM3 normally share IRQ 4. So why not just put the modem on another IRQ, say IRQ 5? Well, that would be fine except IRQ 5 is probably being used by your sound card. To make matters worse, IRQs 0, 1, 2, 8, and 13 aren't even available, and modems generally can't use anything above IRQ 7. But IRQ 7 is used for the printer port, and IRQ 6 is used by the diskette controller. Let's see now, that leaves IRQ 3. IRQ 3 is used by COM2 and COM4, so if you're using either one of those for anything, you don't have a lot of choices. You'll probably have to arrange things so that your modem uses a port and IRQ that doesn't conflict with something else on a COM port. In case you weren't listening earlier, using an external modem is the easiest way to solve this problem.

Sudden disconnects

Even after you get your modem installed, tested, and working correctly, you'll probably be faced with another frustrating modem problem — suddenly being disconnected for no apparent reason. This is the worst type of problem you'll have because it will strike when you're feeling confident that all the problems have been solved, and because no one will give you any help solving the new problem. Oh sure, people will say they'll look into it, but in reality, you're going to be on your own solving this one. You can try calling your Internet Service Provider (ISP), but don't expect too much.

A number of things can cause sudden disconnects. It's up to you to eliminate as many of them as possible:

✔ Never use a modem on a phone line that has call waiting. If you have absolutely no choice, make certain you know the code to dial to disable call waiting, and be sure to do so at the beginning of each modem call — but remember, this won't work for calls to your modem. Call waiting uses a tone that your modem interprets as the line going dead, and this can easily cause sudden disconnects.

✔ Don't put any extension phones on the same line as your modem. Otherwise, people can pick up a phone and start pushing buttons while you're in the middle of transferring several megabytes of important data.

✔ Check the phone line for noise by calling someone and asking the person to put you on hold for a few minutes (just make sure they don't have music playing when you're on hold). Listen for crackling, popping, hum, or static. If the line isn't clean, your modem won't be happy. Be sure to try this several times during the day. If you do hear a lot of noise, take a phone to the interconnect box where the phone lines come into your building and try again. If you don't hear the noise at the interconnect box but you do inside your office, the problem is in your internal phone lines.

✔ If you have a lot of noise even at the telephone interconnect box, call the phone company repair service and complain. Remember that the squeaky wheel gets the grease, and the phone company won't make repairs unless you point out the problem.

✔ Try a different modem. Although you've already been through all the setup and configuration, you won't get too far in the next step of calling your ISP for help until you've tried this.

✔ After you eliminate any problems at your end, call your ISP and ask for help — remember, *you're* the customer here and have a right to demand the service you're paying for!

✔ If your ISP tells you that no one else is having this problem, try out a different service provider. Before people are allowed to work in the tech support department at most ISPs, they have to learn how to say "no one else is having this problem" in their sleep. It's a big lie and they know it, but it's one they love because some people actually believe it.

Some random disconnect problems are inevitable simply because standard phone lines were designed to carry voices, not computer data. If you can immediately repeat your call and not experience the same problems, consider yourself lucky — all you've lost is a little time. On the other hand, if trying to use your modem brings you nothing but frustration, keep telling yourself how much you're learning. It won't help the problem, but it may help you laugh a little.

The Software Wars

Computers aren't really smart. Without software, about all a computer can do is sit there and use electricity. Software tells your PC how to do everything. Telling your system how to communicate with other computers using a modem is one of the things software does.

Because lots of different people create software, you'll find lots of different approaches to doing the same thing. You probably have your own shortcuts to your neighborhood, and some of those shortcuts probably don't follow the same paths other people take. Programmers are like that, too. Just because everyone else thinks method A is the best way to program a task doesn't mean an individual programmer can't come up with a different path — a shortcut — to the same goal.

Different programming approaches produce different programs. One programmer may want to produce the smallest, fastest program, and another may want to produce something that's so easy to use it does everything for you. There's nothing wrong with either person's goals, but sometimes the results conflict.

16-bit versus 32-bit software

When you move from one house or apartment to another, you probably don't use a sports car to haul all your stuff. With a trailer, you can haul more in fewer trips and therefore less time. If you rent a truck, you can haul more in each load and complete the job even more quickly.

The same principle is true in computers, too. The more information a computer can handle at one time, the faster it can accomplish a job. The amount of information a computer can move in one chunk is measured in *bits*. The more bits moved in a certain amount of time, the faster the computer performs, and the more complicated are the tasks it can perform.

The earliest personal computers were 8-bit systems. They were slow and limited, but they did give people a place to start. Later came the 16-bit systems, 32-bit systems, and even 64-bit systems.

Computer hardware and software are often a funny marriage — neither one can do anything without the other, but they're not always at quite the same level. Until Windows 95, for example, most software was 16-bit software even though a large percentage of computers were really 32-bit systems. Windows 95 was designed to run both 16-bit and 32-bit software, and Windows 98 continues that capability. (Windows NT has always been geared more towards 32-bit applications, but it, too, can run most 16-bit software.)

Most of the time, you can run both 16-bit and 32-bit software at the same time and not notice any difference. Anything designed specifically for Windows 95 or later will be 32-bit, but software intended to run on older PCs that use Windows 3.x is usually 16-bit. You won't see a colorful banner on the side of the box that says "this is 16-bit software," but if the system requirements say the software needs Windows 3.x or later, it's a good guess that's the case.

Because most 16-bit and 32-bit software can run at the same time, why should you care? Because of that one word, *most.* When it comes to communications software — anything that uses your modem — a huge divide exists between the 16-bit camp and the 32-bit camp. The 32-bit communications software simply takes over and 16-bit communications software is left for dead. When 32-bit communications software is running, 16-bit communications software can't even tell that a modem is connected to your PC.

Here are some more things you need to know about 16-bit and 32-bit communications software:

✔ Programs such as Microsoft Exchange, Windows Messaging, Microsoft Outlook, Microsoft Outlook Express, Microsoft Personal Fax, and Dial-Up Networking Monitor are all 32-bit applications. When any of these is running, you won't be able to use 16-bit software.

✔ Programs such as FedEx Ship and UPS Online Tracking are 16-bit applications. As Figure 5-2 shows, if a 32-bit communications application is running, these types of programs will try to dial out, but won't get any response from the modem.

Figure 5-2:
16-bit and
32-bit
communi-
cations
programs
don't like
each other.

✔ If you're running Microsoft Personal Fax on Windows NT, you have to use the Services icon in the Control Panel to shut down the Fax service before 16-bit programs can use the modem.

✔ To close Microsoft Exchange, Windows Messaging, Microsoft Outlook, or Microsoft Outlook Express so that you can use a 16-bit communications program, be sure to select Exit and Log Off, not just Exit, from the File menu.

✔ In extreme cases, you may need to restart your computer between using 32-bit and 16-bit communications software. Not all software totally removes itself from memory when the program ends, and restarting the system may be the only way to solve the problem.

It worked before

Installing new software is always a gamble, but installing new communications software is an even bigger gamble. Your computer and modem may have worked out an arrangement in which neither one wanted to be the troublemaker and everything was going along just fine. You were happy, too.

Then someone gave you some new software so that you could access their system and track your packages, check on a supplier's stock, or send in orders. That sounded better than picking up the phone and doing it the old-fashioned way; you figured, "What could it hurt?"

If you're really lucky, your new software works fine and everything that used to work still does, too. If that's true, Mr. Murphy must be sleeping, because life isn't always that simple.

Installing new software, especially communications software, can change various settings in your computer and your modem. Here are some things you can try to prevent the problems these changes can cause:

- ✔ Although it may seem like a royal pain, be sure to write down any settings (such as phone numbers, passwords, and user names) you enter before you install new communications software. This is especially true if you had to get troubleshooting help to get everything working — you don't want to go through the whole "no one else has that problem" cycle again, do you?

- ✔ If something that was working suddenly doesn't, try restarting your computer. It's amazing how many problems are solved this way. If simply restarting your computer doesn't do it, shut everything down for a few minutes and then turn the power back on. (If you have an external modem, be sure to include its power in the shut down.) This may reset things back to normal.

- ✔ Try reinstalling the software that quit working. An important file may have been changed or removed when the new software was installed, and reinstalling the original software may correct the problem.

- ✔ If you're using Windows 98, try the System File Checker utility. If any important files were replaced with older copies, this may solve the problem.

- ✔ When you reach the end of your rope, decide which communications program is most important to you and remove the other one. You'll probably still have to reinstall the software you really want, but you'll have learned an important lesson — sometimes it's best to leave well enough alone!

Beam Me Up

These days, most people think of the Internet when they hear about communicating through computers. It's difficult for most people to believe that except for a few government users and college students, almost no one used the Internet much before about 1994.

The Internet has been around for more than 25 years, but in the early days it was intended as a way for U.S. government agencies to be able to communicate in the event of a nuclear attack. The idea was to create an interconnection between lots of different computers, without a single, central control point that could be knocked out. Messages had hundreds of possible paths from one computer to another, so even if some of the networks were destroyed, communications could still take place on the remaining paths. Later, your tax dollars paid for expanding the network so that college students could do research. But because no one really owned the Internet, no one could stop the inevitable: access for the people who were paying the bills to build and support the Internet (you, the taxpayer).

Today, the Internet has become a giant world where your small business can find customers, buy products, and discover information that can change the way you do business.

Connecting to the Internet

You can connect to the Internet in several ways, but unless you want to spend a lot of money, you'll probably use an Internet Service Provider, or ISP. An *ISP* is a company that provides connections to the Internet, mail servers that enable you to send and receive electronic mail, and news servers browse newsgroups on the Internet. You'll find that there are hundreds of ISP choices, from small local operations to large companies serving millions of users.

You need a modem and a phone line, of course. If you're using Windows 95, Windows 98, or Windows NT, you also need to install a component known as *Dial-Up Networking*. That's just a part of Windows that uses your modem to dial in and connect to the Internet.

Here are just a few of your choices in large ISPs: http://www.aol.com/, http://www.spry.com/, http://www.att.net/, and http://www.us.uu.net/html/products_and_services.html.

Installing Dial-Up Networking

If no one has already set up Dial-Up Networking, take a few minutes now to complete this important step. Then you'll be able to continue connecting to the Internet. Here's how to install Dial-Up Networking on Windows 95. (The steps are similar for other versions of Windows.) You can tell whether Dial-Up Networking is installed by opening the My Computer folder — if you don't see the Dial-Up Networking icon, you need to install it.

1. **Click on the Start button.**

   The Start Menu appears so that you can choose commands by clicking on them with your mouse.

2. **Choose Settings⇨Control Panel.**

   The Control Panel is the nerve center of Windows. All those little icons represent different things you can change, but if you're not sure what they do, leave them alone!

3. **Double-click on the Add/Remove Programs icon.**

   The Add/Remove Programs dialog box appears. This dialog box is handy — you can install or remove programs, and you can add some extras that Windows forgot to install.

4. **Click on the Windows Setup tab.**

   This part of the dialog box enables you to choose the Windows bits and pieces. If you're really bored, you can install the games, but it's up to you to find them!

5. **Select Communications⇨Details.**

   The Communications dialog box appears, as shown in Figure 5-3.

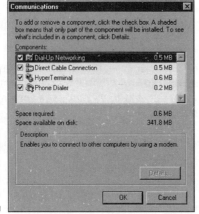

Figure 5-3:
Make sure
Dial-Up
Networking
is installed
before you
connect to
the Internet.

6. **Make certain Dial-Up Networking is checked. If it's not, select it to add a check mark.**

   The remaining three components on the list aren't important right now, but because they don't require much disk space, you can select them if you like.

7. **Click on OK to return to the Add/Remove Programs Properties dialog box.**

8. **If you chose to add Dial-Up Networking or any other new components in Step 6, click on Apply.**

9. **If prompted to insert your Windows 95 CD-ROM to continue, do so.**

10. **Click on OK to close the dialog box.**

11. **If Dial-Up Networking was not already installed, you may see a message telling you that you need to restart your PC.**

Now it's time to continue with the setup by following the instructions in the next section.

Connecting through your ISP

If you don't have an account with an ISP, you need to set up an account before you can continue. If you haven't already chosen an ISP, look in the Yellow Pages under *Internet* — you'll find plenty of choices in most areas.

If your business involves a lot of travel, you may want to consider one of the large national ISPs such as Sprint, SpryNet, AT&T, AOL, or CompuServe. That way, you'll be able to connect no matter where business takes you.

You need a bunch of information from your ISP before you can connect. When you sign up, you should receive a printed list that includes several important pieces of information about logging on to the service. Make sure you keep this information in a safe place so you'll have it when you need it. Here's most of what you'll see on that list:

✔ **Dial-in phone number**. This is the number your computer must call. Make sure you get the number you can call for help, too.

✔ **Your user name.** Be sure to find out whether this is case sensitive — which means you have to use the right combination of uppercase and lowercase characters. You need to use this name to log on to your ISP.

✔ **Your password.** Make sure you know whether this is case sensitive, too. Don't let anyone else know your password. Otherwise, he or she will be able to log on pretending to be you, and can then read your messages and send messages from your account.

✔ **Your e-mail address.** This is how other people address messages they want to send your way. Generally, e-mail addresses look something like `brian@idgbooks.com`.

✔ **IP address.** This address is either a series of four numbers separated by periods, as in 255.12.27.67, or, if you're lucky, the instruction to obtain an IP address automatically from the server.

Considering the direct connect option

After you use the Internet for a while, you'll probably start to think that the whole thing moves slowly. Web pages might take a long time to load, files can take a long time to send or receive, and you may start wondering whether the Internet really is the place for your small business to be trying to do business.

You can get better performance, but it won't be free — or even cheap. Still, if you decide the Internet is important enough to your business to warrant a faster connection, you do have some options:

✔ The keyword in better Internet performance is *bandwidth* — essentially the amount of data you can send or receive over your connection in a given amount of time. The higher the bandwidth, the faster the information will move.

✔ The first step up from a standard modem connection is an ISDN connection.

✔ The next step is a 56K *leased line* — a type of connection that's also called a

point-to-point line. Leased lines are always connected, they aren't switched, and this lowest-level leased line is 30 to 40 percent faster than an ISDN line.

✔ *Fractional T1* lines are the next fastest leased line. These transfer data at 512K, or around nine times faster than a 56K line.

✔ *Full T1* lines are three times the speed of fractional T1 lines — 1.5Mbps.

Leased lines are a lot more expensive than dial-up lines. You pay not only your ISP, but also your local phone company for your leased lines. You'd better have a good reason for needing a leased line — you can probably pay for several dial-up connections for the price of even the cheapest leased line! A leased line *might* make sense if your small business has a Web site that provides a lot of real-time data, or if you have several people who need to access your internal network by going through the Internet.

✔ **Default gateway and DNS addresses.** These are similar to the IP address, and you may not need to enter them if your ISP uses automatic addresses.

✔ **Mail server.** There may be two names: the *SMTP outgoing host* and the *POP* (or *POP3*) *server host*. The outgoing mail host sends messages from you, and the incoming receives messages for you.

✔ **Usenet News Server.** This enables you to view newsgroups.

Get all the information in writing, and make certain it's clear. If you enter any one of the pieces of information incorrectly, you probably won't be able to connect to the Internet, and you'll encounter nothing but frustration trying to correct the situation! It's a lot easier to enter the correct information the first time than to try and figure out what is causing problems later.

After you have all the connection information from your ISP, the rest is easy. All current versions of Windows include an Internet Connection Wizard to help you enter all the necessary information for a successful connection. It will take you only a few more minutes to get connected to the Internet.

Here's how the Windows 95 Internet Connection Wizard works:

1. Double-click on The Internet icon on your desktop.

The Internet Connection Wizard appears, as shown in Figure 5-4.

Figure 5-4:
The Internet
Connection
Wizard
makes
connecting
to the
Internet
easy.

2. Click on Next to continue.

Throughout this setup, you'll be clicking Next each time you complete a dialog box.

3. Click on the Automatic option, and then click on Next.

4. In this dialog box and upcoming ones, you need to enter information from the list you received from your ISP. After you fill in all the information in one dialog box, click on Next to display the next screen.

5. If Windows 95 prompts you to insert your Windows 95 CD-ROM at some point, do so.

6. If you eventually see a check box labeled "Bring up terminal window after dialing," make sure it doesn't have a check mark, unless your ISP has told you that you must log on to the network manually.

Most ISPs support automatic logging on, so you don't have to use the terminal window to enter your user name and password.

7. The final step in setting up your connection is to restart your PC. Remove any disks in drive A and click on Yes.

Fortunately, you probably won't have to go through the setup process again. Make certain, though, that you keep all the information about your connection in case you need to redo any settings in the future.

After your system has restarted, you're ready to give the Internet a try. First, though, mark this page so you'll remember where you were when you come back in a few hours. And remember, too, that you have a small business to run.

Double-click on the Internet icon or the Netscape icon on your desktop to start exploring the Internet.

Make sure you know whether you pay a *flat rate* or a *metered rate* for your Internet connection. With a flat rate, it doesn't matter how much time you spend online, but a metered connection is more like a long distance phone call — you pay for every minute you're connected, whether you're doing anything productive or not.

If you use the Internet only for e-mail, you may be able to save money with a metered connection.

Chapter 6

New Hardware Already?

*Y*ou didn't think that computer would last forever, did you? Even your favorite PC will become obsolete before you know it, but you can breathe new life into tired old systems and extend their useful life by performing a few well-planned upgrades. Whether you upgrade your computer yourself or hire someone else to do it, you can save a lot of time and money by knowing what needs to be accomplished.

I Know Nothing

Computers eat memory for breakfast, lunch, and dinner. There can't be any other explanation for why they're always running out of memory, can there?

Memory is just about the most important component in a PC, and yet most people don't give memory much thought when they buy a computer. Computer manufacturers must know how much memory you'll need, so that's what they put in the systems, right? Actually, no. They usually don't put in nearly enough.

The marketing of computers is a highly competitive business. The extra $100 or so it costs to put in the amount of memory you really need in a new system would have to be recovered by raising the price. The last time you priced computers, did you mentally throw in an extra $100 for systems with extra memory?

You may have better luck getting the amount of memory you really need by buying your PC from one of the computer manufacturers that sells direct to the end user. Good luck trying to get anything changed in an off-the-shelf, boxed system at your local discount outlet!

Figuring out how much memory you need

How do you figure out how much memory you really need? Do you want the short answer or the long one?

The short answer is simple: You probably need about twice as much as what came in your system. That's assuming you bought your computer within the past year or so, and didn't try to be as cheap as possible cutting every corner you could find.

The long answer isn't a whole lot longer: 32MB is a good starting point unless your computer uses Windows NT, in which case you should start with 64MB. If you'll be doing a lot of heavy graphics work, using Adobe Photoshop for example, double those numbers.

Your computer needs a lot of memory for one reason: The more memory it has, the more work it can do at one time. If doubling the memory that originally came in your system saves you half an hour a day because your computer works faster, it won't take long for your small business to recover that extra $100 to $200 investment.

Installing extra memory

Okay, so you've decided that extra memory is probably a good idea. How do you go about installing the extra memory you need to make your computer work the way it should? Is installing memory something a mere mortal can do, or do you have to call in a computer nerd (or worse, a ten year old)?

Yes, you do have to open it up

Yes, you can install memory yourself, but because the memory is installed inside your computer, you do have to open the case.

Opening your computer and diving right in can be a recipe for disaster if you don't use some common sense. You wouldn't go into a fancy gift shop blindfolded and start waving your arms wildly about, and you shouldn't start blindly messing around inside your PC, either. Here are some things to watch out for when you open your computer's case:

✔ Be sure you shut down the system properly before you begin. When your screen says it's okay to turn off the power, do so and then unplug the power cord. After the power cord is unplugged, you eliminate any small chance of contacting any electrical current that can hurt *you.*

✔ Before you touch any components inside your PC, always touch one of the large metal pieces inside the case. That way, you eliminate almost any chance of creating a static electricity charge that can harm the computer's components. Always remember that the electronic components inside the computer are real wimps, and even a small shock can kill them.

✔ Never place your computer where it can fall or be knocked over. Sudden jolts are murder to hard disks and can cause cables to come loose, too.

✔ Every cable and wire inside the system is important, and all of them need to be plugged in correctly for the computer to work properly. But guess what? None of them are labeled, and you'll have a devil of a time figuring out where they go if you unplug them. You can take a Polaroid picture of the inside of the case after the cover is off, but you may find it more practical to make some labels to stick on any cables that may come loose. You can use address labels, and mark where the cable goes on the label. Another idea is to make a list of all cable and wire connections in the system.

✔ If you don't *have* to touch something, don't! You aren't some kid in a store trying to drive your parents nuts, and the less you disturb inside your computer, the less likely you'll cause a problem.

✔ Don't even think about running your computer with the cover off. Dust, dirt, and cats can't resist getting inside an open computer case, and you may cause interference with any radios or TVs in the area, too.

Understanding memory types

If you're going to put more memory into your computer, you have to get the right type of memory. You can't use any old memory in there — your computer may get mad and who knows what it might do then?

You may think memory is memory, but you'd be surprised how many ways the computer engineers can confuse you. Maybe you shouldn't have made fun of that nerdy classmate in high school after all!

Differences in memory types are both physical and electronic. The safest bet is to get an exact match for what's already in your PC, and the easiest way to do that is to have the computer manufacturer install it when building the system. Because you probably didn't do that, you're stuck with trying to figure out what you have and what you need. Here's some information to help you:

TIP

✔ Start by getting out the owner's manual — you know, the book that came with your system that's still wrapped in plastic? With any luck, you'll find something like "adding memory" in the table of contents. Of course, the manual will probably be a poor translation and won't make any sense, but at least you'll be able to say you tried.

✔ Next, try calling the computer manufacturer's tech support line. If you ordered your computer directly from the manufacturer, it probably has a record of what's in your system, and will probably know just what you need. If this works, you won't have to worry about what type of memory your computer uses: Order it from the manufacturer and consider yourself lucky.

✔ Memory comes in several physical sizes. The most common size is a 72-pin SIMM (single inline memory module). Figure 6-1 shows the approximate appearance of a typical SIMM.

✔ Older computers sometimes use 30-pin SIMMs, but you aren't likely to find them in any modern PCs. You can count the little metal fingers that plug into the memory socket if you're not sure what you have, but it's easier to just get out a ruler. The 72-pin SIMMs are about 4¹/₄ inches long, and 30-pin SIMMs are about 3¹/₂ inches.

Figure 6-1:
SIMMs are
several
inches long
and about
an inch
high.

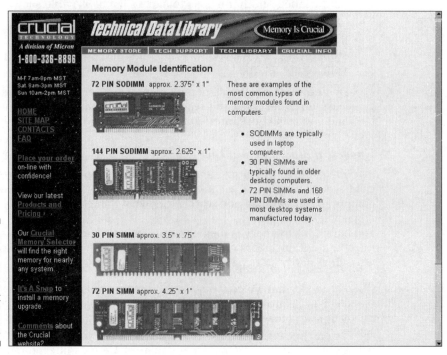

✔ A few computers use other types of memory modules with names such as DIMMs or SODIMMs. These can have 72, 144, or 168 pins. How can you tell if your computer needs these oddballs? If your owner's manual doesn't tell you, try calling a memory expert, such as Crucial Technology at 800-932-4993.

✔ Memory also comes in several electronic flavors. Look in your owner's manual or on the spec sheet that came with your system for a mention of EDO memory. If you see EDO anywhere, you need to buy EDO memory modules, not standard ones.

✔ You also need to know whether your system uses *parity* or *non-parity* memory. Parity memory uses nine bits, and non-parity memory uses eight bits. The extra bit in parity memory helps detect errors, but most computer manufacturers have stopped using parity memory to save a little money. Memory is always listed using a number such as 1 x 32 or 1 x 36. If the second number is evenly divisible by 9, it's parity memory; otherwise, it's non-parity.

✔ Memory speed was once important, but now most memory manufacturers build only memory that's fast enough for today's PCs. If you see a number such as 70ns, that's the memory speed rating, and smaller is faster. Don't buy memory that's slower than what's already in your system; if you're not sure, it's probably safe to get 70ns memory.

✔ Before you buy any memory, you must open your computer. Being very careful not to disturb anything, look for a set of four sockets sitting next to each other. (A few computers may have more than four memory sockets, but four is the most common.) They'll be about 4^1/$_2$ inches long, and two of them will likely have SIMMs already installed. If two of the sockets are empty, you'll be able to add memory without any problem. If all four sockets are full, you'd better get some help because you're going to have to replace two of the existing memory modules.

When you're ready to install new memory modules, be sure to look at the existing modules to see how they sit in the sockets. Your new memory will face the same direction when it's in place. To install the new modules, you need to put them in at an angle and then tilt them up. Be sure to push them all the way down into the socket before you try to tilt them up. If a module isn't all the way in, it won't work correctly.

Recycling your old memory

Have you seen that TV commercial for a gadget you can buy that sorts your pocket change into rolls? The one in which the announcer says, "Stop throwing your loose change away." Do you think people really say to themselves, "Well, I don't have any way to deal with all this loose change, so I guess I'll just throw it away?"

Put that memory in right

Memory manufacturers don't want to deal with returns, so the better ones (such as Micron's Crucial Technology division) include an illustrated instruction sheet when they send you memory modules. Be sure to look over the instructions before you begin, and if you don't feel you can handle the job, wait until your ten-year-old niece or nephew comes around — the memory will be installed in a few minutes! Check out Crucial Technology at `http://www.crucial.com/`.

If you upgrade the memory in your PC, you may end up with something more valuable than loose change — spare memory modules. You can toss them out, or you can find a good use for them.

Most PCs have four sockets for memory modules. When you upgrade the memory, you may be able to simply fill two empty memory sockets and not have leftovers to worry about. Some computer manufacturers, however, fill all four memory sockets with lower-density memory modules. This can be a bit cheaper for the manufacturer, but it also means you may have to junk memory when you want to upgrade.

If all four memory sockets are filled on your system, you have to remove half of the existing memory when you upgrade. If your system has 16MB of memory filling four sockets, for example, and you add a total of 16MB in two modules, you end up with only 24MB of memory, not 32MB. That's one reason to ask how many memory sockets will be filled when you order a computer; you don't want to have to toss out half your memory.

If you do end up with spare memory modules after an upgrade, here are some ideas on how to put them to good use:

✔ Ask if the store accepts trade-ins on memory. This is especially important if you take your system in to have it upgraded. Otherwise, the store will probably "forget" that it removed the old memory modules.

✔ If you have more than one PC, you may be able to use the spare memory in another system. Make sure that both use the same type of memory modules before you try this.

✔ Some printers, especially laser printers, may use standard memory modules. You may be able to use your old memory to increase the memory in your printer.

✔ Even if the store doesn't accept trade-ins, ask whether it will consider exchanging your old memory modules for something you can use. You probably won't get much, but it can't hurt to ask.

✔ You may be able to trade your old memory modules with another small business person who has something you need.

✔ Schools often need donations of computer equipment. If you donate your old memory, you may be entitled to a tax deduction. Other local organizations may also be happy to get your donations, and some may even turn out to be interested in doing business with your company when they find out how generous and helpful you are.

✔ No matter what you intend to do with your old memory modules, don't forget that static electricity can easily destroy them. If you don't have the special conductive bags that memory comes in, wrap the old modules in aluminum foil to prevent static damage.

I Need More Drive

Is your computer feeling tired? Listless? Well, maybe you need some more drive — more hard drive, that is. It seems like no matter how large a hard disk your computer has when you buy it, that disk starts looking small in almost no time.

Just because your hard disk is filling up doesn't mean you need a new hard disk. You could just need to do some housekeeping. Have you filled up your hard disk with a bunch of junk? Are programs installed that you never use? How about sound or graphics files you downloaded from the Internet? Take the time to look around, and you may find several hundred megabytes you could do without. Getting rid of all that stuff is a lot easier and cheaper than adding another hard disk.

You can also increase your free disk space without deleting old files by using disk compression or by changing to a different file system. Here are some options you may have available:

✔ If you use Windows 95 or Windows 98, you can use DriveSpace to compress your hard disk — as long as your disk isn't formatted in FAT32 format. DriveSpace and FAT32 aren't compatible, but you needn't worry about it — you can't apply one if the other is already in place. Compressing your hard disk increases the disk's apparent capacity — that is, it enables you to store more stuff in the same space.

✔ If you use Windows 95b, Windows 98, or Windows NT 5, the good news is that you can use the FAT32 disk format to reduce the amount of wasted space used by each file — resulting in more free space. The bad news is that your disks are probably already using FAT32.

Do you have Windows 95b?

To find out if your system uses Windows 95b — an OEM version of Windows 95 that is available only on systems bought from a manufacturer after 1996 — right-click on the My Computer icon, select Properties, and look for the Windows version number. If it says 950b, you have Windows 95b. You can't buy Windows 95b, so if you don't have it and you want FAT32, you have to upgrade to Windows 98.

- ✔ If you use Windows NT 4 or Windows NT 5, you can use the NTFS disk format to both reduce wasted space and compress your files. You can't use NTFS if you need to access those files using anything but Windows NT, though.

- ✔ No matter what version of Windows you use, you can use WinZip to compress files so that they take a lot less room. With WinZip you can also store compressed files on disks — even if they're too large to fit on a single disk. To make it easier for you, we've not only included WinZip on the CD-ROM but also provided a coupon so that you can get a discount when you register your copy. You can check out WinZip at http://www.winzip.com.

- ✔ If you decide to change your disk format or apply disk compression, make backups of your important files first. You shouldn't encounter any problems converting your files, but the real question is, "Do you feel lucky today?"

Installing additional hard drives

What do you do if you decide that after cleaning out the garbage on your hard disk, you still need to add another? How about a plan to make everything as painless as possible? After all, the better your plan, the fewer opportunities for Mr. Murphy to stick his nose into the process.

By the way, if you have a laptop computer, none of this applies. Laptops generally can use disk drives supplied by the computer's manufacturer, and they usually don't have room for a second hard disk. Sorry, but you just have to go back to the manufacturer for a larger hard disk or do a better job cleaning up your existing hard disk.

Knowing what you have

Some computer geeks have been able to make different types of hard disks work together in a single computer. If you don't eat, sleep, and dream computers, though, it's not worth all the effort and frustration when there's such a simple solution: Buy the same kind of disk drive.

All modern PCs use either IDE or SCSI hard disks. Some minor variations exist in each camp, but you're pretty safe in assuming that your system uses one of these two types. Here are some extra bits of information you may find helpful:

- ✔ IDE drives are sometimes called EIDE or ATA drives, but for all practical purposes, they're really the same thing.

- ✔ SCSI drives come in several minor flavors, too. You may see SCSI 2, SCSI 3, Ultra-SCSI, or Wide-SCSI. Your biggest concern is getting the same variation because that eliminates the need to buy a special adapter. The hard disk vendor should be able to figure out what you need by knowing the model number of what you already have.

- ✔ If someone wants to sell you an additional disk drive, but can't tell what you have from the model number on your existing disk drive, run (don't walk) out the door. How much tech support do you expect to get from someone whose primary experience has been in selling toasters and blenders? You need people who know what they're talking about, not someone whose favorite line is, "Sure, that should work, trust me."

- ✔ Don't trust the spec sheet that came with your computer. Open the cover and look inside to find your existing hard disk. (Find someone who knows computers to help you if necessary.) Your hard disk is connected to a large, flat cable and a smaller cable with four wires for power. Find the label that shows the brand and model number, and write down both; be precise, because a single letter or number may be all that covers major model differences.

Finding room

While you have the cover off your system, look at how the existing hard disk is mounted in the case. Notice that it's screwed into a cage-like mounting bracket. If you will be adding an additional disk drive, you have to find another similar space for the new drive.

An alternative to a new hard drive

If you're out of disk space, you may want to consider an alternative to adding a new hard disk. Drives that use removable media, such as Iomega's Jaz drive, provide virtually unlimited space because when one cartridge is full, you can simply pop in a new cartridge. Recent models of the Jaz drive hold up to 2GB on a single cartridge.

There's probably an open slot similar to the one holding the existing disk drive. Or, the existing drive may be small enough that it's using only the top or bottom half of the mounting cage, leaving room for a similar-sized drive.

If you can't find an open slot for a new disk drive, your only option is to replace your drive with a new, higher capacity disk drive, reinstall your operating system, reinstall all your programs, and restore all your data from your latest set of backups. This is probably more than you'll want to tackle on your own.

Don't even consider mounting a disk drive anywhere except in one of the drive mounting cages. Even if you can make the cables fit (which isn't likely), you run the risk of interfering with airflow or creating an electrical short circuit. In either case, the likely result will be a lot of expensive black smoke announcing that your whole system has just fried.

In one special case, it may be a good idea to run your computer temporarily with the cover open. If you need to add a larger-capacity disk drive because there isn't room for two hard disks, you may be able to transfer files from the old drive to the new drive by connecting both drives while your computer's cover is off. This saves you a lot of diskette swapping by moving your files directly from the old disk drive to the new one. To do this, though, you should have the help of someone who really knows what he or she is doing.

Solving the IDE cable dilemma

You may discover that although there's room for an additional hard disk, the controller cable doesn't have a connector for an additional drive. This is most likely the case if your computer uses IDE drives and a CD-ROM drive is plugged into the cable. IDE controllers can connect to only two drives at a time, whether those drives are hard disks or CD-ROM drives.

Fortunately, you may find that your computer has two IDE controllers. Follow the cable back to the motherboard — the main board in your computer that everything is plugged into. If you see a second connector that's the same size next to where the cable plugs in, you're in luck. You need an extra IDE cable, but the new disk drive may even include one.

If possible, run your IDE hard disks from the primary IDE controller and your CD-ROM drive from the secondary IDE controller. Even if you're not adding a second IDE hard drive, this simple change may speed up your computer for the cost of a second IDE cable. IDE circuits can run only as fast as the slowest component, so your CD-ROM drive may be causing your hard disk to run a lot slower than it should.

Making both drives work

If you've been lucky enough to find a solid home for your new disk drive, you're almost ready to take the final steps toward making everything work together. Before you close the cover, though, you should check out a few things:

> ✔ Make sure all the cables are completely plugged in at both ends. It's pretty easy to disturb cables when you're playing around inside your PC. Many new disk drives that have been returned as defective simply weren't plugged in correctly.

> ✔ Check to see that the power cable — the one with four thick wires — is plugged into each disk drive. Give yourself a dope slap if you have to open the cover again only to find that the problem is that you forgot to connect the power to one of the drives.

> ✔ IDE drives often have little jumpers or switches that need to be set so that two IDE drives can live together. Your main drive should be set as the *master,* and the second drive should be set as the *slave.* Be sure to check the instruction sheet that came with the new drive to see how to make these settings, and don't forget to check the settings on the original drive, too. A drive may work with an incorrect setting if it's the only hard disk in your system, but stop working after you install a second drive.

> ✔ SCSI drives have little jumpers or switches that need to be set. These set the SCSI ID #, and can be in the range of 0–7. Your main hard disk should be set to ID 0, and all other SCSI devices need to be set to a unique number.

> ✔ SCSI cables need to be terminated at the last device on the cable. If you're lucky enough to be able to plug your new drive into the cable between the adapter board and the existing disk drive, you shouldn't need to worry about this. If you plug in the new drive and can't access your hard disks, make sure none of the devices between the adapter board and the last thing plugged into the cable are terminated. The problem is most likely with the last thing you added.

Preparing a new hard disk

Disk drives use letters for names. Drive letters *A* and *B* are saved for disk drives (even if you have only a single disk drive), and your first hard disk is drive *C.* Things get a little complicated after that.

If you have a single hard disk and a CD-ROM drive, your hard disk will always be drive C, and your CD-ROM will be drive D. That is, unless it isn't. Your hard disk may show up as drive C and as drive D, or it may grab more drive letters depending on how your system is set up. Are you confused yet? There's more confusion ahead.

When you add a new hard disk, your computer may rearrange the drive letters just to keep you guessing. At the very least, your CD-ROM drive will be moved to a new letter as the new hard disk takes its place. This can cause programs that worked before to stop working if they look for information on a CD-ROM.

Your new hard disk has to be prepared before you can use it. Preparing a hard disk isn't difficult, but a mistake can destroy all the data on your computer. If you barge ahead ignoring any warnings, you can do serious damage that you can't undo.

Here's how to prepare your new hard disk:

1. **Before you shut down your system to install your new hard disk, check the current drive letter assignments.**

   If you're using Windows, look in Windows Explorer to see which drive letters exist. Most likely, you'll see the diskette drive as A, your hard disk as C, and your CD-ROM as D. If you see additional drive letters, be sure you know what's what!

2. **After you install your new hard disk, see whether a new drive letter has been added.**

3. **If a new drive letter has been added and you can access the drive, you don't need to do anything else: Just start using the new drive.**

4. **If a new drive letter has been added but you can't access the new drive, do the following:**

   a. **Make sure you have a CD-ROM in your CD-ROM drive, and then go to a DOS prompt.**

      In Windows 95 or 98, you find this as MS-DOS Prompt under Programs on the Start menu. In Windows NT, it's called Command Prompt and will also be on the Start menu.

   b. **Type** *letter:* **and press Enter (where letter is the *next* drive letter after your existing hard drive).**

      Don't forget the colon.

   c. **If you see the message** `Invalid drive specification`, **you're in luck; you found the new hard disk. If not, go back to Step 4b and try the next higher drive letter.**

   d. **After you know the correct drive letter for the new hard disk, type** FORMAT *letter:* **(where** *letter* **is the correct drive letter of your new hard disk) and press Enter.**

      Be absolutely sure you use the correct drive letter. Don't forget the colon.

You may see some warnings that this will destroy all existing data on the disk. Don't ignore this warning — if you're not 100 percent certain you have the correct drive letter, get someone to help you (at least then you'll have someone else to blame).

When the formatting is complete, you should be able to access the new drive by typing *letter:* (where *letter* is the drive letter of your new hard drive) and pressing Enter. That's all you have to do to prepare the new drive for use. If your system says it can't format the drive, or if you get any other error messages you don't understand, stop whatever you're doing and *don't continue!* Find a computer expert to come and help you. Otherwise, if you forge ahead, your problems will be much worse.

Adding an Extra Printer

No matter what printer you choose when you first buy your system, you'll probably find yourself wishing you had something else at times. If you bought a laser printer, you may be thinking a color inkjet would be nice. If you bought an inkjet, you may find yourself waiting for long print jobs to finish, and wishing you had a laser printer. Or maybe someone just introduced a new 3-D, color, holographic printer that you want.

Adding an extra printer should be simple. Plug it in, connect the cable to your computer, and off you go. There's just one snag, however: Your PC has only one printer port, and you're already using it for your original printer. You have to be creative if you want to add a second printer to your system.

Using a printer switch

One solution to the problem of not having enough printer ports is to add a special switch box between your PC and the printers. Your computer connects to the switch box, and you flip a switch to choose the printer you want to use. Some switch boxes have enough brains to automatically switch to the correct printer when you send a special command to the switch.

Although using a switch box is an easy solution, it may not be the best choice. Here are some facts to consider about switch boxes:

✔ With a switch box, you can use only one printer at a time. If you start sending a large print job, such as a high-resolution color image, to a slow printer, you have to wait for that print job to finish before you can switch to the other printer.

✔ Some switch boxes can damage your printers or your PC if you switch while the printers are turned on. High-quality printer switches shouldn't have this problem, but it's hard to be sure your switch is safe without trying it — and just testing could blow out your printer.

✔ Unless you check every time you print, you may end up sending a lot of print jobs to the wrong printer. In most cases, different types of printers use different printing commands, so you may end up wasting a lot of time and paper each time you mess up.

Adding a printer port

Another option for adding an extra printer connection to your system is to add a second printer port. Adding a second printer port isn't too difficult, and is more convenient than using a printer switch. (You can't add a second printer port to all systems, though.)

If you're considering adding a second printer port to your computer, you should know the following:

✔ To add a second printer port, you must open your PC and install a card in one of the expansion slots. If you already used up all your standard expansion slots, you can't use this option.

✔ Some printer adapters can cause conflicts with the existing bits and pieces inside your system. If possible, make certain the printer adapter you buy can be configured so that it doesn't require either an IRQ or a DMA. If the vendor can't guarantee this, ask for return privileges if the board doesn't work for you.

✔ Most printer adapters cost about half the price of a printer switch, plus you save the cost of the extra printer cable that's needed from a computer to a switch box.

✔ With a second printer port, you can print to both printers at the same time. If one printer is doing a long, slow print job, you can still get some quick output from your other printer.

✔ Be sure to set the printer you use most as the default printer. That way, print jobs automatically go to that printer unless you specifically choose to use the second printer. You can set the default printer by right-clicking on the desired printer in the Printers folder and selecting Set as Default. Choose Settings⇨Printers from the Start menu to open the Printers folder.

In addition to printer switches and extra printer ports, you can go for a creative solution such as using a serial-to-parallel adapter or buying a serial printer. In both cases, you use an unused COM port for printing. Don't give these ideas too much consideration unless you're desperate. Serial printing is a lot slower than using the standard printer port, but that may be the least of your problems. In addition, you may find that your printer can't tell your computer when it's out of ink, out of paper, or has a paper jam.

I Told You to Go SCSI

When you start trying to add new pieces to your system, you discover that one of the most severe problems in modern computers is their limited expandability. There just aren't enough expansion slots, IRQs, and other resources to support a lot of extra gadgets.

The worst offenders are laptops. In some cases, if you want to use your diskette drive, you have to swap it with the CD-ROM (which means you have to remove your CD-ROM drive). But even desktop systems can be hard to expand, especially if you just had to buy that one with the slim little case that fits neatly under your monitor. Like your mama always told you: "Forget style; bundle up or you'll catch a cold."

If you spent a bit extra and made sure that your system had a good quality SCSI adapter, such as the Adaptec 2940AU, sit back and gloat. Your cheap brother-in-law can't add a scanner because his system is already jammed full, but you have room to add a scanner, extra hard drives, and a Jaz drive — with room to spare.

SCSI adapters are an excellent choice if you want to be able to expand your PC. Because a SCSI adapter uses only one IRQ but can connect either 7 or 14 devices (depending on the adapter), you can add lots of SCSI devices to a system that wouldn't be able to accept any additional non-SCSI devices.

Each item you connect to a SCSI adapter needs a unique ID number. Usually setting the ID number is simply a matter of turning a small switch or moving some jumpers. Also, the entire SCSI *chain* — the devices connected in a daisy chain fashion to the SCSI adapter — needs to be terminated at each end. Terminating the chain is often automatic, but in some cases you need to set a switch.

Even though SCSI is really the way to go, it costs a bit more than systems that don't include SCSI adapters. Because most people don't know the advantages of going SCSI, computer manufacturers don't build too many computers with SCSI adapters and components. Manufacturers have recently realized, though, that people eventually do want to expand beyond the basics.

Recently, computers have started to show up with USB (universal serial bus) ports. USB ports promise to make adding peripherals easier, because you can just run a cable from your computer to the first USB peripheral, then run the next cable from the first peripheral to the second, and so on. Sounds pretty easy, right?

Well, there's a catch. Right now, it's difficult to buy printers, scanners, and other components that connect to USB cables because, until very recently, there weren't any computers that used USB printers, scanners, or other components. But there weren't any computers that used USB printers, scanners, and other components because there weren't any printers, scanners, or other components. (If you aren't dizzy yet, I could go around this circle a few more times.)

Eventually, you should be able to buy all those USB things. Then you won't need to worry about the extra cost of SCSI or the limited expansion capability of non-SCSI PCs. You'll have to worry only about where you're going to put all those extra USB peripherals and not tripping over all those USB cables!

Part III
Putting It All Together

The 5th Wave — By Rich Tennant

"OH YEAH, AND TRY NOT TO ENTER THE WRONG PASSWORD."

In this part . . .

*N*ow that you have all that neat stuff sitting there in all those boxes, do you feel like you'll have to hire a rocket scientist to put it all together? All those bits and pieces and wires and cables add up to confusion. Well, don't worry — you probably can assemble it all yourself. All you need is a little help and some organization, and this is the right place to find what you need.

Perhaps you also want to string computers together into a network so that you can share files and printers. Look no further. Part III also tells you how to put together that more complicated computer setup.

Chapter 7

It's Not Quite Connect the Dots

In This Chapter

▶ Choosing the right spot for your computer

▶ Putting it all together

▶ Making the cables make sense

▶ Testing it without setting off the smoke detectors

*I*f you like untangling plates of spaghetti, you're going to love putting your new computer system together. With all the wires, cables, bits, and pieces you have to put together just right, you'd almost think computers were designed by pasta companies.

Unless you want to pay someone to put it all together, you'll probably end up assembling the pieces of your computer system yourself. In this chapter, you see how you can make certain everything is properly connected and working correctly.

However, just because the computer works doesn't mean *you're* ready to work. You have to find the right place that lets you be productive, too (and no, that doesn't mean you can relocate your office to the tropics for the winter!). The right place isn't just a location, though — it's also a place that's ergonomically designed so that you can be efficient and comfortable while you're working.

Figuring Out Where to Put Your Computer

Bringing a new computer system into your small business can be like bringing a new baby into your family — you'll be surprised at all the changes something so small can require.

It's a good bet that you don't have a lot of office space, especially if you're getting your small business off the ground. This section lists some things to keep in mind as you figure out where to put your PC:

✔ Your computer needs power. That spare closet may seem like just the right spot — you can close the doors and hide the whole mess, but where will you plug in the computer? Stringing an extension cord across the room looks tacky, and you'll be ready to kill the first time someone unplugs your power cord to plug in a vacuum — while you're in the middle of your monthly billing.

✔ Find a spot where you don't need to worry about an overloaded electrical circuit, too. Some printers, especially laser printers, use a lot of power when printing. Put your coffeepot on another circuit.

✔ Computers represent a lot of money in a small, fairly portable package. Thieves love it when they can grab and run, so don't put your system where it's easy for someone to pick it up and be gone in seconds.

✔ The view out your window may be invigorating, but your computer can't stand rain or dust. You shouldn't really be spending your time looking out the window anyway — you have a business to run!

✔ Speaking of windows, don't forget that glare can make reading a computer screen almost impossible. Don't put your computer desk where you'll face directly away from a window. Place your screen perpendicular to the window. That way, you'll be able to sneak an occasional peek out the window but won't be fighting glare coming in over your shoulder.

✔ If your small business is a retail business, make sure you can watch your shop while you're working on the computer. That way, you'll be able to do some computer work during slow periods rather than waiting until the shop is closed.

✔ When positioning your printer, make sure you leave room to open any of its doors or trays.

Choosing your computer desk

You didn't really think your old kitchen table would make a good computer desk, did you? Oh sure, it's probably big enough to give you a good-sized work surface, but that's about all it has going for it. If you will be spending any time at all working with your computer, you need something a whole lot better. What to do with the old kitchen table? Well, you'll probably need some place for lunch, won't you?

When you're looking for a desk or a workstation for your computer, keep the following in mind:

✔ Try out any desk and chair combination before you buy. What fits someone else may prove to be a torture machine to you. If possible, buy a desk and chair that have plenty of adjustments so that you can find a combination that fits your size.

✔ Make certain your computer desk has room for your system. If your computer has a tower-type case or a large-sized monitor, it may not fit on some computer desks — especially hutch-style desks with shelves above the desktop.

✔ Computers have lots of cables. Desks with closed backs can make connecting those cables difficult. Of course, you may enjoy being on the floor under a dark desk trying to figure out where everything goes.

✔ Make sure you've got plenty of room to spread out your work. At a minimum, your computer desk should be at least 60 inches wide and 30 inches deep. Don't forget you need room for a telephone, books, and whatever paperwork your tasks require in addition to space for the monitor and keyboard.

✔ Don't think about putting your printer on your computer desk. Not only would that eat up most of the space you need for working, but printers tend to shake while they're working.

✔ Your printer needs supplies such as paper, toner, cartridges, or ribbons. Buy a printer stand that has room for at least a small supply of these items so that you don't always have to go to your storeroom whenever your printer needs supplies.

Ergonomic basics

It's hard to accomplish much when you don't feel well. If you ignore the *ergonomic* factors when you set up your computer workstation, you'll soon discover what a mistake that can be. The last thing you want to do when your back, shoulders, arms, or hands hurt is to work on your computer. Ignore those pains at your own risk — they're trying to tell you that you're doing serious damage to yourself!

Ergonomics may seem pretty far down on your list when you're struggling to get your small business going. Lots of important things are competing for your limited resources — can't fancy desks and chairs wait until you've made a bunch of money?

Well, you don't have to spend a lot of money to make your office ergonomically correct. Here are some suggestions to keep you from ending up with an aching back:

✔ Make certain your chair and desk are set up so that you can type without having your hands raised in the air. An adjustable keyboard platform is one of the easiest ways to do this, but you can adjust your chair height and angle to help, too.

✔ Don't forget to have a wrist rest in front of your keyboard. You may even find that a folded towel provides the extra support and padding you need.

✔ Don't be tempted by those surplus office chairs some big company is selling for $5 each — if they're too worn out for the big company's office, do you really think they'll do your back any good?

✔ Make sure your chair provides good lower back support, and is adjustable to fit your size. The chair that's perfect for a 5-foot, 100-pound woman won't work for a 6-foot, 230-pound man.

✔ Consider getting an adjustable foot rest if your feet don't sit flat on the floor.

✔ Place your monitor high enough so that you aren't bending your neck over all the time. The top of the screen should be about level with your eyes.

✔ If your printer stand is a bit lower than your computer desk, you'll be able to access your printer without getting up from your chair.

✔ If your office is carpeted, get a chair mat so that you can roll your chair easily. The mat also helps prevent damage to your carpeting.

The Leg Bone's Connected to the Knee Bone

You'll probably be excited and impatient when your system is delivered. Getting a new computer can be a lot of fun, and it's hard to postpone the excitement of seeing the screen come to life the first time. Still, you'll save yourself trouble and extra work if you follow a few steps when your small business computer arrives, even if the computer store delivers and sets up the system for you:

1. **Find the packing list first, and verify that all the pieces were delivered and weren't damaged in shipment.**

   Checking off all the items on the packing list is also a good way to familiarize yourself with the names of the components. Tech support people will be able to help you more quickly if you aren't calling everything a thingamajig or a doohickey!

2. **Locate all the manuals and instruction sheets, and collect them in one place.**

   If something says "read this before installation," read it before you install the component. A lot of components have special shipping brackets that must be removed before you turn on the power — otherwise you may damage something.

3. **Gather all disks and CD-ROMs and keep them in a safe place near the system.**

   You need many of these when you set up your computer, and you may need them in the future, too. Keep all documentation, disks, and CD-ROMs together so you know exactly where to find them.

4. **Make certain you keep all the cables and power cords with the correct components.**

   You may even want to make temporary labels such as *printer* and *monitor* so that you know where each cable belongs.

5. **Temporarily put your computer on a table where you have good lighting, and examine the back of the case.**

   You'll see lots of connectors and jacks on the back of the system. Each connects to a particular cord, and it's easy to get them confused, especially when you're plugging cables into the back of the computer while you're on your back on the floor or leaning over the top of the case. You may want to make a diagram so that you know where each cable plugs in.

   Some connectors are identical, or nearly so. For example, the mouse and the keyboard connectors are usually right next to each other, and both use the same jack and plug. The monitor jack is usually the same size as a serial port connector, but the monitor plug has three rows of delicate pins you can easily damage if you try to force the plug into the wrong connector. Sound boards usually have four identical connectors, and modems have two identical connectors — be sure to read the small labels on the bracket so that you use the correct jacks.

6. **After you identify all the connectors and know where all the cables go, you can put all the pieces on your computer desk, the printer stand, and so on.** *Don't plug in any power cords yet!*

You may want to sit at your desk and check out the location of all the components before you start hooking up the cables. It's a lot easier to adjust the position of the various bits and pieces before they have cables stringing everything together. Also keep in mind that your printer and any other external peripherals must be close enough for you to plug in their cables. Most have limits to the length of their cables.

UPSes

If you have a UPS, you want to make certain your computer and monitor plug into the UPS. But you also want to make certain no one plugs a printer — especially a laser printer — or anything else such as a vacuum into the UPS. If possible, place the UPS on the floor in a location where people would find it difficult to reach to plug other things into.

A power strip provides a convenient place for plugging everything into the power. Just make sure no one finds it convenient for plugging in coffee makers and vacuums.

Making Sense of the Rat's Nest

A rat's nest of cables behind your PC is just one of those things you have to live with. A lot of wires and cables behind your computer, however, doesn't mean it has to be a mess back there. In this section, you find some tips for keeping things organized (your mother would be proud).

Label your cables

Let's see, there's a cable from the monitor to the computer, another from the keyboard, one from the printer, a mouse wire, a telephone cord, probably some wires to your speakers, and a whole bunch of power cords. How will you remember where everything goes when you have to disconnect them to move your system or add a new gadget?

Here are some ideas to help you organize your wires and cables:

✔ Start with your drawing of the back of your computer. Make sure you identify each connector with the name of the peripheral that plugs into the connector or with the purpose of the connector if it's a spare (such as an unused COM or serial port).

✔ You may also want to give each connector a number — you can even write the number on the back panel of your PC or on a stick-on label you place next to the connector.

✔ Make a label for each cable by writing the description of the cable on a stick-on label. Write on one half of the label, and then wrap the center of the label around the cable to form a flag on the wire. If you numbered the connectors of the PC, include the connector number on the flag, too.

✔ After you label all the wires, go ahead and connect them one at a time. As you get each cable connected, leave a small amount of slack, and then use twist ties to neatly take up the excess in each cable.

✔ Don't bundle power cords with any other type of cable — the electrical interference can cause erratic problems that are a nightmare to track down.

✔ You can buy self-stick brackets for the back of your desk to help organize the confusion. Make sure you don't pull the wires too tight — you need some room to adjust the position of things.

✔ If nothing else works, hang an "under construction" sign. You can always claim you're still in the process of getting everything set up and that you'll straighten up the mess as soon as you're finished.

Common cables

Your system should come with all the cables you need to connect everything together. And weekends should always be sunny and beautiful, too. In the real world, your mileage may vary.

Because no manufacturer can possibly know all the different ways people may want to set up their computers, the standard cables may not be enough, and you may end up having to buy some new cables.

Here are some things to know before you spend your money on new cables:

✔ Always buy top quality cables (look for the IEEE label as one indicator of good cables). Cheap cables won't save you much, and in cables you really do get what you pay for. It's especially important that you buy the best cables if you're getting a longer-than-standard cable.

✔ If you put your computer on the floor next to your desk, you may need a keyboard extension cable. Make certain that you get the right type — newer systems all use PS/2 type connectors, which are much smaller than the old-style keyboard connector found on many keyboard extension cables.

✔ Limit printer cables to ten feet if possible. Longer printer cables can cause printing errors that are difficult to troubleshoot.

✔ SCSI cables come in several different types. Make sure you know whether the cable should be narrow (50 conductor) or wide (68 conductor).

✔ SCSI cables also use several different types of connectors. The easiest way to make certain you get the right cable is to bring an existing cable along when you shop for new SCSI cables. Check all your components to make certain you know what connector they use.

✔ Serial cables can have 25-pin or 9-pin connectors, and the cable ends may need to be male or female. Be sure you check both places where you'll be plugging the cable before you buy — don't assume both ends of the cable should be the same!

✔ External modems use serial cables. There's no advantage to using more than eight wires in a modem cable, so nine-pin cables are generally used for modems (one of the pins isn't used).

✔ Macintosh systems use different cables than most other PCs, and they use different cables for modems than they do for serial printers.

Your friend the adapter

No matter how many cables you have, sometimes you still need something just a little different. That's where adapters come into play. Adapters can convert one type of connector to another, or even change the purpose of a cable. Sometimes the only way to solve a particularly thorny problem is to use an adapter.

Here are some types of adapters you may find useful:

✔ Null-modem adapters swap some of the connections in a serial cable connection so that two computers can talk directly through their COM ports. Essentially, null-modem adapters take the place of the modems, so you can swap files quickly between two systems. You use only one null-modem adapter at one end of the cable — not one at each end.

✔ Gender changers make it possible to connect cables that have the wrong types of connectors. Male connectors have the pins, and female connectors have the holes for the pins. Make sure you get the right kind of gender changer — they come with either two male or two female connectors.

✔ Some SCSI adapters use 68-conductor wide SCSI cables, but most SCSI peripherals (except some hard drives) use 50-conductor narrow SCSI cables. You can get a 68-pin to 50-pin SCSI adapter to enable you to plug narrow SCSI devices into a wide SCSI cable. This adapter must be the last thing on the wide SCSI cable because it terminates the top 18 lines of the wide SCSI cable. The last 50-pin SCSI device must terminate the narrow SCSI chain.

✔ External SCSI devices often use an external SCSI terminator. This terminator must be installed on the end of the cable where it connects to the final external SCSI device.

✔ You can buy standard audio adapters, such as Y-adapters, to connect your sound card to external audio devices. Most sound cards use normal $1/8$ inch stereo jacks and plugs.

✔ If necessary, you can get an adapter to connect a mouse to a serial port rather than to a PS/2 mouse port.

✔ Keyboard adapters are also available to allow converting between PS/2 connectors and the larger keyboard connector found on older systems.

No matter what combination of cables and adapters you end up using to tie everything together, don't forget to properly secure all your cables. Some connections use screws to hold the connections together; others use wire snap rings. Always make certain you don't just plug the cable into the connector and forget to tighten the screws or other fasteners. Cables can vibrate loose, causing all sorts of strange problems. If your printer started printing garbage or quit printing entirely, loose cables are probably the last thing you'd think to look for, but they're often the cause of these types of problems.

Getting Ready to Test It All

Okay, it's the big moment — everything is in place and connected, and you're ready to turn on the power. But first, have you paid your insurance, and do you know where the fire extinguisher is located?

Actually, you'll probably discover that your computer works fine when you turn it on. You won't see blue smoke or sparks. That's no guarantee that everything will work perfectly, but at least you won't have to run for the exit.

After you get over the initial rush of seeing something on your computer's screen, it's time to run some quick tests to make sure everything else is working. Start by trying to print something to make sure your printer is working. If nothing comes out of your printer, try these fixes:

- ✔ Make sure the printer is turned on — you should see a lit power indicator.

- ✔ If the printer has an online indicator, make sure it's on. (Some printers have a display panel that reads Off-Line if the printer isn't ready. On-line means the printer is ready to go.)

- ✔ Check the printer cable. Make sure that both ends are plugged in.

- ✔ Check the paper supply.

- ✔ If you're using Windows, click on the Start button, and then choose Settings, Printers to open the Printers folder. If your printer isn't listed, double-click on the Add Printer icon and install your printer.

If your modem doesn't work, try these fixes:

- ✔ Start by checking the phone cord — it may not be fully plugged in at one or both ends.

- ✔ Plug a telephone into the wall jack to make certain you can make a call.

✔ If your modem is an external modem, check to see that it's turned on and connected to your computer. (You didn't forget the modem cable, too, did you?)

✔ If you're using Windows, click on the Start button, select Control Panel, and double-click on Modems. If your modem isn't listed, click on the Add button and install your modem.

If your scanner seems to be kaput, try these things:

✔ It's on, right?

✔ The cable is connected at both ends, isn't it?

✔ Completely power off your system. Turn off the scanner, and then turn the scanner back on. Finally, turn your computer's power back on.

✔ If your scanner is a SCSI scanner, shut everything down, disconnect both ends of the SCSI cable, plug the SCSI cable back into the scanner and then your computer, turn on the scanner, and then turn on the computer.

✔ Make sure the SCSI terminator is plugged into the last SCSI device.

If anything else, such as your monitor, mouse, or keyboard doesn't seem to work, try these suggestions:

✔ Check the power.

✔ Don't forget to check the connecting cable. Even if you're *sure* it's connected properly, it's less embarrassing to find a loose cable yourself than to have a technician find it.

✔ Shut the system down and then restart everything. Sometimes computers seem to forget that extra pieces are sitting out there. When you punish them by turning off their power, they tend to be grateful when you turn the power back on. That's why they'll sometimes find a "lost" component — they don't want you to turn them off again.

Chapter 8

Keeping Your Business Secure

. . . .

In This Chapter

▶ Having a backup plan that works

▶ Preventing crooks from getting in

▶ Keeping your access doors open

. . . .

*H*ave you ever asked yourself how important your small business is to you? What would happen if someone walked in the front door and stole all your products? What if they also took all the special information that gives your business an edge, such as your billing records or customer contact records? It sounds pretty grim, doesn't it? Well, what if no one came in and took anything from you, but you still lost everything because your computer died?

Nothing is more frustrating than losing a lot of time and work due to a system failure. Unless, of course, you consider the possibility of someone stealing or damaging your efforts deliberately. If you don't take the steps necessary to protect your small business from serious computer failure, theft of important information, or outright sabotage, you may as well leave the doors wide open when you go home at the end of the day.

Keeping your computer and the information it holds secure isn't difficult, but it does require a little time and effort. This chapter shows you how to protect your important data files.

Back (up) to the Future

If your computer died, you'd probably be inconvenienced for a day or two while it was being repaired. If something more serious happened and your system were destroyed, you may cringe at the expense, but you could simply pull out your plastic and buy a replacement. For that matter, even if your favorite programs quit working, you'd be able to replace them quickly.

Sure, you may waste some time getting everything back in shape after one of these problems, but your total outlay of time and money wouldn't be enough to threaten your business in the long run.

Suppose, though, that all your customer billing records were suddenly wiped out. You might not be able to tell who owed you money, who had already paid their bills, how much you owed to your suppliers, or even whether your business would be able to meet the bills. Quite simply, losing your vital business information could put you out of business!

Although each small business is somewhat different, it's clear that information is what's important. In addition to billing records, you likely have a lot of other information vital to the success of your business: lists of potential customers who've responded to an ad you placed, credit card information from past customer orders, data on customers who have bought premium priced products in the past, inventory and tax records, and a whole slew of other facts that would be difficult, expensive, or impossible to duplicate. What value could you put on all that?

Creating a backup plan

If you've started to figure out that you really need a backup plan to protect your important data, give yourself a pat on the back. If you're still not convinced you need to worry about it, sit in a corner until you come to your senses.

Anyone who's starting, running, or managing a small business already has plenty of work to do. Therefore, when deciding which backup plan is right for you, take into account how much extra work it will add to your existing workload. If you create a plan that just seems like too much work and trouble, what are your chances of sticking with the plan? If backing up your data takes too much time, you'll probably find excuses for why you just don't have time to do that backup today. Pretty soon you'll find another excuse, and before you know it, Mr. Murphy will come knocking on your door, and you'll be unprepared and unprotected.

Your backup plan needs to consider several factors if it's going to work right for you. Here are some things that you'll want to consider:

✔ Don't include programs in your backups. In the event of a system failure, you can always use the original installation disks to reinstall your programs.

✔ Locate your data files in a separate folder from your program files. That way, it will be a lot easier to back up only your data.

Backup terminology

You'll see a lot of confusing terminology applied to backups. For example, backups of just the files that have changed since your last backup may be called *incremental*, *differential*, or even *partial* backups. You'll also see the term *full* backup applied to both backing up all the files on your system, and to backing up just the data files. In this book, full backups are backups of all your data files — whether they've been changed or not; and incremental backups are backups of only those data files that have changed.

✔ Don't destroy any paperwork until the data generated from it has been backed up. Otherwise, you may be unable to reconstruct data lost since the last backup.

✔ Don't use the same disk or cartridge for all your backups. Have a rotating set of backup disks or cartridges so that if one disk or cartridge fails, you won't lose your entire *backup set* (all the files you've backed up).

✔ After you decide which files need to be backed up regularly, save the backup procedure so that your backup program can reuse the same backup parameters. That way, the computer can remember what needs to be backed up.

✔ Schedule your backups for the same time each day or each week (depending on how much work you'd really like to redo in the event of a failure). By establishing a regular schedule, you're more likely to do the backups instead of "forgetting" about them.

✔ Label the backup disks or cartridges so that you can easily find the latest backup set. If you have a system failure, you'll have plenty to think about without worrying about which backup data to use.

✔ Unless you have a huge amount of data to back up, always do full rather than incremental backups. That gives you the highest level of protection, and probably won't take more than a few minutes extra — especially if you follow the advice to back up only your data, not your programs.

Unless you like playing Russian roulette, you absolutely must have backups of your important business data. Far too many computer users ignore this vital task.

Protecting your backups

Okay, so you have a plan for backing up your important data files on a regular basis and you've been really good about sticking to your plan. That means you're protected, right?

Well, maybe yes, and maybe no. Maybe you have carefully labeled daily backups and you did your last backup just before you went home for the day. But what if later that day, an electrical fire started and wiped out your entire office? You'd have a mess to clean up, but at least you could stay in business by taking your backup disks to another computer and continuing, right? But where are your backup disks? Did you put them someplace in the office, the place where everything was just destroyed?

Obviously, keeping your backup disks in the office gives you far less protection than you expected. Sure, the backup disks are handy sitting right there on your desk, but they're also vulnerable to being destroyed along with your computer. If that happens, you're back to square one (or maybe even worse) because your protection didn't save you.

Here are some ideas you may be able to use to help protect your backups and possibly save your business:

- ✔ If you don't work out of an office in your home, take your backup disks home with you. Just don't put them where your daughter will find them when she desperately needs a disk so that she can save her homework project.

- ✔ If your bank is conveniently located, consider storing your backups in a safe-deposit box.

- ✔ Make a deal with another small business person in your area to be the off-site storage location for each other's business. You can trade off dropping off and picking up each other's backup sets, and you'll have more of an incentive to keep your backups up-to-date. Make sure you choose someone you trust if you decide on this type of arrangement.

- ✔ At the very least, keep a weekly backup set somewhere outside your office.

- ✔ A fireproof cabinet that offers a minimum of one-hour fire protection would also be a good place to store backup disks or cartridges, but that doesn't mean you shouldn't plan on also keeping an off-site backup set. You may want to check with your local locksmith for a recommendation on the right type of cabinet to protect your backup media.

You can probably think of some additional ways to protect your backup disks or cartridges. Remember that your backups should be both protected and easily accessed if a disaster strikes your business.

Who Goes There?

Would you leave your wallet and credit cards on a counter where anyone could come along and help themselves to the contents? Of course you wouldn't. Then why would you let just anyone access the data on your company PC? Billing, payroll, and customer records are only some of the important information you need to protect to ensure the safety of your small business. It doesn't matter what kind of information you're trying to protect: As far as your computer is concerned, everything is the same.

Keeping the bad guys out

You have to keep the bad guys out if you want to protect your data. Who are the bad guys? Anyone who wants to steal valuable information, or anyone who wants to maliciously modify your records, or anyone who may accidentally destroy important data. In other words, the bad guys are anyone who doesn't have a darn good reason to be using your computer.

If you're trying to run your small business from your home, you have to deal with a serious security threat — family members who think they should be able to use your business computer. As difficult as it may be to prohibit them from using your system, allowing them to use it is an all-around bad idea. Not only will you have to fight for access when a son or a daughter needs to finish homework or has reached a record level in some game, but your data may be at risk — especially when someone decides to load a zoomy new program borrowed from a friend. In addition, you won't be able to take your complete business depreciation for your system unless it's used only for business purposes.

Save yourself a lot of trouble and buy a second computer for the family to use. (It can also serve as a backup for your business system in an emergency.)

Here are some things you can do to keep the bad guys and gals out of your computer:

✔ Many computers enable you to set a *password* that must be entered before the system starts up. This first line of defense, however, has a few large holes. After you enter your password and start the computer, anyone can access your files. In addition, a really determined thief can steal your entire computer, pop out the hard disk, and likely gain access to your data by placing the drive in another system.

✔ Some operating systems require you to enter a name and password to log on to your computer. You can create different users who have their own passwords, and in some cases limit people to using specific files. Windows NT is far more powerful in the restrictions you can place on individual users than systems such as Windows 95, Windows 98, or the Mac operating system.

✔ Most computers have a lock on the front panel. Usually, the lock prevents anyone from opening the case and typing anything on the keyboard. A keyboard lock can be fairly effective at keeping people from tampering with your data — if you remember where you put the key (and if you lock the keyboard and take the key with you when you leave your system).

✔ Unfortunately, keyboard locks won't prevent your system from being stolen. After someone has your computer, he or she can drill out the lock and obtain access to your files.

Keeping your laptop covered

Laptop computers are a special security threat. Not only are they portable, but also they represent a lot of money crammed into a small package. If you depend on a laptop system for your small business, here are some special security precautions to keep in mind:

✔ Insist on hand inspection of your laptop system when you go through airport security. Thieves often work security queues in groups. When someone places a laptop on the conveyor belt, one of the thieves gets in front of them in the scanner line and sets off the metal detector. While you're waiting to get through the metal detector, another thief grabs your laptop and disappears.

✔ Some companies make security devices designed to protect laptop PCs. You may want to check out these sites on the Internet: `http://www.trackitcorp.com/`, `http://www.wesecure.com/sp400pp.htm`, and `http://www.compulock.com/`.

✔ If you use a pay phone, public restroom, newsstand, or food vendor while you're carrying a laptop system, keep track of it at all times.

✔ Don't forget that hotels often have digital rather than analog telephone systems. If you plug your laptop into a digital phone line, you blow out your modem at the very least, and may destroy your entire computer.

✔ When traveling, keep a set of backup disks separate from your laptop, such as in your suitcase. That way, you still have your data if someone steals your laptop case.

✔ Consider using security and encryption software to protect important files with passwords. That helps keep your data secure even if your system is stolen.

✔ Most standard insurance policies don't cover laptops. Be sure to discuss your needs with your insurance agent.

I've got a secret

A long time ago, there was a television program called "Whom Do You Trust?" As a small business person, you may need to ask yourself a similar question: Whom *can* you trust? Unfortunately, that question doesn't always have an easy answer. If you have employees, are they being honest with you? Are you getting your money's worth from them?

If you aren't sure of the answers to those questions, you may want to try out one of the tools on the *Small Business Computing For Dummies* CD-ROM. Mr. Burns Productivity Monitoring Package is a *shareware program* that keeps track of how a PC running Windows has been used.

Shareware programs are programs you can try out before you buy them. You find several specially selected shareware programs on the CD-ROM. Shareware distribution keeps the costs down, so in most cases you find that shareware is a bargain. Be sure to remember to register your shareware programs — you not only help keep the shareware authors in business, but you often have the opportunity to get updates and revisions, too.

The Mr. Burns Productivity Monitoring Package software creates a *log,* which is a special file that tells you which programs have been run, how long they were running, and how much keyboard activity took place while the program was running. This enables you to monitor how someone has been using your office PC. You'll be able to tell if he or she has been working or goofing off.

The shareware version of the Mr. Burns Productivity Monitoring Package displays a message telling users they are being monitored. When you register the software, you can run the program without displaying the message. You may want to check with your attorney regarding any notices you may be legally required to provide to employees to advise them that they may be monitored.

Here's what you need to do to use the Mr. Burns Productivity Monitoring Package:

1. **Copy the Mr. Burns Productivity Monitoring Package files from the CD-ROM into a new folder on your hard disk.**

   You need to place the files on your hard disk instead of trying to run them from the CD-ROM, because the software creates the log files in the same folder where the program files reside. Because you can't create any files on the CD-ROM, you have to run the Mr. Burns Productivity Monitoring Package from your hard disk.

2. Double-click on Mrbadmin.exe to load the program.

If you use Windows 98 or Windows NT 5, you may be able to start programs with a single click, depending on how your system is set up. If so, just ignore the instructions that tell you to double-click.

Figure 8-1 shows how Mr. Burns looks when you first load the program.

Figure 8-1:
Use the Mr. Burns software to keep track of how your office PC is being used.

3. Click on the Configure Mr Burns button.

The Configuration dialog box in Figure 8-2 appears.

4. Click on the options that pertain to the activities you want to track, and then click on OK or Save.

Mr. Burns keeps a less detailed log if you don't use any configuration options.

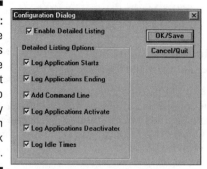

Figure 8-2:
Tell the Mr. Burns software exactly what you want to track by clicking on the check boxes.

5. **If you want Mr. Burns to run every time your PC is used, click on the Load Automatically at Startup option.**

   You can also click on the Run Now button to start Mr. Burns manually, and click on the Stop button to stop the monitoring.

6. **To see how the system has been used, click on the View/Convert Data Logs button.**

   The first time you click on this button, the log is empty, as shown in Figure 8-3. That's because you need to load a log file to see what's in it.

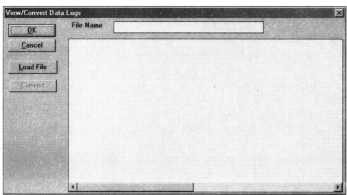

Figure 8-3:
You have to
tell the
Mr. Burns
software
which log
file you
want to see.

7. **Click on the Load File button to choose the log file you want to view.**

8. **Select Tasklist.1 to see a condensed log, or Verbose.1 to see a more complete log. Then click on OK.**

   Figure 8-4 shows an example of Verbose.1.

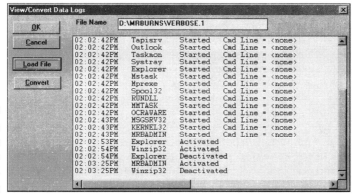

Figure 8-4:
Mr. Burns
can be
verbose.

9. Click on OK to stop viewing the log, and then click on Quit to close the Mr. Burns window.

As a small businessperson, you have a right to know how your employees are using your PCs. Still, it's probably not a good idea to be too heavy handed. If someone isn't typing constantly, it doesn't necessarily mean he or she is goofing off. The person may be answering the phone, taking a customer's order, or looking up important information. Of course, if the only program that's being used while you're out of the office is Freecell, you probably do have a problem.

Using passwords

Another important element in a security plan is the use of *passwords* — words or phrases you need to type to gain access to files. Passwords are like the combination to a safe.

Passwords are no good if everyone knows the password. If you use a simple password that everyone can guess, such as your dog's name, you may as well skip the hassle of using passwords and leave everything open for anyone. Another common mistake people make is to write down their password on a sticky note they put on the front of their monitor. You may as well leave the key under the doormat, too!

One security analyst reported that users often leave their passwords written on a notepad in their desk drawer. When he does a security check, the first place he looks is in the desk drawers. If he finds a password, he uses it to access the person's account and change the password, leaving the person unable to use the computer. A thief would do something a lot more harmful than simply inconveniencing you by changing your password. Don't leave your password where it can be easily found.

A lot of programs let you use a password to protect your files. To see a typical example of using passwords, try out WinZip, a useful shareware program on the *Small Business Computing For Dummies* CD-ROM. WinZip enables you to compress files so that they take less disk space and can be sent more quickly over a modem. WinZip also enables you to easily open *ZIP* files (ones with a ZIP file extension).

Although WinZip allows you to use passwords, the password protection in WinZip isn't 100 percent secure. To maintain compatibility (and because the U.S. government limits the export of secure encryption technology), WinZip can't use extremely strong encryption methods. Unless you're in the spying business, though, WinZip should be good enough to protect your files.

To try out using a password to protect a WinZip file, follow these steps:

1. **Double-click on Winzip95.exe on the CD-ROM to begin installing WinZip.**

   Go ahead and accept all the standard suggestions while you're install-ing WinZip. This well-designed program won't do anything to cause you problems.

2. **After WinZip is installed, click on the Start button to display the Start menu.**

   The Start menu is similar whether you use Windows 95, Windows 98, Windows NT 4, or Windows NT 5. You can run most of your programs by selecting them from the Start menu.

3. **Move the mouse up to Programs and then over to the menu that appears to the right. Click on the left mouse button when WinZip is highlighted.**

   WinZip starts, as shown in Figure 8-5. (The screen is different if you're using the WinZip Wizard, but you can always get to this window eventu-ally after you step through the wizard screens.)

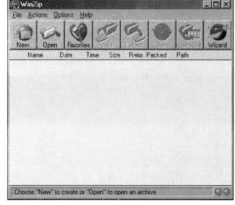

Figure 8-5:
You can try
out using
passwords
with
WinZip.

4. **Click on the New button so that you can name a new WinZip file.**

   The New Archive dialog box appears, as shown in Figure 8-6.

5. **In the File name box, type a name, such as** Test**, and then click on OK.**

   You have to name the WinZip file before you can use a password. You also have to provide a password before you add files to the WinZip file. Some programs that use passwords work a little differently than WinZip. In general, however, you enter a password when you save a file, and then type the same password later to reopen the file.

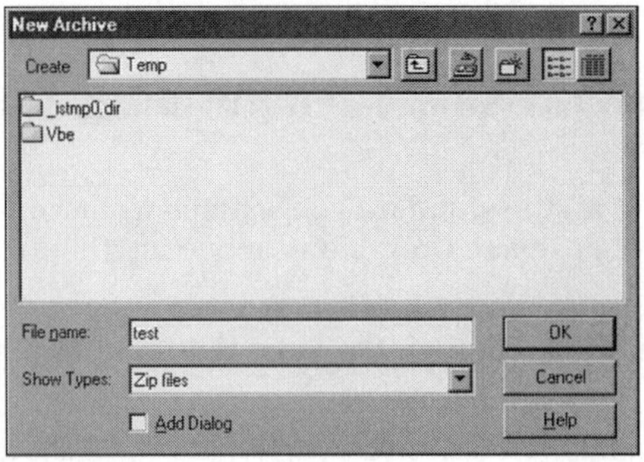

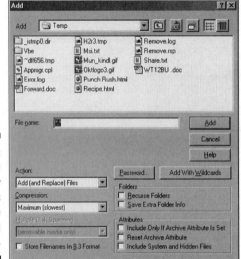

Figure 8-6:
You can specify how you want to create the WinZip file.

6. Click on the Add button.

The Add dialog box appears, as shown in Figure 8-7.

Figure 8-7:
You'll eventually add files using the Add dialog box.

7. Click on the Password button.

WinZip displays the Password dialog box, as shown in Figure 8-8.

8. In the Password text box, type the password and then click on OK.

If the Mask Password option is checked, your password won't appear on the screen.

Figure 8-8:
Passwords
apply only
to files you
add to the
WinZip file
after you
enter a
password.

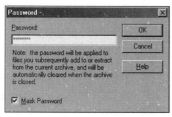

9. **Type the same password again to confirm the password you entered, and then click on OK.**

10. **Add any files you want to the WinZip file by clicking on them and then clicking on the Add button.**

   The original files remain on your hard disk.

11. **Click on the Close button (X).**

   You need to close WinZip before you can test your password.

12. **Open WinZip again by clicking on the Start button and choosing WinZip from the Programs menu.**

13. **Click on the Open button, select the WinZip file you just created (mine is Test.zip), and click on Open.**

14. **Click on the Extract button, and then click on the second Extract button.**

   The second Extract button appears so that you can choose where to put (extract) the files so you can use them. After you click on the second Extract button, WinZip asks for the password.

15. **Type the same password you used when you saved the file.**

   WinZip extracts the files so that you can use them.

You can use a password also when you start your PC, but that password works a little differently than the ones used by individual programs. In general, the password you use when you log on to your system gives you access to your computer. If you've also used individual passwords, you must enter those when you want to use the files that they specifically protect. Individual passwords also protect files you send with your modem or on a disk. The person receiving the protected files must also know the password to open the files.

Who Has the Master Key?

Passwords can provide a lot of protection — sometimes too much! If you forget or lose your password, you may as well kiss your data files goodbye, because you're probably not going to be able to open and use those files. But isn't that exactly what you want? Someone who doesn't know the correct password shouldn't be able to open your files, right? In most cases, yes. But password protection isn't a completely black-or-white issue. Before you use a password, think about the following:

- ✔ No matter how good you think your memory is, you should have a written list of all your passwords. Be sure to indicate the exact case of your passwords because most are case sensitive. For example, if you type BRIAN as the password for a file, you won't be able to open the file by typing brian.

- ✔ If you have a written list of passwords, store it in a safe, secure location, such as your safe-deposit box. Although this may be inconvenient when you need to look up a password, it also means someone else can't casually look over your list.

- ✔ Make certain you are kept informed of any passwords your employees are using. You could be in big trouble if someone suddenly quits and he or she is the only one who knows the password to certain files, such as your accounting files.

- ✔ Test the passwords your employees provide from time to time. That way, you'll be able to catch the error if they "accidentally" give you the wrong password.

- ✔ Change any default passwords as soon as possible. Criminals usually know the standard account names and passwords supplied with most software packages, and if you leave these unchanged, it's like leaving the back door open.

- ✔ Don't use the same passwords forever. People are sometimes careless with their passwords; the longer you use the same passwords, the more likely it is that the wrong people will know them.

- ✔ At the very least, change your passwords when an employee leaves.

- ✔ Be reasonable in using password protection. If you try to protect everything, or use too many different passwords, no one wants to use the passwords because it is too much trouble. Use passwords only on files you really need to protect.

Making sure you can get in

Imagine what would happen if the person who enters all the billing information into your accounting software suddenly disappeared. Now imagine that your accounting files were password protected, and you didn't know the password. If you don't have a headache yet, suppose you also just received a letter from the IRS telling you they wanted to audit your books next week. Do you have a plan to protect your small business from this scenario, or would you just give up and hop the next flight to Brazil?

You may not be able to completely trust the people who work for you. An employee could clean out your bank account without warning. Someone could decide to hitchhike across Mexico, and forget to tell you the passwords before leaving. Or you may be the culprit by entering a password differently, locking yourself out of your files.

You should make certain that you have an accurate list of all passwords. But how can you be certain your list of passwords is up-to-date? How can you know if Sally decides to change the passwords used to access your important company files just before she skips town?

Using Password Thief

Password Thief, another shareware program on the *Small Business Computing For Dummies* CD-ROM, may be your answer to the password problem. This software has one purpose: It keeps track of virtually all the passwords anyone enters while using your Windows PC. The passwords are stored in a hidden file that you can open when you need to see what passwords have been used. The shareware version of Password Thief lets the computer's user know that Password Thief is running. To prevent this message from appearing, register your copy of Password Thief.

No program, not even Password Thief, can track *every* password entered. For example, the password you enter when you start your system can't be tracked because the program has to be running before it can track passwords, and the program can't run until you start your computer.

To try out Password Thief, follow these steps:

1. **Copy Thief.exe and Pwthook.dll from the *Small Business Computing For Dummies* CD-ROM to the C:\Windows\System folder.**

   You can copy files using Windows Explorer. Click on the Start button, and then select Windows Explorer from the Programs menu. Right-click on the files you want to copy, select Copy, and then right-click on the C:\Windows\System folder. Select Paste to copy the files to the folder. If you didn't get both files in one step, go back and get the second file.

2. **Copy PWTManager.exe to a folder on your hard disk.**

   That way, you can run the program even when the *Small Business Computing For Dummies* CD-ROM isn't in your CD-ROM drive. You *can* run the Password Thief Manager (PWTManager.exe) directly from the CD-ROM, but you need to have the CD-ROM in the drive whenever you want to run the program.

3. **Double-click on PWTManager.exe to run the program.**

4. **Click on the Run Now button to start monitoring any passwords that are entered.**

   If you want the Password Thief to run automatically the next time you start your PC, click on the Load Automatically at Startup option. This won't run Password Thief right now, though, so you need to either restart your system or click on the Run Now button.

5. **Run another program, such as WinZip, and enter a password.**

   Your password log won't have any entries until you enter at least one password in another program.

6. **When you finish, click on the Password Thief window to return to Password Thief.**

7. **Click on the View Password Logs button to see the details on any passwords that were entered.**

   Figure 8-9 shows an example of the log that Password Thief creates when testpassword is entered as a password.

8. **Click on OK to close the password log, and then click on Quit to close the Password Thief window.**

If you don't want anyone else to be able to view the password logs, you may want to keep PWTManager.exe on a disk and run the program from the disk.

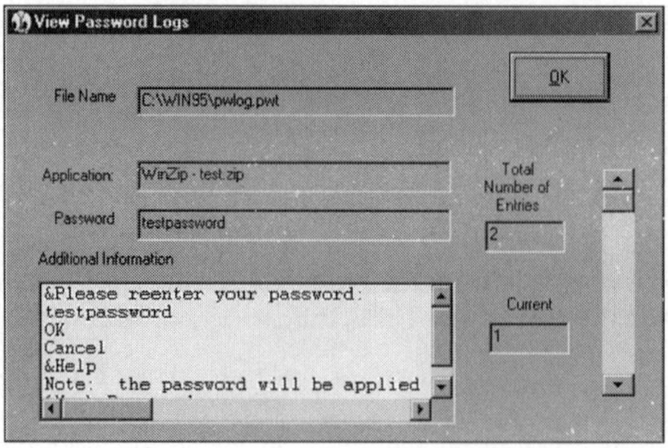

Figure 8-9:
If you used
a password
when
Password
Thief was
running, the
password
log shows
the
password
you
entered.

View Password Logs		[OK]
File Name	C:\WIN95\pwlog.pwt	
Application:	WinZip - test.zip	Total Number of Entries: 2
Password	testpassword	
Additional Information		
&Please reenter your password: testpassword OK Cancel &Help Note: the password will be applied		Current: 1

Chapter 9

Small Business Networks Simplified

- -

- -

*A*s soon as your small business needs more than one computer, you'll probably start thinking about connecting the systems in a network. Connecting your computers makes a lot of sense. Why should each PC be isolated when it's so easy to bring them together?

Installing a network doesn't require the services of a rocket scientist. You can probably do it yourself, but even if you decide the job is more than you want to take on, it's a good idea to understand the basics. This chapter shows you how to put in a network so that you can share files, printers, and other resources.

In the few pages available here it just isn't possible to cover all aspects of small business networking. If you need more information than you find in this chapter, check out *Small Business Networking For Dummies* by Glenn Weadock (published by IDG Books Worldwide, Inc.).

Dancing in a Line

Imagine a big dance hall full of people and music. Now suppose that each person was dancing around with a boombox blasting out a favorite piece of music. The result would be chaos, with little cooperation between competing groups. Now change the scene a little bit. Throw out all those boomboxes and bring in a band so that everyone is dancing to the same music. You don't have to be a dancer to know that this scenario works a whole lot better. Instead of people doing their own thing, everyone is cooperating.

A *network* can make your computers work together a whole lot better than if they're all disconnected and doing their own thing. Networks just make a whole lot of sense, and there's no arguing the idea of everyone in a business working together!

Networks for small business

There are all sorts of networks. Radio and television networks send out what they call entertainment. People often use their network of friends to build business and social contacts. Telephone networks enable people to talk to each other no matter how far apart they're located. Computer networks do the same sorts of things and lots more.

Here are some of the things a network can do for your small business:

- ✔ *File sharing* lets everyone on the network have the same information. If everyone is getting their information from the same file, it's much easier to keep everybody playing the same game. Your salespeople won't be selling your products at a loss because they're too lazy to put the updated pages in their catalogs.

- ✔ *Printer sharing* may make it possible for your business to afford a higher quality printer than if everyone needs his or her own printer. A $3,000 color laser printer probably doesn't belong on every desk, but if half a dozen people share it, the price isn't nearly so bad.

- ✔ It's much easier for two or more people to work on the same project if they can easily share information over a network. Suppose you're creating a new marketing brochure to help launch your newest product. You may be great at describing the product in words, but another employee may be far more artistic. You can quickly trade ideas on the network and get the project finished on time.

- ✔ You can use scheduling software, such as Sidekick 98 or Microsoft Outlook, to schedule staff meetings by automatically checking everyone's schedule over the network. It's up to you, though, to make sure the meeting is lively enough that you don't hear snoring from the back of the room!

- ✔ Some networks enable you to share modems so that everyone won't need a modem or an extra phone line. This works best if your online access needs aren't too high.

> ✔ Backups are much easier to organize if your company's important files are all stored in the same place on the network. You won't have to hunt for the files that need to be backed up, and you can make backups part of someone's job description.
>
> ✔ Certain games have options to allow people to play against other users on the network. They often have a "boss key" that players can push to make it look like they're working on a spreadsheet or a document. *Your* employees would never do something like that, would they?

After you have a network, you'll probably think of plenty of other ways to use it. A network almost makes all your computers work together like a much bigger computer — except that your individual computers can still keep on working if one of the other computers has a problem.

Network types and the bottom line

Years ago, in the dark ages of computers, people had a much harder time connecting their systems together in a network. PCs were *personal computers* and networks were something else. You needed special networking software, fancy hardware, lots of cables, and someone with a pocket protector to put it all together. You didn't expect two different types of networks to work together, and the network administrator seldom spoke with ordinary people — such as the people who had to use the network.

Computer networks have come a long way since those times. Most PC operating systems now have the necessary bits and pieces for networking built in, and the hardware is much more standard, too. Oh, you'll still have plenty of cables, but they're mostly hidden behind desks anyway.

Networks are usually classified as being either *peer-to-peer* or *client-server* types. Basically, in a peer-to-peer network, all workstations are equals on the network. In a client-server network, one powerful system controls the network applications and a bunch of workstations run applications. Most small business networks follow the peer-to-peer model.

Just because a network is a peer-to-peer network doesn't mean that all the computers have to be the same. Some workstations can be more equal than others, and others can even serve some of the needs of other workstations.

Choosing your network

Before networking was built into modern PC operating systems, choosing a network was complicated. Today, you hardly have to give it a thought — most computers already have all the networking software you'll need.

If you haven't bought your PCs yet, you can make some choices that will have a direct effect on the network you'll eventually want to create. Here are some of the things that may help you make a better decision:

- Windows 95, Windows 98, Windows NT, and the Mac operating system all have networking components built in. You won't need to buy any additional networking software if your system uses one of these.

- Although you can share some files between Windows and Mac computers on the same network, the two types of computers use different software. This can make sharing some types of files difficult at best. Check to see whether the applications you want to use can share files.

- All versions of Windows NT have more robust networking components than you find in any version of Windows 95, Windows 98, or the Mac operating system. If you need to control who can access certain network resources, make sure those resources are on a system running Windows NT.

- Windows 95 and Windows 98-based computers are quite content to run on Windows NT-based networks.

- You can connect up to ten other computers to a PC running Windows NT Workstation. If your network is larger than that, get Windows NT Server.

- A few programs won't run on Windows NT. Mostly, these are programs that try to get direct access to your hardware — some games, for example. Ask yourself whether you want these types of programs running on your business computers, and whether you can find an alternative, if necessary.

- Windows NT is often up to 20 percent faster than Windows 95 or Windows 98 at running 32-bit software, which includes most software you can buy today. You need a bit more memory for Windows NT — 64MB is a good round figure — but that's a cheap price to pay for faster computers, isn't it?

Network cabling simplified

Choosing network software isn't the only thing that's become a great deal easier in recent years. Choosing the type of wires to connect it all together is simple, too. You have two basic choices (and a bunch of details you don't have to worry about too much).

When you wire your network, you connect all the computers together with cables. PC networks use either a thin coaxial cable similar to the cable that brings cable TV into your house, or a small, flat cable similar to a telephone cord. You use one type of cable throughout a single network.

Here are some considerations to help you decide which type of cable will best suit your needs:

✔ If you use coaxial cable, each computer connects to the next system in a daisy-chain fashion. For example, if three computers are on the network, computer A connects to computer B, and computer B connects to computer C. No direct connection is needed (or even allowed) between computers A and C, but that doesn't prevent them from sharing files just as if they were directly connected.

✔ If you use the flat telephone cord type of cable, each computer must be connected to a special box called a *hub* or a *concentrator*. None of the computers can be connected directly to each other.

✔ Although coaxial cable costs more per foot than telephone type cable, using coaxial cable is generally much cheaper because you don't need to buy a hub. If your network has only a few PCs, coaxial cable is probably the best choice.

✔ Each computer connected to a coaxial cable-based network must be connected using a T connector. In addition, the two computers at each end of the cables must also have a special terminator attached to the unused end of their T connector.

✔ Flat type cable is also called *UTP* (unshielded twisted pair) or *STP* (shielded twisted pair) and uses RJ-45 modular connectors.

✔ The coaxial cable used for computer networks is generally RG-58U, and the connectors are called *BNC*.

After you decide on the type of network and cabling you're going to use, you need to run the cables (or have someone run them for you). Installing the cables isn't just a matter of getting a bunch of wire — you also have to figure out where to put the cables. Here are some things you need to know about installing network cabling:

✔ Although you can save some money buying bulk cable and installing the connectors yourself, you run the risk of creating intermittent network problems if your connections aren't perfect. Buy pre-made, high-quality cables to prevent this problem.

✔ Network cables laid across the floor can be a safety hazard. You can get rubber channels to protect the cables where they cross open areas and to prevent people from tripping.

✔ Never place cables in heating or ventilating ducts. Not only is this a fire hazard, but it may void your insurance policy in the event of a fire — even if the cables didn't cause the problem.

✔ All networks have restrictions on the total length of cables on the network. Make sure your cables are long enough for easy connections, but don't get cables that are a lot longer than necessary.

No matter which type of cable you choose, try to plan your network so that people and cables don't have to mix. If you can cluster your computers, or at least place them so that the cabling will be out of the way, everything will be much neater.

Network security

It's easy enough to see whether someone is sitting down at your desk and messing around with your computer. After you have a network, though, someone can access your system across your network and, if you're not careful, through your modem as well.

Regardless of which operating system your computer is using, tools are available to help keep track of who's doing what on your computer. In addition, you can specify passwords that users must enter to access folders.

Controlling passwords can be confusing. Generally, after someone has entered a password that gives the user access to a network folder, the password is remembered as long as that user remains logged on. This can be dangerous if a user leaves his or her desk for a time without logging off. Even if that user has closed a password-protected network folder, anyone who sits down at the user's PC will usually be able to access that same folder without having to reenter the password. Needless to say, this throws your security right out the window. Network users need to be trained to log off the network whenever they will be away from their desks.

Figure 9-1 shows the Windows Net Watcher you can use to see who's connected to your system. In this case, the computer named Darlene is accessing the D:\BOOKS folder — a folder whose network access is controlled by passwords. You can reach Net Watcher from the Start menu by selecting Programs⇨Accessories⇨System Tools⇨Net Watcher.

Use the security tools

Windows NT is far more secure than any other version of Windows or any version of the Mac operating system. If your network has an open door that provides easy access to the network, do yourself a big favor and let Windows NT control that access door. But even Windows NT can't protect you if you're careless, so make certain you use the network administration tools properly.

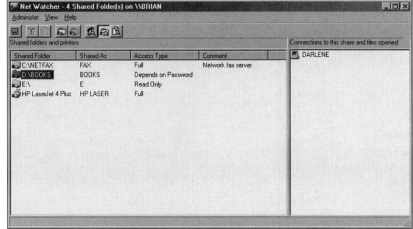

Figure 9-1:
The Net
Watcher
shows you
who's
accessing
your
computer
over the
network.

Although you can use Net Watcher to control which folders and printers on
your computer can be shared by others on the network, it's usually easier to
use Windows Explorer to share folders. You can control printer sharing in
the Printers folder.

Figure 9-2 shows how you can use Windows Explorer to control the sharing
properties for a folder. To display the Properties dialog box for a folder,
right-click on the folder in the Windows Explorer window, and then click on
the Sharing tab.

The Not Shared and Shared As options are *radio buttons;* you can choose one
or the other but not both at the same time. Unless you specify otherwise,
folders are not shared with other users on the network:

- ✔ If you want other users to see a name different than the folder's actual
  name, type the name you want them to see in the Share Name text box.

- ✔ You can add a note to the Comment text box so that other users can
  understand the purpose of the shared folder. For example, you may use
  this option to tell people that the folder is read-only, meaning they can't
  save files in this folder.

Use the Access Type options to control how much access other users have
to the folder:

- ✔ *Read-Only* means that people can view the contents of the folder but
  can't make any changes. This prevents them from modifying or deleting
  any files in the folder or saving any new files in the folder.

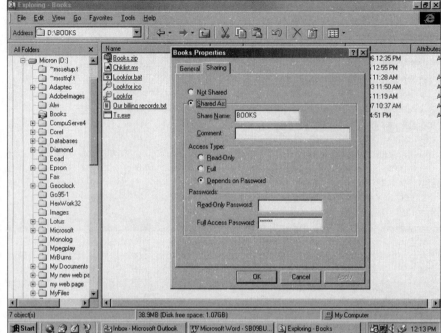

Figure 9-2:
Use the
Sharing tab
of a folder's
Properties
dialog box
to control
how other
people on
the network
can access
your files.

✔ *Full* means anyone can do anything they want in the folder. They can modify, add, or delete — whether you like it or not! You probably wouldn't place important or sensitive files in a shared folder that allows full access.

✔ *Depends on Password* controls access using passwords. You can specify one password that allows read-only access and another that allows full access. Or you can leave the read-only password blank but require a password from anyone who wants to make any changes.

Be careful about which folders you share. Any folders contained in shared folders are also shared — unless you specifically designate them as not shared. If you shared the root folder, C:\, for example, anyone on the network would be able to visit any folder on your entire hard drive. If you enabled full access, then anyone who wanted to could delete files, change records, or even plant a virus.

Always make certain that the folders you share don't contain any folders or files you don't want shared. You can't easily control access to individual files, and you may forget to specify that certain folders should not be shared. It's much safer to simply create a new folder containing only those files you really do want to share, and allow network access only to that new folder.

It's best to provide the least amount of network access that will allow your employees to do what they need to do. If other people need only to get information from your PC, then provide read-only access, not full access. Don't find out the hard way that some people don't know what they're doing — make sure they can't do any damage!

Are You Being Served?

Computer terminology is often confusing, isn't it? Just when you thought you understood the difference between client-server and peer-to-peer networks, this section talks about *servers* for your peer-to-peer network. What's the deal?

Well, as confusing as it may seem, peer-to-peer networks *can* have servers without becoming client-server networks. You see, not all servers are the same. The server on a client-server network is sometimes called an *application server* because that's where the main program, or application, runs. The servers you find on a peer-to-peer network provide different types of services.

Do you need a server on your peer-to-peer network? That depends. If you're going to throw a bunch of parties, it would be nice to have someone serve your guests food and drinks. If you want to share a bunch of files or expensive hardware on your network, you should at least think about some special servers, too.

File servers

File servers are just computers on the network where everyone accesses certain common files, such as inventory files. Imagine how much fun you'd have if everyone had his or her own inventory files. At the end of every day, you'd have to consolidate everyone's work so that you'd have some idea of how much stock you really had. If everyone works from a shared inventory file, however, the records always reflect the actual events.

Here are some other ways that file servers can help your small business:

✔ Large information files can take up a great deal of space. If those files are shared on the network file server, everyone won't need to dedicate so much space to duplicated data.

✔ Information that needs to be updated on a regular basis is much easier to maintain when there's only one copy that everyone shares.

✔ You can have more than one file server on your network. In fact, every computer on the network can function as a file server. You don't need to do anything special to create a file server — except share the folders you want to share, of course.

✔ If you want to allow outside access — perhaps using a modem — to some files, you can isolate that access to a file server to prevent unauthorized people from going places they shouldn't be on your network.

✔ You can extend the life of some older PCs by using a network file server. By storing many of the larger files on the server, you won't need to upgrade that shrinking hard drive quite so soon.

Print servers

Print servers are another option you may want to consider for your network. As you've probably guessed, a print server is just a fancy name for a computer that has a printer it shares on the network.

Here are some print server considerations for your small business network:

✔ If you have limited space, a single shared printer takes up less room than printers attached to every PC.

✔ It's much easier to justify the cost of a high-quality printer when it's shared by everyone on the network.

✔ A single shared printer can be a real pain to use if different jobs require different paper. You may find that it's a whole lot handier to have two or more printers — each dedicated to a specific type of printing.

✔ You may want to make a policy about checking printer supplies so that the same person isn't always stuck filling the paper tray. Anyone who runs a large print job should check that the printer tray isn't nearly empty at the end of the job.

✔ Large capacity paper trays and print cartridges are important on shared printers. Sometimes you can buy larger-than-standard trays and cartridges as options.

✔ You may notice that the print server runs programs a bit slower when big jobs are printing. Print jobs are *spooled* — stored on the hard disk and doled out to the printer in bits and pieces. Any slowdown is far less noticeable on faster computers than on slower ones and isn't noticeable at all on a system that no one is using for anything else.

✔ Printer cables generally can't be more than about ten feet long, so a network print server may be the most effective way to move a noisy printer away from your workstations. You can hide the print server and printer in a closet so that no one has to listen to the racket.

Fax servers

Fax servers aren't nearly as common as file and print servers, but they can be handy as well as economical. Fax servers aren't for everyone, though. Here are some pluses and minuses you'll want to know about fax servers:

- ✔ A shared fax needs only one phone line — not one for each PC — so you may save on your phone bill by creating a fax server.

- ✔ Outgoing faxes are no problem for shared fax modems. Anyone on the network can simply send a fax to the fax server, and the fax goes out when the line is available.

- ✔ Incoming faxes are another matter. Most simple fax software lacks the capability to forward incoming faxes to the correct network computer. Some more sophisticated — read that as expensive — fax sharing software can direct faxes across the network, but you have to spend some time finding software with all the features you want.

- ✔ The most capable fax sharing software runs only on Windows NT. That doesn't mean you *can't* share a fax modem if you aren't running Windows NT, but you simply won't have as many neat features. Here are some Web sites you may want to check out: http://www.blkbox.com/~jonk/ and http://www.gfifax.com/index.htm.

CD-ROM servers

You can share CD-ROMs on your network, too. This may be especially important if your business uses information distributed on CD-ROMs and the sets of discs are too expensive to buy a copy for everyone on the network. You may, for example, subscribe to a service that provides government filing records on frequently updated CD-ROMs. With a *CD-ROM server,* everyone on the network has quick access to the latest information.

Here are some additional facts about CD-ROM servers that you may want to consider:

- ✔ Some software licenses specify that a CD-ROM may not be used on a network. Check before you spend the money to install a CD-ROM server.

- ✔ Sharing CD-ROMs on a network works best when everyone needs to access the same discs. If users often need to access many different discs, it is much more efficient to have them load the disc they need on their own PC.

- ✔ Some companies make special CD-ROM servers that can load a few different discs at the same time by using separate CD-ROM drives. One of the best is made by Plextor, which you can find at http://www.plextor.com/product.htm.

✔ If your users need to access a small number of different CD-ROMs frequently, you may be able to avoid getting a dedicated CD-ROM server by keeping the discs loaded in different systems on the network and sharing those drives. Of course, this won't work if employees can't keep their hands off their CD-ROM drives.

✔ Although some companies make CD-ROM changers, these probably aren't a good choice for sharing on your network. Imagine what would happen if two employees needed to use information from discs in the CD-ROM changer at the same time — but they needed information from different discs. Whoever got there first would be the winner, and the other person would simply have to wait around until the first person was finished.

Don't Drag Me Down

How much time can you afford to waste today? If your network isn't working correctly, you may be wasting a whole lot more time than you'd like. And worse, everyone on the network will be wasting time that could be better spent making money for your business.

But aren't computers supposed to be really fast? Don't they do everything at lightning-fast speed? Well, the longer you use a computer, the slower it will seem. It's true that computers can do a great deal of work in a remarkably short period of time, but plenty of things can slow them down.

A long time ago, PCs did one thing at a time. If you wanted to type a letter, you turned on the computer and loaded your word processor. When you were finished writing, you told the system to print your letter — and you waited while the letter was printed. If you wanted to work on a spreadsheet, you saved your work, closed the word processor, loaded the spreadsheet program, and then started your spreadsheet work. If you then needed to send a file to someone, well, you first had to save your work, close the spreadsheet program, and load the communications program. Changing from one process to another took a long time, and you ended up waiting for the computer quite a bit.

It's probably a good guess that swapping between programs wasted at least a minute every time you needed to do something else with those early PCs. You probably wouldn't be too far off figuring that early PC users lost a few hours a week because of this wasted time. Today's PCs are much faster and can do several things at the same time. Even so, those annoying little delays start to add up. A couple of seconds here and there may not seem like much — unless you're paying for all that lost time and realize how much it's costing you.

Watch out for that 486 anchor

If you have an old 486-based PC sitting around, it's tempting to think it would make a good file, print, or fax server, isn't it? After all, that old boat anchor is too slow for anyone to use, and if it's just sitting there handling some of those jobs no one else wants, you can get some use out of it.

That idea has one major flaw: Putting that old piece of leftover junk on your network will slow things down for everybody. Unfortunately, there's no way around the problem, either.

Virtually all modern PC networks are known as *Ethernet* networks. These types of networks run at either 10Mbps (millions of bits per second) or 100Mbps. You don't need sophisticated math skills to recognize that one of these is ten times as fast as the other. Can you guess which one your old 486 system would use?

Almost all 486 systems are limited to 10Mbps for one simple reason: To run at 100Mbps requires a network adapter that plugs into a PCI expansion slot. Your old 486 probably doesn't have PCI slots, so the 486 and the rest of your network are stuck at 10Mbps. If you've ever sat near the back of an airliner, it's easy to understand the problem. When the plane lands, someone in front of you always walks about as fast as paint dries. You can't get around the slowpoke because the aisles are too narrow. It doesn't matter that you're in a hurry — until that person is off the plane, you're stuck going at a snail's pace. That's the way an old 486 works on your network — everyone else has to slow down to the same slow rate for transferring data across the network. With a 486 on your network, you get about 10 percent of what you paid for — quite the bargain, wouldn't you say?

So how can you speed up the network without dumping your classic 486? You haven't been listening, have you? Find someone who doesn't know anything about PCs and give them that antique — your business can't afford to keep it around!

Networks are notorious time-wasters. When you start thinking about putting in a network in your small business, you'll probably be thinking about only how much time the network will save. It's true that networks can save a lot of time, but it's also true that they can waste a lot of time.

How can this be? Well, you may do many things that can waste your time and money. Here are some bottlenecks you want to avoid:

✔ It can be tempting to try to save money by installing one copy of a program and having everyone on the network run that copy. This is generally both illegal and stupid. Running that one copy of the program requires each PC to download the program across the network, putting a lot of unnecessary traffic on the network.

✔ Programs that aren't designed for network use often lack the sophisticated methods of providing data access included in real network applications. The result can be that an entire file, rather than a single record, may be locked when someone is accessing data — preventing more than one person from working with the data at a time. There's a big difference between applications designed for network use and applications that simply say they will work on a network!

✔ Poorly designed programs may send too much data at one time. If all you need is someone's phone number, you probably don't need a complete record of what they bought from your company over the past year.

✔ Video and other types of graphics files can be huge. If someone on the network is downloading real-time video files, there won't be much network capacity left for anyone else to use.

Open the Door and Let Me In

Your network doesn't have to stop at your front door. If anyone who's part of your small business does business away from the office, you want that person to have remote access to your network. If you can call in and get the latest information right on your laptop PC, you can give your customers immediate answers.

You don't need a huge network to provide remote access. In fact, you don't need a network at all. You can use the same technique to provide secure access to a single PC as you use for an entire network — which is lucky, because you won't have to change much when your business grows.

Controlling access

The last thing you need is for just anyone to be able to get into your system — whether you have a network or a single PC. Those who call in from outside should have to identify themselves and should get through the front door only if you give them authorization. In other words, outside access should work just like network access. If you don't know the correct password, you shouldn't get in.

One way that remote network access differs from local network access is that remote access typically is far less secure. To log on to your network locally, you probably need to enter both your user name and a password. To log on to your network remotely, you probably need to enter only a password. Even though this may seem somewhat backward, it's not. You'll likely have only one modem set up for remote access, so anyone who needs to call in will have to call that same modem. A single dial-in account is much less work to administer, and with reasonable caution on your part, it should handle your needs.

If you allow remote access to your small business network, remember that many dishonest people are out there playing with computers. Many have programs that can cycle through thousands of password attempts in a few seconds. If you use an easily guessed word for your remote access password, don't be surprised if someone gains unauthorized access to your network. Make sure you use a password that would be hard to stumble across. Security experts typically recommend using passwords that contain uppercase and lowercase letters as well as numbers. It's much harder to guess a password such as 4rAnDOM32 than one such as ralph.

Don't forget to change the remote access password often, too. Be sure to change it immediately when an employee leaves or if someone outside your company has had a chance to find out the password. At the very least, change the password every month.

Enabling outside access

To allow someone to dial in and access your system remotely, you need software that manages that remote access. In Windows, this software was originally called the Remote Access Service, or RAS. Now it's more commonly called the Dial-Up Networking Server. You can obtain similar software for a Mac, including one product called Timbuktu.

Windows NT includes a version of the Dial-Up Networking Server that allows several callers to access your network through different connections at the same time. For most small business needs, this is probably overkill — at least in the beginning. You can try out a version of the Dial-Up Networking Server that allows one caller at a time to access your system if you have either Windows 95 with the Plus! add-on or Windows 98 (which doesn't need the Plus! add-on).

The Dial-Up Server is an optional Windows component. If you try the following steps and don't see the Dial-Up Server option, you can add it using the Communications option on the Windows Setup tab of the Add/Remove Programs dialog box.

Here's how you can set up the Dial-Up Server so that you or someone else can dial in to your PC:

1. **Double-click on the My Computer icon on your desktop.**

   In Windows 98, you may need to click only once, depending on how your computer is set up.

2. **In the My Computer window, double-click on the Dial-Up Networking icon.**

   The Dial-Up Networking window has icons for any connections that are set up for you to call other computers — such as a connection to the Internet.

3. Choose Connections➪Dial-Up Server.

The Dial-Up Server dialog box appears, as shown in Figure 9-3.

Figure 9-3:
The Dial-Up
Server
allows
someone to
access your
PC or the
network
through
your
modem.

4. To enable someone to call in, click on the Allow Caller Access option.

Remember that radio buttons are mutually exclusive — when you select one radio button, the other radio buttons in the same group are deselected.

5. Click on the Change Password button.

The Dial-Up Networking Password dialog box appears, as shown in Figure 9-4.

It's important to configure the Dial-Up Networking Server to require a password; otherwise, anyone who calls in can access your files.

Figure 9-4:
Don't forget
to set up a
password.

6. In the New Password text box, type a password.

If this is the first time you're using the Dial-Up Networking Server, you won't need to enter anything in the Old Password text box. Otherwise, you need to know the old password before you can change it.

7. **In the Confirm New Password text box, type the same password you typed in the New Password box.**

   Because the password won't be visible when you're typing it, this gives you the chance to make certain you typed the correct password the first time. Make sure you know exactly what you typed — you wouldn't want to be visiting a customer and find out you didn't know your own password!

8. **Click on OK to close the Dial-Up Networking Password dialog box.**

   If you decide not to change the password, click on the Cancel button.

9. **Click on the Server Type button.**

   The Server Types dialog box appears, as shown in Figure 9-5. (You may need to remove the checks from the Enable Software Compression and Require Encrypted Password options if you have trouble connecting when you dial in.)

Figure 9-5:
You may
need to
disable the
Advanced
options.

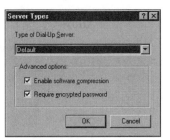

10. **Click on OK to return to the Dial-Up Server dialog box and then click on Apply to make your system accessible.**

    The Status indicator changes from `Idle` to `Monitoring` to indicate that the Dial-Up Networking Server is waiting to answer incoming calls. At this point, anyone can dial in to your modem, enter the remote access password, and access any shared resources on your PC.

11. **When you no longer need to allow access through Dial-Up Networking, be sure to select the No Caller Access option in the Dial-Up Server dialog box and click on Apply.**

    Until you do this, your modem is an open door into your system. That's why it's so important to specify passwords when you set up the Dial-Up Networking Server. Unless you have password protection, anyone can dial into your PC and do whatever he or she likes!

Don't forget to share the folders that the caller needs to access. If you haven't shared any folders (or printers), people can call in but they can't do anything. In fact, it will seem as though your Dial-Up Server isn't even working because the caller won't be able to see anything on your system.

Unless you have the Dial-Up Server window visible, you won't have any good way to tell when someone is accessing your system remotely. Be sure to check the Dial-Up Server Status indicator before you shut down your system or take other actions that could disrupt someone who's dialed into your network.

Part IV

Choosing Your Software

In this part . . .

Computers can't do much without software — except for making pretty good paperweights. In Part IV, you discover how to choose the right software that will make your computer a real working business partner. You even get a taste of putting your business on the Internet so that millions of potential customers can find you.

And with software comes software upgrades, so this part also shows you how to win at the software upgrade game. Software companies want your money, but why let them call all the shots? Why not decide for yourself when to stay put, when to upgrade, and when to jump ship and try something new?

Chapter 10

Finding the Best Small Business Software

*A*fter you put together the perfect computer for your small business, what's next? Software, that's what. I have some good news: The right small business software will save you plenty of time and money.

Getting the right software isn't too hard. Still, you should be armed before you dive in to do battle with the office store clerk. You'll find several general types of software useful in your business:

✔ People have taken to calling certain packages of software *office suites*. It's probably better than calling them bananas, but don't you wish for something more creative? In a typical office suite, you find a word processor, a spreadsheet, a graphics program, and a database program. Office suites take the Swiss Army knife approach: They do a bit of everything.

✔ Accounting software helps you keep track of who owes you what and what you owe. Although accounting software isn't fun, it's better than telling the IRS that you have the receipt in a shoebox somewhere.

✔ It's probably a safe bet that you'd like your business to grow. If so, you'll want a business plan, especially if you intend to borrow money.

✔ *Information managers* — programs that help you keep track of your contacts and your schedule — can save you all sorts of embarrassment, and they can make you look pretty smart, too.

✔ Much of what a lawyer does is fill out forms full of legal mumbo jumbo. You can save a bundle by doing it yourself with your PC and the right legal software. You can even skip the lawyer jokes!

Making a Deal on a Bundle

Everyone likes to get a good deal. Manufacturers like to make you think you're getting a good deal, too, because maybe then you'll overlook what else they're trying to do to you. That's one of the reasons that PC manufacturers bundle software with their systems. "Just look, Marge, they're giving me a free cookbook on CD-ROM when I buy this computer for only $1,999.99." Never mind that the computer is an overpriced, obsolete 486 system — it's that "free" deal that's important, right?

Magicians use a similar technique called *misdirection* to get you to watch their right hand while they secretly palm a silver dollar in their left hand. All of a sudden, the coin is in the hand that you'd swear was empty a second ago. When you're buying your computer system, you don't want to be the one to end up empty-handed!

Software bundles *can* be a good deal, but only if they add something to the package. Even the best software bundle can't make up for a lousy deal or junk hardware. You can get some idea of the bundle's value if you consider these points:

✔ Any software in a bundle should be something you really can use. Otherwise, it will sit on your shelf taking up space. In figuring the value of the bundled software, reduce the value to half what the manufacturer says it's worth.

✔ Software bundles should contain the most current versions of the software. If you have to upgrade to get the newest release, reduce the bundle value by one and a half times the cost of the upgrade to make up for the hassle of upgrading.

✔ Bundles often include "lite" versions, which don't include the complete range of features or which you can use only for a limited time. In figuring the value of the bundled software, reduce the value by the full cost of buying the full version to replace any lite versions.

✔ Get a written promise that you can return the system with no restocking charge if the software you want turns out to be incompatible. Manufacturers often "forget" to tell their prospective customers that a system is incompatible with the newest software version. Sometimes only one piece of hardware is incompatible, but it may be the one that's important to you.

✔ Bundled software usually doesn't include printed manuals. If the PC manufacturer won't give you the printed manuals, reduce the bundled software value by half for any software you don't already know inside and out.

✔ Make certain all the bundled software is really intended for the operating system you'll be using. If you want to run Windows NT, for example, you may not be able to run that DOS-based game they're throwing in. Reduce the bundle value by the value of the software if the manufacturer won't guarantee that every piece will run on the operating system you prefer.

✔ Unless you want to spend a lot of time reading condensed or cutesy articles, consider most bundled encyclopedia software best suited to use as a coaster under your morning coffee.

Okay, does this mean you should avoid software bundles? No. You should, however, be aware that the deals aren't usually what they seem. Much of the software in a bundle is there simply to inflate the "retail" value of the package. But the PC manufacturer didn't pay retail, so neither should you! When you're shopping for a PC, make sure you discount the software add-ons in figuring the real value of the whole package.

What if you find the right PC, but it has the wrong software package? You probably won't have much success getting the software package switched to a different package, but you'll never know unless you ask. You might also ask what kind of discount you would get if you skipped the software package.

Skip the Ordinary Room. I Want a Suite.

Included software isn't all snake oil and empty promises; some good deals are out there. *Office suites* — bundles of the most common business applications — are worth more than what you'll probably pay for them.

Office suite sweet deals (try saying that fast three times!) are the result of a battle between three huge companies that all want to own your desktop: Microsoft, Corel, and Lotus. You can choose any one of them and be perfectly happy or completely miserable. However, you'll probably end up somewhere in the middle.

Office suites

You can buy office software suites from each of the three major software companies. You may find the choices a little confusing, though. Microsoft offers Microsoft Office in standard, professional, and small business editions. Corel offers WordPerfect Suite in standard, pro, and several specialized editions. Lotus has one primary edition of SmartSuite.

Why are the three giants so interested in getting you hooked on their office suites? They want to build brand loyalty so that when it's time for you to buy more software or upgrade your existing software, you'll spend your money on their software.

Although each of the three major office suites includes little extra bits and pieces, you'll use the main programs the most. Each suite includes the same types of main programs: a word processor, a spreadsheet, presentation graphics, and, optionally, a database manager.

If you do choose Microsoft Office, you may want to pick up *Small Business Microsoft Office 97 For Dummies* by Todd Stauffer and Dave Johnson (published by IDG Books Worldwide, Inc.) to find out more about using this office software suite.

A trend in office suites is to blur the distinction between general office software and specialized packages through the introduction of specialized versions of office suites. Corel, for example, has a medical edition of its WordPerfect Suite, and Microsoft has a small business edition of Microsoft Office. You may want to check out these specialized versions if one is aimed at your type of business. Just be sure to watch out for the pieces that may have been left out of the package. You may want to compare the packages to see what's included before you make a decision.

Working with words

Word processors are just very fancy typewriters. Well, maybe a typewriter crossed with an English teacher is more like it. Even if you're a lousy typist, can't spell, and don't know the difference between *its* and *it's,* a word processor can help make your letters look good. (Content, however, is an entirely different issue.)

All modern word processors can check your spelling and grammar. The latest versions can even check for and correct errors as you type. The effect can seem a little funky the first few times you see mistyped words magically correct themselves, but you get used to it quickly.

No word processor can turn you into the next Hemingway, but then, even he said, "We are all apprentices in a craft where no one ever becomes a master." As long as your business correspondence looks professional, you're halfway there.

The three office suite word processors are called Microsoft Word, Corel WordPerfect, and Lotus Word Pro. All three have been around for quite some time (Word Pro used to be called AmiPro), and, not surprisingly, their features are pretty much interchangeable — if you can type a letter in Word, WordPerfect, or Word Pro, the others will be a snap to use, too. Figures 10-1, 10-2, and 10-3 show how much the three look like each other.

Even though each of the three word processors starts out with a different appearance, you're not stuck with that look. With some playing around, you can make Word look as sparse as Word Pro, or make WordPerfect or Word Pro look as cluttered as Word.

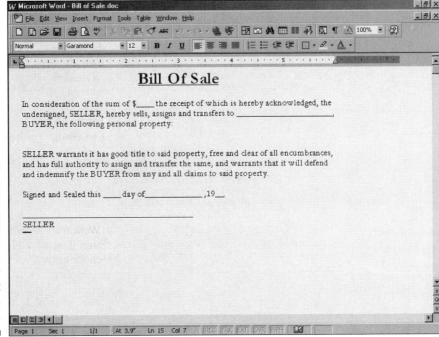

Figure 10-1: Microsoft Word loads plenty of tools and information about your document on the screen.

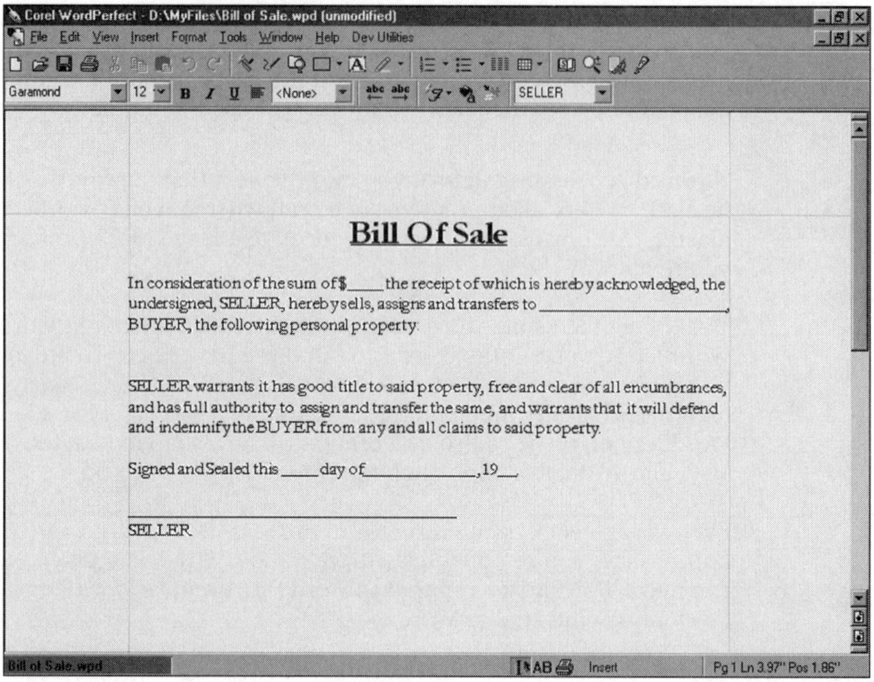

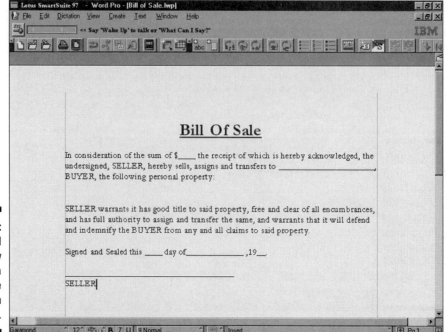

Figure 10-2:
Corel
WordPerfect
shows the
page
margins,
too.

Figure 10-3:
Lotus Word
Pro now
includes a
voice
dictation
option.

Most of the time, it doesn't matter which word processor you choose. Your letters look similar whether you type them in Word, WordPerfect, or Word Pro. If you work alone, it's hard to make a good argument in favor of one of these word processors over the other — unless you happen to own stock in Microsoft, Corel, or IBM, which owns Lotus.

Sometimes, however, it does make a difference which word processor you use:

✔ If you need to share document files with someone who uses a different word processor, everything may not come out quite right when he or she opens your files. Each of the three software companies *claims* to be able to open the other's files, but the results aren't always the greatest!

✔ If you need to use *templates* (special files with styles, macros, and other stuff most people don't care about), you'll probably have to use the same word processor. None of the three word processors can use the others' template files correctly.

✔ If you want to automate a document using programming, you're stuck again because each of the three word processors uses its own programming language.

✔ Lotus Word Pro is the only one of the three that currently includes voice dictation software in the box. You can buy voice dictation software separately for Word and WordPerfect, though.

✔ If you decide to get into programming your documents, you're in for another rude awakening. Even if you stick with one word processor, the programming languages may not work when you upgrade to a newer version of the same word processor.

Playing with numbers

If *spreadsheets* make you think of geeky folks with pocket protectors, slide rules, and tape on their glasses, you're not alone. Who else could love a program devoted to solving strange equations like the ones you see on the blackboard in the mad scientist's lab in every old science fiction movie? Accountants, that's who!

Spreadsheets are like word processors for numbers. You put in a bunch of numbers, throw in some formulas, and out come the answers. If you're creative with spreadsheets, you may be able to convince yourself that the numbers make sense. Now *that's* scary!

The Microsoft Office spreadsheet is called Excel, the Corel WordPerfect Suite spreadsheet is called Quattro Pro, and the Lotus SmartSuite spreadsheet is called 1-2-3. All three have been around for some time.

If you thought the word processors looked similar, you won't be surprised at the appearance of the spreadsheets, either. If you've seen one spreadsheet, you've seen them all. If you *have* seen them all, take two aspirin and don't call me in the morning! Figure 10-4 shows a typical small business spreadsheet as it may appear in Excel.

Here are some things you'll want to know about spreadsheets:

✔ You guessed it, there is one important difference between Excel, Quattro Pro, and 1-2-3. Although they can do most of the same calculations, they can't run each other's spreadsheet programming language. Each one speaks only its own language. That may be important if you need to use someone else's spreadsheet in your business.

✔ If you're really into numbers, you may be interested to know that Quattro Pro has a few more built-in *functions* (calculations you can use in a formula) than Excel or 1-2-3. Most of the extra functions are pretty funky, though. After all, do you really care what your checkbook balance would be in base 17?

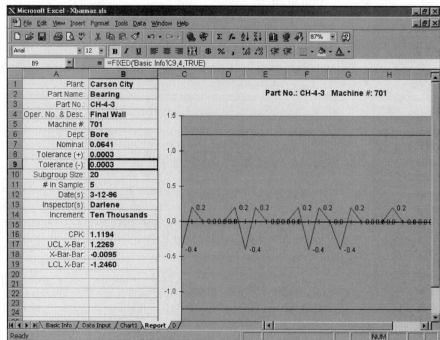

Figure 10-4: Spreadsheets analyze numbers so you can impress your accountant.

✔ If you do need to create your own functions for some off-the-wall calculation, Excel is probably the best choice. You can create special functions using VBA (Visual Basic for Applications), which is the programming language Microsoft would like everyone in the world to use.

✔ It's a little easier to create graphs in Quattro Pro than in Excel or 1-2-3, but all three are pretty handy for creating charts.

✔ It can be difficult to modify charts in Excel. In fact, it's often easier to just start over, making sure you get it right the second time.

Producing pictures

The third major piece of software in each of the office suites is called *presentation graphics,* which is a fancy way of saying "pictures." You'll probably think of these programs as sign makers, because that's what people do with them the most.

Presentation graphics programs started out as a way to make slides shown on overhead projectors in boring meetings where nearly everyone except the speaker dozes off. Maybe that's why most speakers bring along copies of their presentation — so you'll know what went on during your nap!

The Microsoft Office graphics program is PowerPoint, the Corel WordPerfect Suite graphics program is Presentations, and the Lotus SmartSuite graphics program is Freelance Graphics.

You don't have to be an artist to make signs or other graphics with these programs (it may even be better if you aren't!). Each comes with a set of *clip art,* pre-made images that vary in quality from "My kindergartner can do better than that" to "Say, that's not too bad for an amateur." Figure 10-5 shows a sign created in Corel Presentations.

All three presentation graphics programs will probably do everything you need, but you'll find some differences. Here are some things you'll want to know about presentation graphics programs:

✔ You can create self-running slide shows with any of the presentation graphics programs. This can be a great way to show off your company's products at a trade show, at a flea market ("Yes, I'll take that yellow-striped flea, please"), or even right in your shop window.

✔ Don't plan on using a file from one of the three presentation graphics programs in one of the others. Even if they can open a file, you won't like the problems you'll have, especially if you try to run any slide show programming in the file.

✔ Corel Presentations is the clear winner if you want a lot of free clip art, because it generally includes 10,000 or so clip art images on the CD-ROM. The other suites have nowhere near that amount of clip art.

Database programs

Database programs are the remaining major office suite application. A database is simply a method of storing information so that you can access the information in an organized fashion. Your address book is a typical database; you probably have it organized to let you look up people and companies by name.

Although each of the office suites has a database program available, both Microsoft and Corel offer versions of their office suites that don't include a database program. Lotus includes its database program in every copy of its office suite. If you need to organize data, be sure the office suite version you buy includes the database program. Otherwise, you have to spend extra to add the program.

Microsoft's database is called Access, Corel's is called Paradox, and the Lotus database is Approach.

Figure 10-5:
A few minutes with some clip art and you have a sign.

You may be pleasantly surprised by some of the pre-built applications included with database programs. For example, Figure 10-6 shows an order management application you get for free with Approach. The other two database programs include similar but not identical applications.

The most useful databases are *relational* databases. Relational databases use a series of tables (or files) to organize related information in an efficient manner. For example, an address list may have a table that stores company information. If the company changes its address, you need change the address only once for all the company's employees, instead of having to change it for each employee individually.

Here are some important considerations in choosing a database program:

- ✔ Each of the three uses its own file format. Although each claims to be able to read files from the other two, they can't always read the most current versions. Approach 97, for example, can read Paradox 4.5 files, but not Paradox versions 5, 7, or 8 files.

- ✔ Even if you can read the data from a different database program, don't expect to be able to use the forms, reports, or queries from another program.

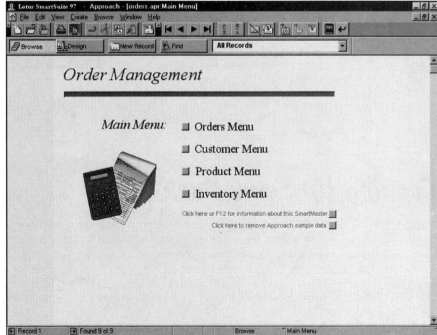

Figure 10-6: The other two database programs include bonus applications similar to the Order Management system from Approach.

✔ You can't use any programming from a different database program. If you need to use a database application that someone has created, you need to have the right database program and probably the correct version, too.

✔ If you have to share database information and aren't sure which program someone else may use, save the data in dBASE format. The dBASE format lacks some of the fancier data types and a few other bells and whistles, but it's considered a more or less universal database format for sharing data.

Let's get compatible

Compatibility in your computer is important. If your programs don't get along with each other, the computer, or the operating system, you have a big mess. That's the main reason that most people who'd like to remain sane don't try to mix Windows-based PCs with Macs: They just aren't very compatible. For the most part, Mac software won't run on PCs, and Windows software won't run on Macs.

Here are some important compatibility issues to consider:

✔ It's safer to assume that products within a single office suite are more compatible with each other than with other programs.

✔ Add-ins that enhance an application program are almost never compatible with different programs or even different versions of the same program. You can't expect Excel add-ins to work with Quattro Pro, for example.

✔ Converting a file from one format to another often produces some strange changes. A carefully laid-out document may end up pretty disorganized.

Cooking Up Some Books

You can't run a successful business without keeping some books: records of your income, expenses, and other basic financial facts. If you're starting out with a small business, perhaps you think that keeping track of all that stuff isn't necessary. If so, you're making a big mistake.

Good accounting records are important for many different reasons, such as the following:

✔ Unless you know what's coming in and what's going out, you can't be certain it's even worth your time to run your business. You won't make up losses on every sale by increasing your volume; you'll just lose your shirt that much faster!

✔ The tax people want accurate income and expense information. You won't get away with saying "I guess I about broke even last year" when you're called in for an audit.

✔ Don't think about trying to borrow money for your small business unless you can show that the business can make a profit. Bankers have less of a sense of humor than the folks at the IRS.

Accounting the hard way

There's an easy way and a hard way to do almost anything. If you're just getting started in a small business, you probably do many things the hard way because you don't know about the easier way.

One of the surest ways to make keeping your books hard is to try to reinvent the wheel. After all, you have an office suite and it includes a spreadsheet program, so why not create an accounting system in a spreadsheet? Because it's too hard, that's why!

Many years ago, in the early days of personal computing, the large company I worked for asked me to set up an accounting system using a spreadsheet. Having nothing better to do (and wanting that paycheck to keep coming in), I worked on a program with the help of our chief accountant. Many months later, we had our spreadsheet: a monster so huge that a printout of it covered the walls of my office.

Was that the end of it? Could I start working on more interesting projects? Of course not! Over the next several years, we stroked, refined, cussed, and wheedled that monstrosity as we tried to kill all the subtle errors and add needed updates. Any money you think you'll save by trying to create your own accounting system in a spreadsheet will quickly disappear when you realize how much time you've wasted.

Accounting the easier way

A relatively painless way exists to keep the books for your small business. Dedicated small business accounting software is the answer to keeping track of who you owe, who owes you, and all the other picky financial details.

QuickBooks and QuickBooks Pro are some of the most popular small business accounting packages. Because you were smart enough to buy this book, you'll find trial versions on the *Small Business Computing For Dummies* CD-ROM. Chapter 13 has some information on using QuickBooks to help keep your books.

QuickBooks and QuickBooks Pro are similar. The Pro version includes a few extra reports, more advanced job costing and budgeting, estimates and bids, and time tracking for people who bill by the length of time they spend on a project. All basic accounting functions are the same in both versions, so if you don't need the extra features of the Pro version, the basic version should be right for you. To make things a bit less confusing, I use *QuickBooks* to refer to either version unless there's an important difference you need to know about. To find out which version best suits your needs, visit http://www.intuit.com/quickbooks.

If you've ever tried to talk with an accountant, you know that the accounting field has its own jargon — most of which seems designed to make ordinary people feel stupid. Accountants talk about *accounts receivable, accounts payable, aging, credits, debits,* and so on as if anyone really cared. You're much more interested in knowing what bills you have and who owes you money.

QuickBooks doesn't force that jargon on you. Oh sure, you'll probably pick up a little as you use the program, but that's optional. Figure 10-7 shows the main QuickBooks screen you see after installing the program.

In addition to just keeping your books (although that's quite a bit by itself), QuickBooks can do much more. Here are some of the small business functions QuickBooks can handle to make your business run more smoothly:

- ✔ QuickBooks can prepare professional-looking invoices. You don't need to buy special and expensive forms, calculate sales taxes, or worry about costly math errors in your billings.

- ✔ You can use online banking and bill payments and even transfer money between bank accounts right from QuickBooks.

- ✔ If you have employees, QuickBooks can handle your payroll chores. You won't have to struggle with all those tax and deduction calculations.

- ✔ QuickBooks makes inventory and purchase order tracking a snap.

- ✔ If you use TurboTax to figure out what you owe the government, the information you enter in QuickBooks won't have to be reentered when you figure your taxes. It won't make paying taxes any more fun, but at least you won't have to spend so much time doing it.

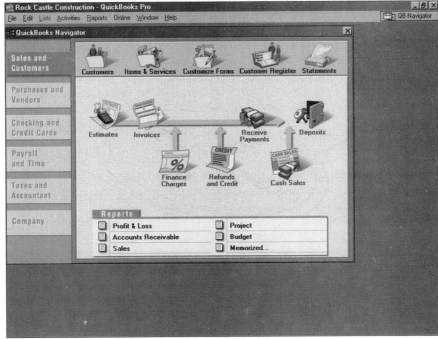

Figure 10-7: QuickBooks is designed for ordinary people to keep the books for a small business.

QuickBooks and QuickBooks Pro aren't the only small business accounting programs you can get for your computer, but they're some of the easiest to use and most capable packages around.

Making Some Plans

Do you have a business plan? No, I don't mean "I plan to make tons of money selling these widgets." I mean a written business plan that you could present to your banker or a potential investor. If the answer is no, start thinking about creating a business plan.

Writing a good business plan is difficult. In many ways, a business plan is like a resume for your business — and you know how hard it can be to write a good resume. You have to be honest, but you also have to throw in some promotion. You have to tell the reader not only what you've accomplished, but also where you're going.

There's no reason that you can't sit down with your word processor and spreadsheet and create your business plan, but you need to know where to begin, what to say, and what to include. That's where something like Jian BizPlanBuilder Interactive comes in. Using this software to create your business plan is almost like having a wise old business manager standing at your side, helping you create your plan. You'll find BizPlanBuilder Interactive on the CD-ROM. If you decide it looks right for you, you can call Jian for the code you need to unlock the program so that you can use it right away.

Figure 10-8 shows the beginning of a sample business plan in BizPlanBuilder Interactive. You can find out much more about this software in Chapter 12.

You can visit the Jian Web site at http://www.jianusa.com/ to find out more about its other products. All of Jian's software seems to have one goal: making things easier on the small businessperson.

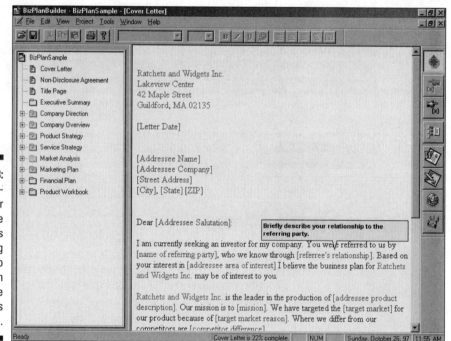

Figure 10-8: BizPlan-Builder Interactive has everything you need to create an effective business plan.

Staying on the Right Track

Do you ever get the feeling you're drowning in information? Between to-do lists, phone numbers, your events calendar, and all the other information that hits you every day, there's hardly time to run your business. An *information manager,* or *PIM* (Personal Information Manager), can help you organize and keep track of all that information. With the many choices of PIMs, you should be able to find one you love.

One of the best-known PIMs is Sidekick. Figure 10-9 shows a sample contact list in Sidekick 98. Sidekick 98 has a feature you won't see in other PIMs: a moving world time display that constantly shows your local time and the time at several other locations around the world. You can download a full-featured trial version of Sidekick 98 from http://www.starfish.com.

The *Small Business Computing For Dummies* CD-ROM includes a few shareware PIMs you can try out: 2do and Executive Desk. Each takes a different approach, so try them all to see which one you prefer.

If you have one of the office suites, you'll find additional variations on the information manager theme. Microsoft Office includes Outlook, which is shown in Figure 10-10. Corel WordPerfect Suite 8 includes CorelCENTRAL, and Lotus SmartSuite includes Organizer. Windows 98 and Windows NT 5 include a "lite" version of Outlook called Outlook Express.

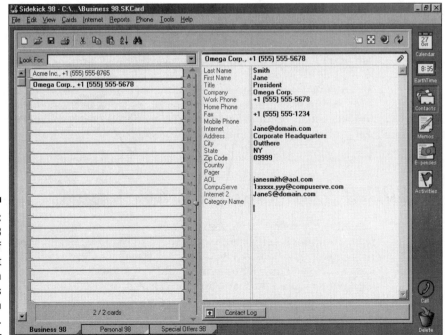

Figure 10-9: Sidekick 98 is one of the best information managers you can find.

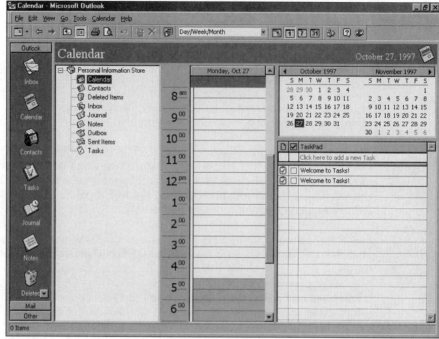

Figure 10-10:
Each major
office suite
includes a
PIM, such as
Microsoft
Office's
Outlook.

Sidekick 98 has one feature you'll really appreciate if you're going to create a Web site for your small business. The Web Publisher makes it easy to publish calendars and contact lists in *HTML*, the language of the Web. This feature is handy because you won't have to do anything special to keep your Web pages up-to-date. After you update your Sidekick 98 calendar or contact list, you're just a few mouse clicks away from updating your Web pages, too.

All three major office suites include e-mail features connected with their PIM. Microsoft Outlook (and Outlook Express) as well as CorelCENTRAL work as e-mail centers. SmartSuite includes a separate e-mail program that will probably be part of Lotus Organizer in a future version of SmartSuite.

Keeping Your Agreements Legal

Sometimes it seems as if small-business owners are buried in legal require-ments. Although software can't handle all your legal needs, it can help reduce your legal costs. Why should you pay a lawyer to create a standard form such as a contract or agreement from scratch when you can create legal agreements with just a little help from your PC?

Jian's Agreement Builder is an example of legal documentation software for small businesses. It creates contracts that use plain English (that language lawyers seem to hate). Agreement Builder has more than 100 small business contracts and agreements you can use for the majority of your contract needs. Each contract is a template you can customize in your word processor. Figure 10-11 shows another type of agreement in Agreement Builder — Articles of Incorporation. You can also find employment agreements, sales contracts, contractor agreements, and so on in this package. The Agreement Builder manual provides a mini-course in contract law to help you understand what the agreements mean — try that with the typical contract written by a lawyer! You can find out more about using Agreement Builder in Chapter 14.

You can find out more about Agreement Builder at http://www.jianusa.com. You may also want to visit http://members.aol.com/bmethven/index.html, a Web site dedicated to business law. If you need to find a lawyer, check out http://www.wld.com/.

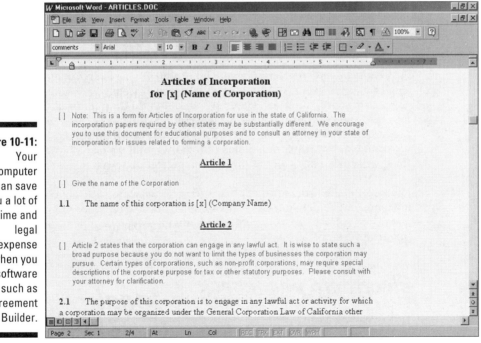

Figure 10-11: Your computer can save you a lot of time and legal expense when you use software such as Agreement Builder.

You still need a lawyer

Software isn't a substitute for a lawyer. When you create an agreement or a contract using legal agreement software, you may want to have your lawyer review the agreement before you present it. This is especially true if the contract involves a lot of money or if you have any questions about what the agreement means.

There's More?

I've only scratched the surface of what your PC can do for your small business. One of the great things about having a computer is that it won't complain when you ask it to do lots of different jobs. This section describes some other types of small business software you may find pretty neat.

Project management software

Project management software isn't something you're likely to need in a really small business. After all, if you do everything, it's easy to schedule who's going to work on a project. "Let's see, should I do that job or should I assign it to me?" When your business grows, you may discover that multi-person projects are harder to manage. You need to know when the right people will be available, how their schedules fit together, and how much the whole thing will cost. That's where project management software comes in.

Microsoft makes some project management software with the really surprising name of Project. You can find out more about Project at `http://www.microsoft.com/project/`, and you may even be able to download a free trial version.

Electronic phonebooks

Who would pay good money for information they can get for free in their phonebook? Anyone who understands the value of having that information in a usable format, that's who. *Electronic phonebooks* are huge databases full of much more useful information than you'll find in any printed phonebook. Here are some of the reasons an electronic phonebook may be useful to your small business:

✔ If you want more than the phone numbers in your local phone company's phonebook, an electronic phonebook is for you. Every published phone number in the country is contained on several CD-ROMs.

✔ Do you need a reverse listing so that you can find out who a phone number belongs to? Your phone company won't tell you, but an electronic phonebook will.

✔ You can use an electronic phonebook to create a mailing list for everyone in a specified radius of your business, in a specific ZIP code, or in an entire city. If you've ever priced mailing lists, you'll know what a bargain electronic phonebooks are.

✔ If you need to search for someone and all you know is the person's name, an electronic phonebook may be able to find that person. You can use several Internet services — such as Bigfoot, Four11, InfoSpace, SwitchBoard, Verisign, and WhoWhere — to try to locate people, but none is quite as convenient as an electronic phonebook on CD-ROM.

✔ You can search an electronic phonebook using the SIC code (a standard business classification) to locate businesses that may be potential customers or competitors.

✔ Some electronic phonebooks include demographic information so that you can target your marketing efforts in areas where people may need your products or services.

✔ Electronic phonebooks generally include street-mapping programs, too. If your company makes service calls or deliveries, you can easily pinpoint your customers' locations without having to ask them.

You can find out more about electronic phonebooks by checking out the one offered by ProCD, called Select Deluxe, at `http://www.procd.com`.

Web publishing programs

It seems that you can't be in business today without being on the Internet. You need to have a Web site so your customers can find you and your products (well, maybe not if you run an ice cream stand at the beach). It's easy to find high-priced consultants who'll be happy to build you a Web site. Or you may want to save some money and look into Web publishing software.

The *Web* is short for the World Wide Web, the graphical part of the Internet. Making the Internet graphical and yet compatible with many different types of computers required a new computer language, *HTML* (HyperText Markup Language). The only reason any of that matters to you is that your Web pages need to be created using HTML. If you don't want to worry about using HTML, use a Web publishing program, which creates the HTML for you.

The *Small Business Computing For Dummies* CD-ROM includes several shareware Web publishing programs you can try out. LiquidFX and WebMania are two programs specifically for making your own Web pages. WebForms, Banner*Show, CGI*Star Pro, Guestbook*Star, and Site*Sleuth are additional Web site tools you may find useful after you create your Web site.

Figure 10-12 shows a simple Web page created in about ten minutes in FrontPage Express, a simple Web publishing program from Microsoft. You may want to create something a bit more fancy for your business, but you don't have to pay someone tons of money just so that you can have a Web site.

You find more about creating your own small business Web site in Chapter 15.

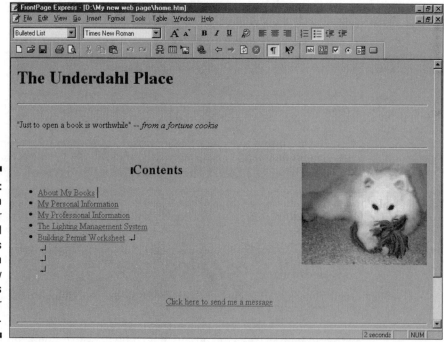

Figure 10-12: You can create your own small business Web site in a few minutes on your own PC.

Chapter 11

Putting Your Office Software to Work

. . . .

. . . .

*W*ith the right software working for you, your small business can remain on track and grow. But you need to know how to make the software work for you so you don't waste all your time working on the computer instead of working on your business.

Don't lose sight of an important point: Your computer is just another tool that's there because of what it can do for you. If you're starting to look for things to do on the computer rather than simply seeing the PC as a faster way to do necessary tasks, you've lost your focus, which should be to make your business more profitable.

This chapter shows you how to use some of the most important software tools that will make your computer time more productive.

Getting It All in There

If you bought your computer with all the software already installed, that's great. But you'll still want to know how to make sure that you have everything you paid for. You'll also want to have an idea of how to install new software and change the options for what you already have.

Most software now comes on CD-ROM discs, but the software seldom fills the entire disc. This often leaves plenty of room for extras that the software manufacturer throws on the disc as a bonus. Often, though, you need to hunt a little to find these goodies, because the main installation program may not even mention them. Be sure to look at anything the manufacturer labels as "free stuff," "bonus programs," or something similar — you may find some real gems.

In the old days — before CD-ROM drives showed up on nearly every PC — installing software could be a chore. You had to sit there swapping disks while the program slowly installed the software. One of the office suites, for example, had nearly 30 disks!

Installing software today is much easier. Throw in the CD-ROM, sit back and answer a few simple questions, and off it goes. Figure 11-1 shows what you'd see shortly after inserting the Corel WordPerfect 8 Professional CD-ROM in your drive.

If you've never installed software on a PC, here are a few pointers that may help you through:

✔ You may be asked to accept or reject a license agreement at some point. Don't even think about saying no — if you don't accept the agreement, the software won't install.

Figure 11-1:
Installing software from a CD-ROM is easy — just a few mouse clicks and you're finished.

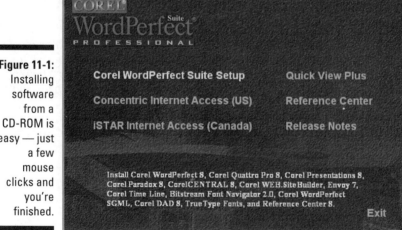

✔ You may get a choice of what to install. Your options will probably be something like these:

> **Typical:** The normal installation. It includes most standard features but may not include some options that will be important to you. For example, you may not get all the help files that are available or that French spell checker you need.

> **Compact:** Sometimes called *portable* or *laptop,* this option installs a bare minimum of the features. Don't choose this unless you're really short on disk space.

> **Custom:** Sometimes called *advanced,* this option enables you to choose exactly what you want to install. Even though the screen may warn you that this is for advanced users only, this is really your best choice if you feel comfortable deciding what should be installed.

✔ You don't have to accept the suggested installation folders. You'll probably see a button that says Browse or something similar. That's your key to putting everything where *you* want. If you have more than one hard drive, for example, you may want to choose the drive that has the most open space. Usually, though, you can just accept the suggested location.

✔ Many installation programs insist on restarting your system when they're just about finished, so make sure that you don't have any other programs open when you install a new one.

✔ You may want to see whether installing the new program added anything to your Start Up folder. If it did, whatever junk was added to that folder will always be running whenever your system is on. You can safely delete any shortcuts in the Start Up folder (you can always start programs when you want them started). For more information on the Start Up folder, you may want to pick up a copy of *Small Business Windows 95 For Dummies* by Steve Nelson (published by IDG Books Worldwide, Inc.).

Writing a Masterpiece

Your business can't afford to look like it's composed of a bunch of uneducated yokels, sending out misspelled or ungrammatical letters. Even if you're not a great speller or you fell asleep when your teacher was talking about grammar, you'll be able to produce professional-looking correspondence with your word processor.

Business letters

When you sit down to write a letter and are faced with a blank page, do the words refuse to come? Or do the words come out, but they're all wrong?

Wouldn't it be nice if there was a way to write business letters without having to actually write them? Well, it's not going to be quite that easy, but word processors have templates ready to help. *Templates* are standard layouts for all sorts of documents, including business letters.

Remember that I told you that you should use the Custom option when you install your software? Many useful business letter templates may be skipped if you choose the Typical option.

The following example uses Corel WordPerfect 8 to show you how word-processor templates can help you create professional-looking business letters in a flash. (Microsoft Word and Lotus WordPro have similar features.) Here's how you can create a letter accepting someone's credit application:

1. **Open Corel WordPerfect 8.**

   It doesn't matter how you start your word processor. Choosing it from the Start menu or clicking on the desktop icon both work.

2. **Choose File⇨New to display the New dialog box.**

   The idea here is to open the list of templates so that you can choose the type of letter you want to create. The New dialog box gives you numerous choices of different types of documents.

3. **Scroll down the list until you find Letter, Business and click on that option.**

   In Word and WordPro, find a variation of this type of document.

4. **Click on the Create button.**

   If you haven't used Corel WordPerfect 8 before, you have the chance to fill in your identification information before you start the letter. That way, the program can automatically fill in the letterhead for you.

5. **Click on the Change the Body button.**

   All you need to do to complete your letter is to fill in the blanks.

6. **Make sure that Accepting Requests appears in the box at the top of the list of letter templates and then choose one of the Accept Credit Application choices from the scrolling list.**

   If Accepting Requests isn't in the box, click on the down arrow at the right edge of the box and choose it from the list.

   Some types of letters have more than one template. For example, there are four different credit application acceptance letters.

7. Click on the Apply button.

Whichever letter is selected when you click on Apply appears in the document window. Figure 11-2 shows the second credit application acceptance letter.

8. Click on the Fill In Entry Fields button.

The highlight jumps to the area where you need to type something — skipping right over all the *boilerplate* text. Boy, this business letter writing stuff isn't so hard after all, is it?

9. Type text to replace the highlighted text.

In the credit application acceptance letter, you first type the terms you offer to your customers. When you finish with that item, click on the Fill In Entry Fields button again to move to the next place where you need to put in something.

10. Finish your letter by typing the customer's name, address, and so on.

You can also use the buttons labeled Fill in Heading Info, Fill in Closing Info, Change the Look, and so on to finish up most of the rest of the letter.

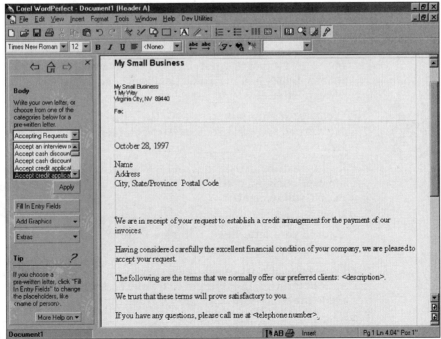

Figure 11-2:
By using one of the existing letter templates, you can have most of the letter written automatically.

11. Click on the Finish button.

12. Save the letter.

Before you print or fax the letter, it's a good idea to save it. You should check the spelling, too.

Are you thinking that using prewritten letters makes it seem as though you're taking shortcuts? Don't let that idea bother you. Your customers won't know that your computer has been helping out (how many credit acceptance letters will you be sending to the same customer?), and you can count on your letters having a professional tone. Besides, if you have enough time to write each business letter individually, you're not spending enough time looking for new business — get up from that computer and go make some money!

Letterheads

If you want your letters to be noticed, you need a *letterhead*. Why pay someone to create and print fancy letterhead paper for your small business, when you can create your own with your computer? Here are some things to consider:

- ✔ Letterhead is generally used only as the first page of a letter. Therefore, if you use letterhead to start your letters, you automatically print the letterhead design only on the first page because the letterhead appears only at the top of the first page of the document. That's much easier than manually loading a sheet of preprinted letterhead at the beginning of each letter.

- ✔ Create your letterhead as a template rather than as a standard document. Then you can use your letterhead template as the basis for new letters.

- ✔ If you create an artistic design for your letterhead, use the same design for your business cards, too. That way, you create a company image people will remember.

- ✔ If you have a color inkjet printer, consider adding a small splash of color to your letterhead. Don't get extreme — just throw in a small amount of color.

- ✔ If you have clip art (most office suites do), you can use it to enliven your letterhead. Don't forget that you can resize the clip art so that it fits in the letterhead.

- ✔ Your letterhead should include your complete contact information: company name, address, phone number, fax number, and e-mail address if you have one.

✔ If your business has a Web site, be sure to show that address in your letterhead, too.

✔ Don't forget to keep the letterhead compact — you need room to write letters, too!

✔ Before you use your new letterhead, print a sample and try making a photocopy. If everything isn't clear in the photocopy, adjust the type sizes and colors and try again. You may want to try faxing a copy, too. If customers can't read photocopied or faxed copies of your letterhead, they may have trouble contacting you.

✔ Take a hint from the templates that came with your word processor — add a date field just above the space for the customer's name and address. You can insert fields by using commands such as Insert⇨Field from your word-processor's menu. You may want to make two copies of your letterhead template — one with the date field and one without — so that you can use your letterhead for things other than dated letters.

Figure 11-3 shows an example of a small business letterhead template you can create in just a few minutes.

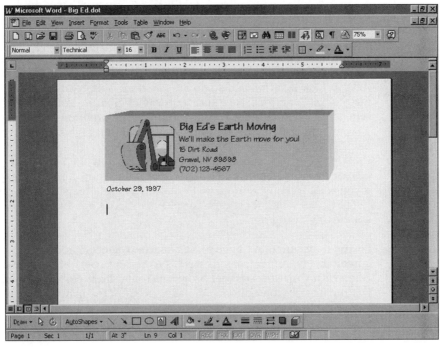

Figure 11-3:
Create your own letterhead to give your small business the image it needs.

Playing with the Numbers

Much of your business is about numbers; how much did you make on that last deal, what does it cost to produce your products, what were your expenses for the week, and so on. When it's time to play around with numbers, start with the spreadsheet component of your office suite package.

Spreadsheets are made up of *columns* and *rows* (and sometimes pages, if you want to go three-dimensional). Columns are generally designated by using letters, and rows are numbered. The intersection of a column and row is called a *cell*. The cell in the upper-leftmost corner of a spreadsheet is labeled A1, meaning it's in the first column and the first row. The next cell down is A2. The top cell in the second column is B1, and the next cell down in that column is B2.

What happens when you get to the 27th column? Well, that's a little tricky. The alphabet has only 26 letters, so you have to add extra letters to designate columns further to the right. Column 27 is AA, column 28 is AB, and so on.

When you enter a formula, you refer to the cell address or addresses in the formula. If you want cell B10 to have the total of cells A1 through A5, you use a formula like this: +A1+A2+A3+A4+A5. But suppose that you wanted the total of cells A1 through A100. Whew! You'd be there all day just typing in the formula. How about a simpler version: =SUM(A1..A100).

AVG, AVERAGE, SUM, and so on are *functions* — spreadsheet formula building blocks. Functions are a shortcut way of creating complex calculations. When you use functions in your formulas, the program figures out the answer, and you don't have to remember all that high school algebra.

Creating your own spreadsheets can be a lot of work, and you need to know a great deal before you begin — far more than there's room to explain here. If you want to know more about creating spreadsheets on your own, visit http://www.idgbooks.com to see what books are available for your spreadsheet program.

Fortunately, you don't have to be a math whiz or an accounting geek to use spreadsheets. A great way to start is to try out some of the templates that came with your spreadsheet program. You did remember to choose the custom installation option and make sure that the sample spreadsheets were installed, didn't you?

Spreadsheets need formulas

If you want to create your own spreadsheet, you have to work with formulas. Spreadsheet formulas tell the program how to manipulate numbers. For example, to average five numbers in a column, you might use a formula like this in Excel: =AVERAGE(A1..A5). In 1-2-3 or Quattro Pro, the formula would be a little different: @AVG(A1.A5). Either way, you're telling the program the same thing: Add the numbers in that range and divide by the number of entries to find the average.

The following example uses a spreadsheet template in Lotus 1-2-3. Microsoft Excel and Corel Quattro Pro have similar templates. Here's how you can create an expense report in Lotus 1-2-3:

1. **Open 1-2-3.**

   Select the program from the Start menu or click on the program icon on your desktop.

2. **In the opening dialog box, click on the Create a New Workbook Using a SmartMaster tab.**

   SmartMaster is the Lotus 1-2-3 name for templates. If you don't see this dialog box or you're using a different spreadsheet, you can find a similar option by choosing File⊅New from the menu.

3. **Choose Create an Expense Report, and then click on OK.**

   All three spreadsheet programs include some variation on the expense report theme. You may need to examine the options in your spreadsheet program to find the one that suits your needs.

4. **Click on the sheet icon to create a new page for your expense report.**

   The sheet icon looks like a file folder. When the expense report opens, you see the following message near the top of the spreadsheet: Use the sheet icon at the far right to create your own copy of this sheet. Do not make changes to this sheet.

5. **Fill in your company name, your name, and some mileage figures in the yellow shaded areas.**

   Figure 11-4 shows how the spreadsheet looks after several items have been completed.

If the selected cell contains a formula, it appears here.

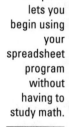

Figure 11-4:
The
expense
report
template
lets you
begin using
your
spreadsheet
program
without
having to
study math.

Don't type anything in unshaded cells. Otherwise, you could overwrite a formula, making the spreadsheet incapable of calculating results.

6. Choose File⇨Save.

If you make any changes without saving them and then try to exit, the program asks whether you want to save your changes.

You find tons of different spreadsheet templates you can use. If you're experimenting, remember to save your experiments using a new name so that you don't destroy the original template. When you've settled on a spreadsheet you'll be using on a continuous basis, choose one filename and always use it when you save the file. When you need a new report, such as when you've finished your October expenses and want to work on November's, use a new name for the new file so that you don't overwrite your old file. You may want to use a descriptive name, such as Expense report for October 1998 to make finding your saved reports easy. See *Small Business Windows 95 For Dummies* for more information on how you can name files in Windows 95, Windows 98, and Windows NT.

Strutting Your Stuff

Presentation graphics mean different things to different people. The traditional view of presentation graphics programs is that they're best suited to creating those boring sets of slides used in countless meetings. As the owner of a small business, you probably have the benefit of not having to sit through too many meetings.

You're more likely to use your presentation graphics program to create neat signs. If you've priced custom signs lately, you know how much that will save you!

If you're using an inkjet printer, note that some ink isn't waterproof. Be sure to check yours before you put a sign out where it may get wet.

The following example uses Microsoft PowerPoint to show you how to create a sign in a presentation graphics program. Corel Presentations and Lotus Freelance Graphics are similar.

1. **Open PowerPoint.**

2. **Choose Template and click on OK.**

   It's your old friend the template. By using a template, you start with a fancy design and won't have to do everything yourself. It's nice when someone else does the work, isn't it?

3. **Click on the Presentation Designs tab.**

   This tab offers some of the best options for signs.

Making signs with graphics programs

Presentation graphics programs are oriented toward fulfilling the needs of people who are creating slide shows. Therefore, you'll have a bit of extra work using them to create signs. You won't find templates designed for signs, but don't let that throw you. You can create your sign as if it were a single slide in a show. You still have the benefit of professional designs — you're just using them in an unconventional way. But then, you're used to that — after all, you're in small business!

4. Choose Professional and click on OK.

You want a professional look, so why not start with a template called Professional? Actually, you can choose whichever template best suits your style. As you click on each template, you see a small preview of the design in the window at the right side of the dialog box.

5. Choose the Clip Art & Text layout (in the second column of the third row), and then click on OK.

Here, too, you can choose a different layout, but a sign with some clip art and text would look nice.

6. Click on the various places on the template where you can add text and graphics.

When you click on a text box, go ahead and type the text you want. If you click on a clip art box, you can choose one of the pieces of clip art you installed. If you didn't install the office suite using the custom option, you won't have nearly as many choices, but you'll be able to import additional clip art if you like.

7. When you finish creating your sign, be sure to save it.

Figure 11-5 shows a completed sign. You can create your own signs in just a few minutes — if you quit playing around and simply choose a standard design!

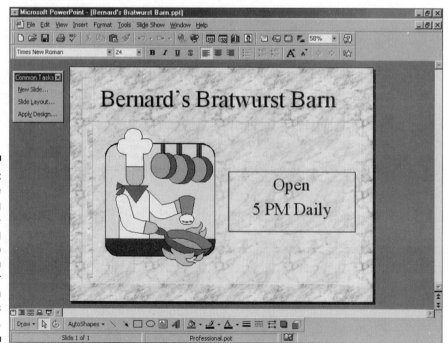

Figure 11-5:
You'll be creating professional-looking signs in no time with your presentation graphics program.

If you have a laser printer, you can add color to your signs by printing them on colored paper. Be sure to get paper that's designed for laser printers, though, so you don't get stuck with paper jams in the printer.

You may want to check out some of the fancy paper products available at http://www.paperdirect.com. They even have plastic sign holders that can improve the look of signs printed on light paper stock.

Keeping Track of All Your Marbles

Running a small business can be tough sometimes. People expect you to keep track of all sorts of information — everything from how much product you have in stock to who owes you how much.

Databases are supposed to be the solution to keeping track of lots of information. And they would be, too, if they weren't so darned complicated to create. The problem occurs after you create a simple database. The task was so easy that you start thinking it should be easy to do more. It's often not, though, as the following example demonstrates.

Suppose you want to create a database that keeps track of your customer orders and inventory. At the very least, you'll have two tables of information: one containing your inventory records and one for customer orders. Adding items to inventory as they're received is a straightforward process. All you need to do is find the item in the inventory table and add the newly received quantity to the existing quantity. If you had 15 pieces in stock, and 20 more came in, you'd change the on-hand level to 35.

Now suppose that you want to enter a customer order for 10 pieces. You enter the new order in the customer orders table, but how do you reduce the on-hand level from 35 to 25? You have two choices. You can manually change the inventory table (and hope you aren't distracted between entering the customer order and changing the inventory level), or you can write a computer program that automatically does what you'd do manually. Is this starting to sound like fun?

Fortunately, there's another choice. You can use a database someone else created. QuickBooks, for example, is a specialized database program designed to help you run your small business. A PIM (Personal Information Manager) such as Sidekick is also a sophisticated database program (with lots of built-in bells and whistles) that helps you keep track of your contacts and your schedule. Of course, most of the time, people don't think of programs such as QuickBooks and Sidekick as databases, but they are. The difference is that they're already programmed for you, and you don't have to start from scratch.

If your office suite includes a database program, it probably includes some sample databases, too. In some cases, these samples are simple — just templates with no real programming. In others, the samples are sophisticated programs just waiting for your data.

It's not a good idea to stake your whole business on a free sample database. Free samples are provided as examples — not fully developed applications. For example, one inventory database example lacked the programming necessary to adjust inventory levels when stock arrived — it relied instead on creating new inventory items unrelated to the existing stock.

The following example shows how you can use one of the sample databases that comes with Lotus Approach. Microsoft Access and Corel Paradox have similar samples you can use.

1. **Open Approach.**

   You find Approach in the SmartSuite folder in the Programs section of the Start menu.

2. **Click on the Create a New File Using a SmartMaster tab.**

   When you start Approach, you have the choice of working with an existing file or using a SmartMaster to create a new database. Because you want to create a new database, the Create a New File Using a SmartMaster tab is the place to start.

3. **At the right side of the SmartMaster types list box, click on the down arrow and select Templates from the list.**

   Approach has two types of SmartMasters: applications and templates. The difference between these two types of SmartMasters is fairly simple. Applications include programming so that the resulting database can perform more complicated actions, such as a survey builder that calculates survey results and presents complex reports on those results. Templates are simpler databases that don't need or include any programming.

4. **Scroll down the list of templates and select Customer Contacts.**

   When you select a template or an application, the dialog box shows a description of the selected option, as shown in the right side of the dialog box in Figure 11-6.

5. **Click on OK to continue.**

   Approach displays the New dialog box, shown in Figure 11-7, so you can name your new database file.

6. **Click on Create to prepare your new database for use.**

   When you click on Create, Approach builds all of the forms, reports, and tables that make up the database. Figure 11-8 shows the customer contacts database.

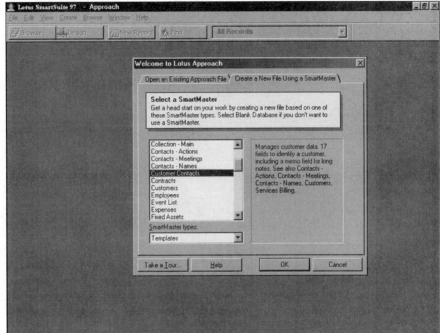

Figure 11-6:
The SmartMasters include a number of useful choices so you don't have to start from scratch.

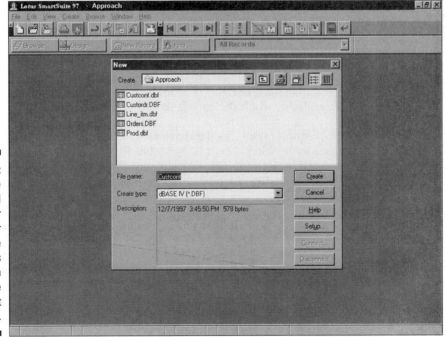

Figure 11-7:
The suggested name for your database file is shown in the File name text box.

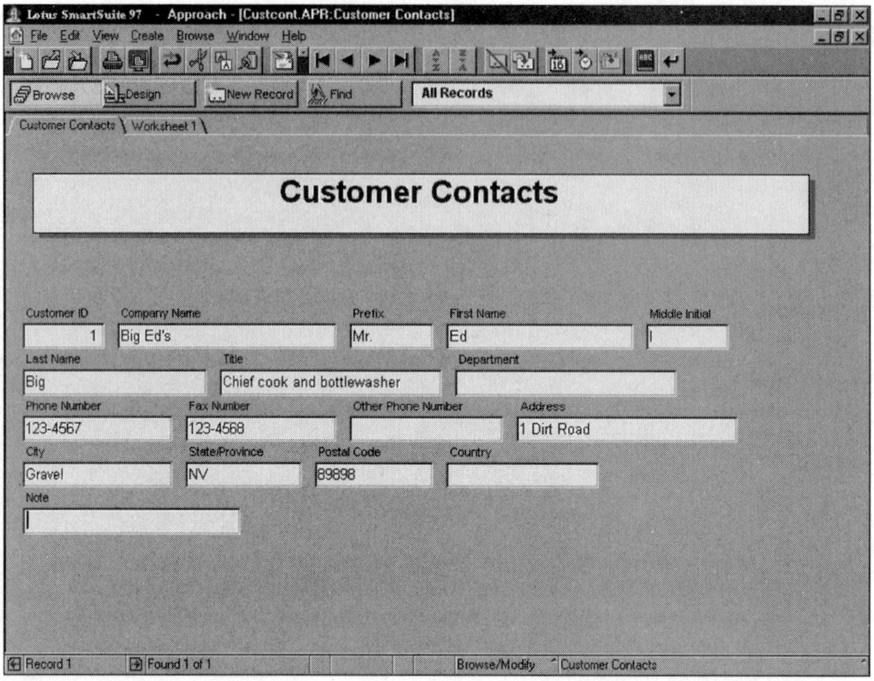

Figure 11-8:
A simple
sample
database
may serve
your needs
if you don't
expect too
much.

A simple database such as this, which uses a single table, is reliable but limited. Still, if all you want to do is keep track of your customers, this type of database may work.

If you're getting the impression that it makes much more sense to buy a specialized database program than to try to create your own or use one of the free samples, you're right! Here are some more reasons that these simple samples probably won't do the job your small business needs:

- ✔ The customer contacts database sample is a *flat-file database*. That means everything is kept in one table. If your database contained several contacts at a certain company, for example, and the information for that company changed, you would have to change each record manually.

- ✔ The sample databases aren't an officially supported product, so don't expect support.

- ✔ If you spend a lot of time putting information into one of the sample databases, you may find that when you finally buy a real application, you can't import the data from the sample into your new program.

- ✔ Specialized programs such as QuickBooks or Sidekick are so inexpensive that it's not worth wasting even a few hours trying to reinvent the wheel.

Reading the Mail

Electronic mail, or *e-mail,* has changed the speed of business messaging. Up until a few years ago, businesses had three primary choices for sending messages long distance. You could mail a letter and hope it arrived in less than a week; you could send an overnight express package and pay a lot of money; or you could call someone and hope that person was available.

It's now possible to send a message around the world in seconds. You also don't have to worry whether it's the right time to make a phone call, because e-mail makes the differences in time zones and office hours meaningless. To send and receive e-mail, you need an *e-mail client*, which is just a fancy way of saying you need e-mail software.

These days, using e-mail generally means you're sending and receiving messages over the Internet. This means that you need an account with an *Internet Service Provider,* or *ISP,* to use e-mail.

You can find many different e-mail programs, but if your PC runs some version of Windows, you have an e-mail program that came free with your system.

The e-mail messages you create usually consist of long lines of text that automatically wrap to a new line to suit the width of the text editor window. Many e-mail programs commonly used on the Internet, however, don't wrap long lines of text to a new line. This can make it difficult for some people to read your messages. If someone complains about not being able to read your complete messages, consider pressing Enter at the end of each line to place the following text on a new line.

In the following example, you see how you can use the free e-mail program in Windows to create an e-mail message. If e-mail hasn't been installed on your system, these steps won't work.

1. **Double-click on the Inbox icon on your desktop.**

   Depending on your version of Windows, this icon may be called Outlook, Outlook Express, Windows Messaging, or Mail.

2. **Choose File⇨New⇨Mail Message.**

   A text editor appears to let you type a message. If Word is installed, it may open as your message editor.

3. **In the To text box, type an e-mail address.**

   E-mail addresses look like someone@company.com. Type someone else's address to send them a message. (If you don't know anyone else's e-mail address, type your e-mail address in the To box.)

4. In the Subject text box, type the subject.

Use a subject line that's easy to understand — otherwise, some people may not bother reading your messages.

5. In the body of the message, type the text of your message.

If you want to send a file along with your message, click on the icon that looks like a paper clip — it's the Attach File icon. Browse your folders until you find the file you want to send, and double-click on it to add it to your message.

6. Click on the Send button to place the outgoing message in the Outbox folder.

Until it leaves your Outbox folder, you can reopen the message by double-clicking on it in the Outbox folder. You may need to do this if you create a message and then discover that you forgot part of the message. You also can cancel messages in the Outbox folder by selecting the message and clicking on the Delete button. After a message leaves the Outbox folder, however, you can't stop its delivery.

7. To send the message, choose Tools⇨Deliver Now Using⇨Internet Mail.

You may see a slight variation on this command, such as Tools⇨Check for New Mail or something similar.

You don't have to use the menu to send each message individually. You can configure the Internet Mail service to automatically log on, check your mail, and send any pending messages. Look for Internet Mail in the Tools⇨ Services menu for the scheduling options so that you can set this up.

Even if you haven't configured Internet Mail to automatically log on and check your mail, you can wait until you have several outgoing messages before logging on and delivering them.

Chapter 12

Creating a Business Plan

. . . .

In This Chapter

▶ Deciding where you want to go

▶ Creating your plan

▶ Building a market

▶ Creating a budget

. . . .

*L*ots of people go into business without a formal business plan. But lots of people never make it very far in business, and in many cases, they're the same ones who thought they didn't need a plan.

A business plan is vital to your small business venture. Fortunately, creating a business plan isn't quite as complicated or hard as it sounds, especially when you have your PC to help you. In this chapter, you see how to use your computer to help develop a plan so you know what to expect from your business.

Here, I use BizPlanBuilder Interactive — which requires Windows 95 or later — to show you how to create a business plan. BizPlanBuilder also comes in a template version that will work on a Mac or any other type of PC. You can find out more about BizPlanBuilder at http://www.jianusa.com.

What a Plan!

Success can be measured many ways, but most small businesses measure it by how much money they make. To make money, you have to put together a winning combination of the right products or services, funding so that you can bring your products to market, the right people to help you accomplish the work, and a clear understanding of what everyone needs to do. A business plan is the place to start.

How fancy of a business plan do you need? That depends on how you're going to use it. Here are a few things that may influence the level of the business plan you need to design:

✔ If you'll be asking for funding, your business plan should be as formal and complete as possible.

✔ If you are using only your own financial resources for your small business, a business plan mainly helps you keep your business on track. You can probably get away with a bare-minimum business plan.

✔ If you're adding other people to a business you've been running on your own, your business plan should at least show your business philosophy. This will help new people get up to speed at doing business your way and give them the opportunity to point out areas for improvement. This part of a business plan is sometimes called a mission statement, and should certainly be shared with your employees.

✔ If your small business is experiencing a sudden growth spurt, your business plan should include an analysis of your ability to handle growth. Too-rapid growth can kill a small business unprepared for the consequences.

Setting Your Goals

Before you start to create your business plan, you need to set reasonable goals for your small business. Set your goals as promises to yourself, taking into account how hard you're willing to work to achieve those goals.

Here are some questions to answer when setting goals for your small business:

✔ Do you have reasonable expectations for growth? Is the market ready for you to expand your business? In some cases, such as a food concession at an annual public event, your growth may be limited by factors beyond your control — the size of the crowd, the length of the event, and restrictions on the products you can offer.

✔ Are you planning to remain an active participant in the business, or is your goal to make the business a success, sell it, and move on? If you're hoping to sell the business after it's a success, you need to set a goal of making the business attractive to potential buyers.

✔ Will you be trying to borrow funds or apply for special grants? If so, you need to set goals that make your business one that's worth the investment.

✔ Are your goals realistic? If you're breaking into a new business, getting a good share of the market will probably take a lot of hard work, plenty of great service, and a lot of time.

✔ Will your partners or employees support your goals? If you set goals that require too much work from other people without providing an incentive for them to reach those goals, your plan is doomed.

✔ Do your goals include a plan for paying back your investors?

✔ Do you have both near-term and long-term goals? Short-term goals are important for keeping on track toward your long-term vision.

Developing Your Plan

After you set your goals, you need to decide how to create a business plan. If you have a lot of spare time, you can start from scratch, use your word-processor and spreadsheet programs, and do it all yourself. If you're a bit more practical, use a program designed to lead you through the process. In this section, I show you how to create a business plan using BizPlanBuilder Interactive.

If you'd like to use Jian BizPlanBuilder Interactive to create your business plan, you can obtain a code to unlock the version on the *Small Business Computing For Dummies* CD-ROM by calling a toll-free number and using your credit card. A discount on the purchase price has been arranged, too. (See the "About the CD" appendix for more details.)

Choosing a type of plan

BizPlan Builder Interactive defines three types of business plans — *complete, summary,* and *operational.* Fortunately, just about anything you do to create one type of business plan can be carried over to a different plan if you change your mind.

Here are some considerations you can use to figure out which type of business plan you need:

✔ **Complete business plans** require the most work, but they include everything a potential investor would want. Choose a complete business plan if you intend to go out and borrow a lot of money.

✔ **Summary business plans** require a lot less work, and don't include nearly as much detail about your business. A summary business plan may be good enough if you're trying to get your rich relatives to loan you some money — this type of plan is impressive enough to show that you mean business, but it is not so detailed that it will put everyone to sleep.

✔ **Operational business plans** are short and are intended to get everyone in the company focused on the same set of goals. You wouldn't use this type of plan to try to borrow money — but if everyone follows the plan, you may not have to!

Getting started on your plan

Okay, so you can't wait any longer — it's time to begin your business plan.

BizPlanBuilder Interactive includes a sample business plan. Take a few minutes to see what the sample looks like before you spend too much time on your own business plan. BizPlanBuilder Interactive also has a quick tour you can take to become acquainted with the program. Figure 12-1 shows you a sample of the quick tour.

You'll probably follow the same preliminary steps when creating a business plan, although the details for each plan will differ. Here's a quick view of how to begin:

1. **Open BizPlanBuilder Interactive.**

   If you use the Start menu, note that BizPlanBuilder Interactive is included in the Jian folder. When BizPlanBuilder Interactive opens, you have several options, as shown in Figure 12-2.

2. **Choose the Start a New Project option to create a new business plan.**

   If you've been viewing the sample or the quick tour, choose File➪New Project. If you've already been working on your business plan, open your existing plan instead by choosing Open Your Last Project.

Figure 12-1:
The BizPlan-Builder Interactive quick tour takes only a few minutes.

Click on these buttons to move through or exit the tour.

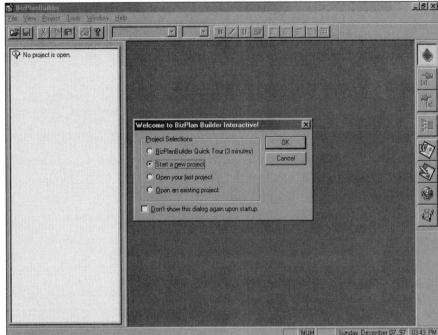

Figure 12-2:
BizPlan-
Builder
Interactive
starts by
asking what
type of
project
you'd like
to use.

3. Enter your company information.

BizPlanBuilder Interactive tries to help you by showing the registration information you entered when you installed the program, as shown in Figure 12-3. You'll want to check to see that this is correct for the business plan you're creating.

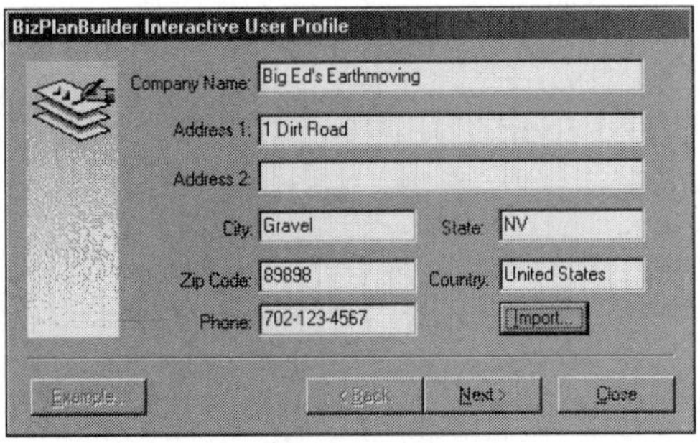

Figure 12-3:
BizPlan-
Builder
Interactive
uses your
registration
information
to begin
your
business
plan.

Type only in the places in the documents where the text is blue. If you enter anything anywhere else, you run the risk of screwing up the business plan project.

4. Click on Next to continue.

BizPlanBuilder Interactive displays the PowerPrompt dialog box shown in Figure 12-4. As you continue through the interview, this dialog box helps gather the information necessary to create your basic business plan.

Figure 12-4:
The BizPlan-Builder Interactive interview uses dialog boxes to help you create a business plan.

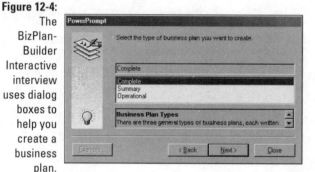

5. Choose the type of business plan you want.

If you're not sure what you need, choose a complete business plan — you can always skip or delete items you don't need when you create your plan. If you start with a complete business plan, you can be certain that no important documents are missed.

6. Click on Next to continue.

BizPlanBuilder Interactive asks you to indicate your type of business, as shown in Figure 12-5. You can use the arrows at the right edge of the list box to see all the choices.

7. Choose your business type.

Try to fit your business into one of the listed types, if possible. That way, BizPlanBuilder Interactive can do a better job of helping you create your business plan.

8. Click on Next to continue.

9. Choose what your business will provide — products, services, or both.

10. Click on Next to continue.

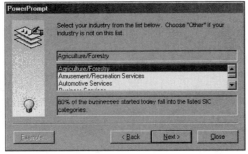

Figure 12-5:
The list of business types may include a choice appropriate for your small business.

11. **Finish answering the questions that define your business.**

For example, if your business provides services, BizPlanBuilder Interactive asks you how many services your business provides, as shown in Figure 12-6. If you don't understand what's being asked, look in the tip box for more information.

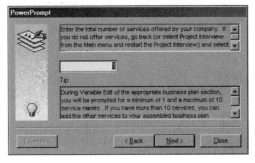

Figure 12-6:
BizPlan- Builder Interactive asks you questions necessary to create your business plan.

12. **Click on the Finish button when you have answered all the questions and reached the final interview screen.**

BizPlanBuilder Interactive uses your answers to create the basic business plan template for your business.

13. **Right-click on one of the items in the document tree (at the left side of the screen), and choose Open to start work on that document.**

Figure 12-7 shows the basic cover letter ready for your personal touches. Each item inside brackets is a *variable* — something you need to enter to complete the letter.

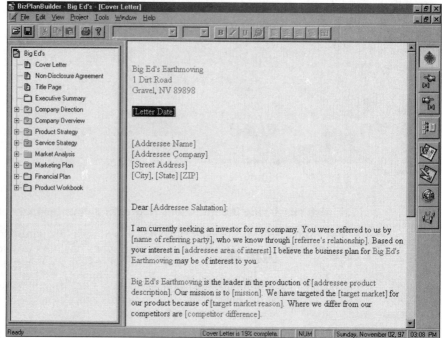

Figure 12-7:
Just fill in
the blanks
to create
your
business
plan.

14. **Choose File⇨Save Project.**

    Save your business plan project often so that you don't lose any work.

15. **To work on another document, right-click on it and choose Open.**

    Documents and folders that are yellow are part of your business plan project. Those that are gray won't be a part of your business plan. Click on an item with the left mouse button to change it from gray to yellow, or yellow to gray. You probably won't need to add or remove items from the project, but you can do it if you think it's important.

16. **Choose File⇨Close Project.**

    You can return to your business plan later by choosing File⇨Open and selecting your business plan project file.

BizPlanBuilder Interactive uses the word processor, spreadsheet program, and Web browser installed on your system. As you change to different documents within the business plan, the BizPlanBuilder Interactive menus change to include some items from those other applications. Unless you want to take a chance of really messing up your business plan project, don't try to use those extra items — stick with BizPlanBuilder Interactive to finish the project.

Don't forget to go through each document that will be included in your business plan. BizPlanBuilder Interactive uses sample values in a lot of the variables to give you an idea of the kind of information to enter. If you don't replace those sample values with real information, your business plan will be full of bogus data.

Creating a Marketing Strategy

No matter what product or service your small business provides, a marketing strategy is an important part of your business plan. You have to figure out whether there's a market for what you have to offer, who will buy it, and how to let them know you're there.

Figuring out your market

The first part of defining a marketing strategy is figuring out your market. This can be one of the hardest parts of a business plan, and is probably the place where it's easiest to fool yourself because your enthusiasm can cloud your thinking. Here are some things to keep in mind when analyzing your market:

- ✔ Figure out what market segment your business fits into. If you intend to sell office supplies, for example, will you be targeting large companies, small businesses, or the home office market?

- ✔ What type of competition are you facing? It can be tough to make a living in a saturated market.

- ✔ Who is your target audience, and are you in the right location to serve that market?

- ✔ What are the weaknesses of your competition? Can you exploit those weaknesses to make your business successful? If your competitor has poor parking facilities and no room for expansion, for example, you may be able to find a convenient location with good parking.

- ✔ If you've used census data to see whether you're locating in the right place, is the information current? If an area is changing rapidly, you don't want to rely on outdated data.

- ✔ Have you visited your competition — perhaps even made a small purchase to see how they treat customers? You can learn a lot about your competition by doing business with them.

- ✔ How long has your competition been in the market, and what kind of track record do they have?

✔ Check with the Better Business Bureau to see whether it has any complaints on file about your competition.

✔ Is your product or service allowed in the area where you intend to set up shop? Check to make certain no new laws ban or restrict your product or service. For example, if you intend to rent or sell gasoline-powered equipment near a major recreational area, make sure that the government isn't planning on turning the area into a nonmotorized activity area.

✔ If your business will need the services of other businesses, can you find those services when and where you need them?

Figuring out your marketing plan

After you have a good idea of your market, it's time to figure out how to take advantage of that market. How do you get people through the door and spending money?

You need to figure out how to make your product or service stand out, and how to make people want to do business with you rather than with your competition. You have to figure out the right price, how you're going to get your product or service to your customers, what kind of advertising to do, and lots more.

When you work on your marketing plan, don't forget these factors:

✔ Perception is often more important than reality. Your product may be better than the competition's, but if you're the new kid on the block, no one but you may know that.

✔ The lowest price isn't always the best marketing strategy. Your product may be seen as junk because it's less expensive.

✔ A higher price may give the impression of higher quality, or it may make cost-conscious shoppers buy from your competition if they feel you're charging too much.

✔ You may be able to make a higher profit by offering additional service as an add-on. Just don't expect that every sale will generate the add-on sale.

✔ Your competition won't ignore your entry into the market. They may have deep enough pockets to withstand losses longer than you can.

✔ Offering something your competition doesn't, such as easy payment plans or more convenient service hours, can give you the market edge you need.

✔ Make sure you know the most likely audience for your products or services. That way, you can spend your advertising money wisely.

If you are seeking investors, your marketing plan must thoroughly address a broad range of issues so that potential investors can see that you understand your market. You're selling more than your product: You're selling your company's capability to market that product successfully.

To work on your marketing plan and sales strategy, follow these steps:

1. **Open BizPlanBuilder Interactive.**

2. **Choose Open Your Last Project to open your business plan project.**

   If you have more than one business plan project, choose Open an Existing Project, and then select the project you want to open.

3. **Make certain the Marketing Plan item is yellow, which indicates that it is included in your business plan project.**

   If the Marketing Plan is gray, click on the Marketing Plan in the document tree to change it to yellow. Only items shown in yellow will be part of your business plan project.

4. **Click on the plus sign to the left of the Marketing Plan item to expand the document tree.**

   You need to expand the document tree to select which marketing plan items will be included in your project.

5. **Make certain that Sales Strategy is included in your project.**

   When you add documents to your business plan project, they appear in the document window when you have the appropriate document folder open. For example, Figure 12-8 shows the open Marketing Plan folder, which includes the Sales Strategy document.

6. **To complete your marketing plan and sales strategy, click on the first of the variables — the items shown in blue inside square brackets — in the document window.**

   When you begin filling in the variables, BizPlanBuilder Interactive displays a dialog box to help you understand what you need to add. For example, Figure 12-9 shows the dialog box that appears when you click on the [product marketing strategy] variable.

7. **Click on Next to continue.**

8. **Continue through the document, filling in the variables and clicking on Next to continue after each one.**

9. **When you have completed all the variables, click on Finish to close the dialog box.**

   You can also click on Close if you'd rather not complete all the variables during the current session. If you don't complete all the variables, you can pick up where you left off the next time you work on the document.

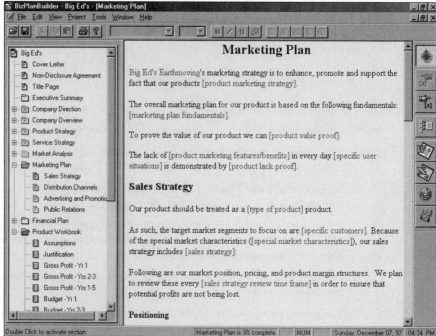

Figure 12-8:
The Sales
Strategy
document
appears
when the
Marketing
Plan that
contains it
is opened.

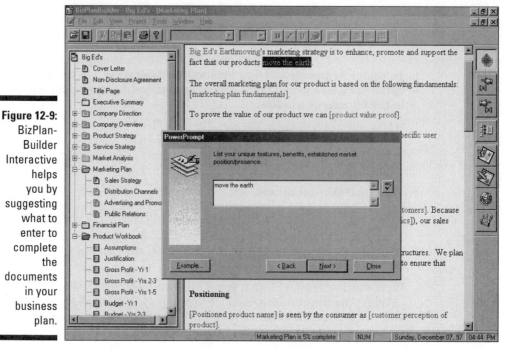

Figure 12-9:
BizPlan-
Builder
Interactive
helps
you by
suggesting
what to
enter to
complete
the
documents
in your
business
plan.

10. Choose File⇨Save Project.

Always make certain you save the business plan project before you leave BizPlanBuilder Interactive.

You can work on the other documents in your business plan project the same way you worked on the marketing plan. Right-click on a document or a folder in the document tree to display the document in the document window.

Setting a Budget

Call it what you like — a budget, a financial plan, the bottom line. The financial details section of your business plan is what everyone wants to see. Here's where you put together all the numbers that answer the most important question about your company: Can it make enough profit to succeed in business?

The financial part of your business plan includes a lot of stuff your accountant would include. Who else but an accountant would talk about balance sheets, ratio analysis, and COGS (cost of goods sold) as if they were normal topics of daily conversation? The financial plan section of your business plan has several components. Here's a look at a few of the more important ones.

Making assumptions

Making financial assumptions can be fun. That's where you get to project all the money you'll be making if everything goes your way. Too bad a person can't live on assumptions — otherwise, we'd all be living in big houses on warm beaches with lots of people to attend to our every need.

Here are some of the things that make up the assumptions portion of your business plan's financial section:

✔ How much product or service will you sell? Here's where you'll probably do the most to deceive yourself, by basing your assumptions on what you hope to sell rather than on what's likely to sell. You may want to do these calculations twice — once with the numbers you like, and a second time with those numbers cut in half. If you can live with the lower number, maybe you should settle on something between the two. Just make certain the numbers you use are reasonable.

✔ What will your products or services cost you? This is COGS (cost of goods sold), and includes all sorts of things that are easy to forget, such as shipping and handling.

✔ How much will it cost you to keep the doors open even when you're not selling anything? This is called the *operating expense* and includes rent, electricity, phones, and a bit of salary so you can afford to keep coming in every day.

✔ Will the money come in quickly enough — *cash flow* — so you can pay the bills and keep operating? As a new business, you may need to pay cash for a lot of the things you buy, but you may need to wait for the money for things your customers buy. If you have to put money out a lot faster than it comes in, you could go broke even if people owe you tons of money.

✔ What will happen to your business if the economy goes boom or bust? In other words, how sensitive is your business to factors beyond your control?

Putting the numbers on paper

Financial statements look deceptively simple — until you try to create them yourself. Your business plan needs lots of financial statements — everything from formal budgets to balance sheets.

Some financial statements are projections. Budgets, for example, are based on assumptions about what it will cost you to do business. Other financial statements are real-life, bottom-line numbers. Profit and loss (or income) statements show what you've already accomplished.

Figure 12-10 shows a portion of the financial statements part of a business plan created in BizPlanBuilder Interactive. If you're just starting out, you may not be able to show meaningful numbers in this report.

Even if you haven't been in business long enough to produce a profit and loss statement, you still need a balance sheet, which is a current view of how much your business is worth. You'll have *assets* (things the business owns) and *liabilities* (bills you owe).

In BizPlanBuilder Interactive, most of your financial statements are under a category called *Product Workbook*. You can fill out the statements by right-clicking on a statement in the document tree and selecting Open. Look for the values in blue, and type your real numbers to replace the sample numbers. A better way to complete the financial statements is to select Project⇨Workbook Interview and follow the prompts. That way, you'll be sure to put in all the numbers.

When you're working with financial statements in BizPlanBuilder Interactive, move your mouse pointer over a variable to see what type of information you need to enter. For example, Figure 12-11 shows the assumptions work-book when the mouse pointer is over the beginning year variable.

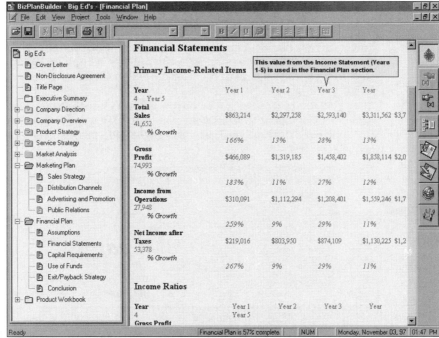

Figure 12-10:
Your
financial
statements
show
whether
you're in
the right
business.

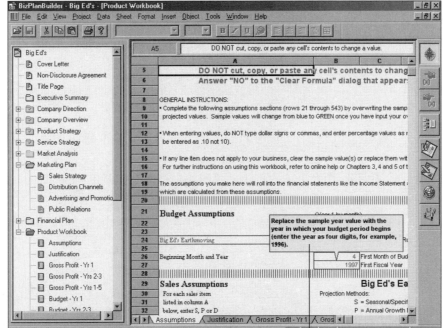

Figure 12-11:
BizPlan-
Builder
Interactive
helps you
complete
workbooks
by
displaying
prompts
over
variable
cells.

This tells you what you need to enter.

Finishing Your Business Plan

Your business plan will include a lot of different documents. Make sure each document is complete before you print your final copy by looking on the status line at the bottom of the BizPlanBuilder Interactive screen.

After you complete your entire business plan, choose Project⇨ Assemble Document to print your plan. You may want to have your accountant look over the final business plan before you present it to potential investors.

Chapter 13

Keeping Your Books

. . . .

In This Chapter

▶ Setting up your books

▶ Getting paid for your work

▶ Keeping track of what you have

. . . .

*N*ow that your business plan is in place, you need to keep track of how you're doing and make sure people are paying you. For that, you need some accounting software such as QuickBooks (or QuickBooks Pro if you bill customers by the hour). QuickBooks is a great accounting program for your small business, and in this chapter, you get a quick look at it.

The *Small Business Computing For Dummies* CD-ROM includes a trial version of QuickBooks and QuickBooks Pro you can use up to 25 times before you must register the program. (See the "About the CD" appendix for more information.)

Where to Begin

You can't discover everything about QuickBooks in a few pages, but you can get a feel for its major features — and that's all you need to get started using QuickBooks to manage your books. Don't worry if this chapter's overview of QuickBooks seems like a whirlwind tour — QuickBooks is made for ordinary small-business people like you and me. Before long, you'll be keeping your books like an old hand!

When you start QuickBooks, you have an option of seeing an introduction to the program. Doing so won't take long and will give you a feel for some accounting terms you have to confront sometime. Don't worry — you won't end up talking like an accountant!

To start QuickBooks and see the tour, follow these steps:

1. **If you haven't already installed the QuickBooks trial version, do so now.**

   You can find the trial version on the *Small Business Computing For Dummies* CD-ROM.

2. **Click on the Start button.**

3. **Choose Programs⇨QuickBooks (or QuickBooks Pro if you installed the Pro version)⇨QuickBooks.**

   The first time you start QuickBooks, the introductory tour runs automatically.

When you finish the tour, you can continue to the next section. Take your time with the tour, though — using QuickBooks is much easier after you're a bit more familiar with the program.

Starting a business file

After you take the quick introductory tour of QuickBooks, you're ready to begin setting up your business. You'll customize a file in QuickBooks for your company, including only the items you need. (That way, every time you use the program, you won't have to wade through a bunch of options you don't need.)

To begin setting up QuickBooks for your business, follow these steps:

1. **Start QuickBooks.**

   You can find QuickBooks in the QuickBooks folder in the Programs section of your Start menu.

2. **Click on the Set Up a New Data File for a Company option.**

   If this option doesn't appear, choose File⇨New Company. The option box may not appear if you've already used QuickBooks and closed the option box.

3. **Click on the OK button.**

   Figure 13-1 shows the QuickBooks EasyStep interview. Down the right edge of the screen are sections, such as General, Income & Expenses, and Income Details. Within each section are tabs. The tabs in the General section, for example, are Welcome, Company Info, Preferences, and Start Date (as shown in Figure 13-1). This interview process asks you a series of simple questions so that QuickBooks can be tailored for your business.

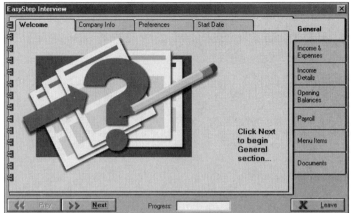

Figure 13-1:
Setting up
QuickBooks
for your
business is
easy — just
answer a
few simple
questions.

4. **Click on the Next button.**

5. **Continue through the interview, clicking on Next after you complete each screen, until you complete the Welcome tab.**

If you make a mistake, click on the Prev button to go back and take another shot at it. QuickBooks warns you if you're about to do something you can't easily change.

6. **After you complete the Welcome tab, click on Next to display the Company Info tab and then type your company name.**

Figure 13-2 shows the start of the Company Info tab. If your business has a *fictitious name* (sometimes called a DBA, or Doing Business As, name), enter that in the Company Name box. If your company has a different *legal name,* enter it in the Legal name box.

7. **Continue through the interview by clicking on Next as you finish each screen (making the correct selections to match your business, of course).**

If you aren't sure how to answer, click on the More button for a bit of extra help. If the help screen is no help — and frankly, some aren't — you can always click on the Leave button in the lower-right corner of the dialog box to end the interview for now. QuickBooks saves your place and lets you pick up where you left off later.

8. **When you've nearly completed the Company Info tab and QuickBooks is ready to save the information you've entered so far, note the name that QuickBooks suggests for your company's filename.**

If you set up more than one company in QuickBooks, you need to know the correct filenames so that you can easily open your company's books when you need to.

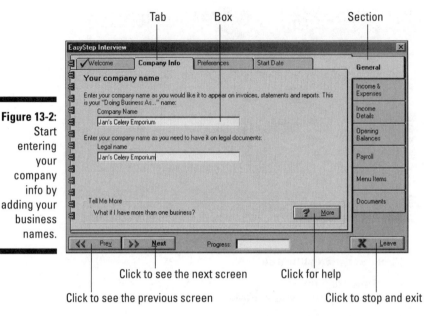

Tab   Box   Section

Figure 13-2:
Start
entering
your
company
info by
adding your
business
names.

Click to see the next screen   Click for help

Click to see the previous screen   Click to stop and exit

9. **When you complete the Company Info tab, click on Next to continue to the Preferences tab.**

   In the Preferences tab, you choose whether to use certain features of QuickBooks. If your business doesn't have to collect sales tax, for example, you won't have to be bothered with that. As you go through the Preferences tab, QuickBooks asks you questions based on your earlier answers.

10. **When you complete the Preferences tab, click on Next to continue to the Start Date tab.**

   Choosing a start date isn't difficult, but your choice may mean more or less work for you in getting QuickBooks ready to use. Basically, you must enter every transaction between the start date and today. That doesn't mean you should take the easy way out and use today's date — QuickBooks won't be able to give you nearly as much detail if you use any date after the start of your *fiscal* year — essentially, your tax year.

11. **When you complete the Start date section, click on the Leave button.**

   The Start Date tab is the last tab in the General section. You still need to complete the EasyStep interview, but take a break before continuing — there's no need to do everything at once!

Adding accounts

Adding accounts is easy, but QuickBooks won't let you remove an account you've used. Don't complain — it's for your own good. If you removed an account that was in use, you could wipe out tons of work and create a nightmare trying to figure out how to recover from the resulting problems. Remember, though, to think about where items *really* belong rather than throwing them anywhere "for now." You could be making trouble for yourself down the road!

Follow these steps to set up the QuickBooks accounts you'll need:

1. **If you closed QuickBooks, open it again.**

2. **Choose File⇨Open Company to open your company file.**

   Although you didn't finish setting up QuickBooks for your company, you'll see lots of unfamiliar stuff when you open your existing company file. Ignore it for now — you'll use it later after you finish the EasyStep interview.

3. **Choose File⇨EasyStep Interview.**

   QuickBooks starts where you left off.

4. **Click on Next to move on to set up your income accounts.**

   You can also click on a section, such as Income and Expenses, to go directly to that section.

   Figure 13-3 shows the typical income accounts QuickBooks offers to create for a retail business. If you need an account that isn't on the list, you can add it now or later. Before creating an account, however, it's usually better to wait and use the program for a while and become better acquainted with its features as well as your needs. That way, you won't create unnecessary accounts — remember, QuickBooks won't let you remove an account after you use it.

Understanding accounts

Accounts are the categories you use to keep track of different types of income and expenses. Accounting programs such as QuickBooks provide accounts set up and ready to use. If you don't find an account that fits an income or an expense, you can simply add a new account.

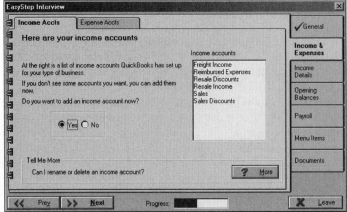

Figure 13-3:
QuickBooks uses accounts to keep track of what's going in and out.

5. **Set up the rest of the income and expense accounts by answering the EasyStep interview questions.**

   Keep the number of expense accounts to a minimum and add them only as necessary. Don't forget that if you use an account, you won't be able to get rid of it!

6. **Click on Next or click on the Income Details tab to continue to the Income Details section.**

   No, you don't get a break *every* time you complete a section.

7. **Choose the type of payment you get from your customers.**

   Unless you're lucky enough to always get paid as soon as the customer has the goods, QuickBooks needs to set up *accounts receivable* — a method of tracking who owes you what. The bad news is that you have to put up with a bit more complication than if you worked on a strictly cash basis, but the good news is that QuickBooks lets you know who the deadbeats are.

8. **If you keep an inventory, enter your stock details.**

   This is probably the most time-consuming part of setting up QuickBooks. At least you have to do this only once.

Show me some balances

Few businesses run on a strictly-cash basis. You probably have bills you owe, customers who haven't paid you, and maybe even a reserve in your checking account. All of these items are known as *balances* (or more correctly, *account balances*).

QuickBooks tracks all sorts of balances. You need to step through the Opening Balances section of the EasyStep interview to set up any accounts that had a balance on the start date you chose earlier. That's why it's a lot easier to start using a program such as QuickBooks when you first set up your new business — if you do it later, you have to dig out lots of old information to get the opening balances as accurate as possible.

By now, you should be comfortable enough with the EasyStep interview process to be able to finish by following along and answering the questions. Although you can correct a lot of items later, it's better to give the best possible answers during the interview. QuickBooks is flexible, but if you're not familiar with accounting practices, you may not realize you're missing something. Remember that you can always put the interview on hold while you go and find an answer.

After you finish the EasyStep interview, QuickBooks creates a customized accounting system for your business. Although different businesses have many similarities — simply because everyone uses certain items, such as invoices — your copy of QuickBooks has only the items you need.

Use the File⇨Preferences command to customize QuickBooks after you complete the interview. The Preferences dialog box gives you lots of ways to change the way QuickBooks looks and works. For example, if you hire independent contractors, you can use the Preferences dialog box to specify which accounts should be included when you print 1099 forms.

Ready to roll

Figure 13-4 shows how QuickBooks looks after you complete the interview. (Okay, I'll admit I did use the icon bar section of the Preferences dialog box to add those neat little pictures to the buttons below the menu items.)

You can use QuickBooks several ways. Here's a quick look at the options:

- ✔ If you like to give orders, you can use the menus below the QuickBooks title bar. For most tasks, though, using the menus is the hard way to do things. You have to remember which menu you need, drop down the menu, and then choose the correct command. This is the way your accountant would probably use QuickBooks.

- ✔ If you know exactly what you want to do but don't want to bother with remembering all those commands, you can use the icon bar to help you do things. The icon bar is that bunch of buttons below the menus. Have fun with the MemTx button!

Title bar   Menus   QuickBooks Navigator   Icon bar

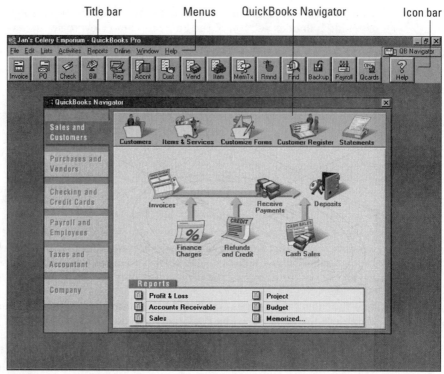

Figure 13-4:
QuickBooks
is easy to
use —
simply click
on an icon
to do a task.

✔ If you don't want to bother with a lot of accounting nonsense, go ahead and use the QuickBooks Navigator. That's the big box in the middle of your screen. It's the easy way to use QuickBooks — click on an item and off you go. In Figure 13-4, for example, it's clear that to create a customer invoice, you need to click on the Invoices item in the Sales and Customers area. If you prefer to use the menus or the icon bar, go ahead and do so. Just try to keep the document flow shown in the QuickBooks Navigator in mind so that you don't forget an important step.

✔ You'll probably use the menus once in a while no matter which way you like to work with QuickBooks. You need the menus to restart the EasyStep interview, for example.

Let's Talk Money

When you get right down to basics, the bottom line for running a successful business is taking in more money than you pay out. Getting money in usually means getting invoices out first. Getting more in than you pay out means keeping track of what you're paying and what you're billing. In this section, you find out how your computer can keep track of all those details.

Getting paid

Getting paid is a lot more fun than paying someone else, so that's a good place to start with QuickBooks. In fact, the entire top section of the QuickBooks Navigator is all about getting paid.

You can save a lot of time with QuickBooks by doing things only when it's absolutely necessary. You *could* sit down and add every customer to your books right now, but in QuickBooks, you don't have to. If you try to create an invoice for a customer who isn't in the records, QuickBooks simply makes a record for that customer. The same applies with almost everything else QuickBooks tracks for you, so there's no reason to do a lot of extra work setting up QuickBooks. Go ahead and use the program, and it will become more attuned to your business as you go along.

Preparing invoices

In this example, you look at how to prepare a customer invoice in QuickBooks. In this case, QuickBooks has been configured for a retail business, but the process is similar for other types of businesses.

Follow these steps to create a customer invoice in QuickBooks:

1. **Make sure the Sales and Customers tab of the QuickBooks Navigator dialog box is selected, as shown in Figure 13-4.**

   You click on the tabs on the left side of the QuickBooks Navigator dialog box to make different tabs active, or selected. When a tab is selected, it appears to be on top of all the other tabs, and you can choose the items displayed on that tab.

2. **Click on the Invoices item.**

   The Create Invoices dialog box appears. As you move from box to box on the invoice, QuickBooks pops up a message box to tell you something about what you need to do.

Wait to do it!

When you're using QuickBooks, don't bother adding a lot of information — such as customer names or accounts — until you need the item. If you add something that isn't already in the records, QuickBooks asks whatever questions are necessary to properly include the new item.

3. In the Customer:Job box, type the customer's name.

If you've billed this customer before, QuickBooks fills in a lot of the information for you. If this is the first time you've billed this customer, you have to fill in the address yourself — but QuickBooks remembers this customer for the next time you create an invoice so that you won't have to fill in the address again in the future.

4. Move to the next box by clicking on it or by pressing the Tab key, and fill in the information.

Many boxes have a down-pointing arrow. You can click on the arrow to display a list, and then select an item from the list. Some boxes, such as the Bill To box, show the information QuickBooks already has for the selected customer. If necessary, you can modify the information QuickBooks displays — for example, if you need to temporarily send customer invoices to a different address while someone's office is being remodeled.

If you aren't quite sure what to do, you can always click on the Show Me button to have QuickBooks explain what you need to do. You have to insert your QuickBooks CD-ROM in your CD-ROM drive for this feature to work.

5. Continue to move through the boxes on the invoice until you've added everything.

Although it looks as if there's only room for a few items on the invoice, don't forget that there's a *scroll bar* at the right edge of the invoice amount box. Use the scroll bar to move up and down to see all the items you're billing to your customer.

6. When you finish with the invoice, click on the Print button to create a printed copy to give to your customer.

Figure 13-5 shows a completed invoice ready to print. If you'd prefer to wait until you've finished creating invoices, you can skip clicking on the Print button and choose File⇨Print Forms⇨Print Invoices later when you want to print a batch of invoices.

7. To create another invoice, click on Next. Otherwise, click on OK.

If you're just practicing, or if you created the invoice in error, click on the Cancel button before you leave the invoice. Otherwise, you have to create a credit to reverse the transaction or reopen the invoice. Choose Edit⇨Delete Invoice, and then click on OK to confirm the deletion. Unfortunately, if you choose to delete an invoice, there will be a gap in your invoice numbers — something accountants generally consider unacceptable because there's a missing transaction number.

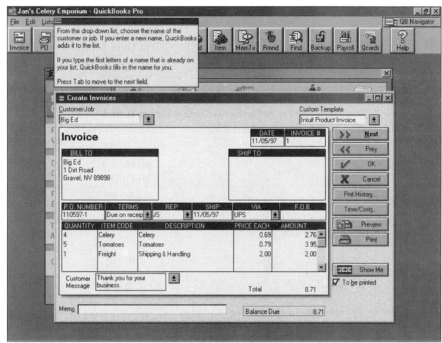

Figure 13-5:
With
QuickBooks,
you can
create an
invoice in
almost no
time at all.

Correcting mistakes

Everyone makes mistakes sometimes. You may accidentally bill the wrong customer, send the wrong merchandise, or even click on the OK button when you meant to click on the Cancel button. Or perhaps a few customers changed their minds about something they bought and want to return it. Any one of these actions (and lots more) can create transactions you'll need to correct.

Why you need good records

You might be tempted to think you could correct mistakes by deleting the incorrect invoice. If you did this, though, you'd soon discover how important it is to have a more formal procedure for correcting errors. Imagine that your salesman Joe decided to start his own little side business selling your company's products to his friends at a big discount. To make everything appear to be on the level, Joe would write out an invoice for the merchandise. Then when his friends and your merchandise were out the door, Joe would simply delete the invoice so that there wouldn't be any record of the transaction. Joe, of course, would put the money in his own pocket, and you'd be out the goods.

Good accounting systems track every transaction very closely. If you generate an invoice, the only acceptable ways to close out that invoice are to post a payment or issue a credit or a refund. Either way, the individual transactions — invoices, payments, credits, and so on — remain in the records so that you can go back and see what happened.

Even if your small business is very small and you work alone, tracking every transaction is a good idea — if for no better reason than to help at tax time. If you have a good record of every transaction, it's a lot easier to prove how much profit (or loss) your business generated.

Issuing a credit or a refund in QuickBooks is similar to creating an invoice, except that you click on the Refunds and Credit item rather than on the Invoices item. Another difference is that you can write a check on the spot by clicking on the Refund button while the Create Credit Memos/Refunds dialog box is displayed.

Show me the cash sale

What businessperson doesn't like cash sales? As soon as the customer gets the goods, you get the dough. You don't have to worry that the customer may take a long time to pay or may not pay at all.

Although cash sales seem to be a simple and straightforward type of transaction, it's not as simple as you may think. In most cases, the customer wants a receipt, and you want to record the sale. If you keep an inventory, you also want to adjust your stock records. With QuickBooks, all these functions are handled automatically.

When you create the sales receipt for your customer, QuickBooks records the sale and adjusts your inventory records — just as it does when you create a customer invoice. In fact, QuickBooks goes a step further on cash sales: The money you take in on a cash sale is recorded as a payment received. Talk about efficient!

If your business accepts credit cards, record credit card sales as cash sales in QuickBooks because you won't be sending the customer an invoice, but you will probably give the customer a sales receipt.

Recording payments

Making sales and sending invoices is great, but nothing else equals getting paid. When you do get paid, QuickBooks handles all the messy stuff, such as adjusting your accounts receivable balances, applying the payments to your customers' outstanding invoices, and adding the funds to your deposits. You get the fun part — figuring out what to do with your profits.

Recording customer payments is easier than creating invoices. An invoice has a lot of details, such as what the customer bought, that are unnecessary when you record a payment. When you record a payment, you need to know who made the payment, how much was paid, and sometimes which invoice was paid.

To record customer payments, use the Receive Payments item on the Sales and Customers tab of QuickBooks Navigator. As soon as you choose the customer, QuickBooks shows you any outstanding invoices for that customer. You choose which invoices are being paid, and QuickBooks does the rest.

You can also choose to apply discounts — such as early payment discounts — to invoice amounts when you're recording customer payments. QuickBooks uses the terms you chose when you generated the invoice to determine the suggested discount, but you can override the suggested discount if necessary. In fact, QuickBooks allows you to override most amounts, such as sales prices, as needed.

Paying your bills

If getting money in is a lot of fun, seeing it go out is the opposite. There's no reason for bill paying to be a chore, though — let QuickBooks do most of the work.

It's common for businesses to use float to keep their operations going. *Float* is the time when you're getting a free loan because of the time for transactions to be completed. For example, if you mail a check for $5,000 to a vendor, your bank probably won't deduct the $5,000 from your account for several days. It will take some time for the vendor to receive your check, process your payment, and deposit the check. If that vendor uses a different bank than you do, it will take a bit longer before your bank receives the check and reduces your balance. Another common type of float is the time between buying something and when you have to pay the invoice. The longer you can keep your vendor's product without paying the invoice, the longer you have to sell the product and receive your customer's payment. QuickBooks can help you manage float time by keeping track of when you need to pay vendor invoices so that you don't pay sooner than necessary.

Know what you owe

What kind of response would you have if a stranger walked up to you and said you owed him or her $50? You'd probably ask for more information before forking over the money, wouldn't you? Well then, why would you pay a vendor's invoice without knowing whether you really owed the money?

With QuickBooks, you can keep an accurate record of what you owe. In accounting terms, this is called *accounts payable* — bills you need to pay. Figure 13-6 shows the Purchases and Vendors tab of the QuickBooks Navigator. This tab has the functions you'll use to keep track of what you owe.

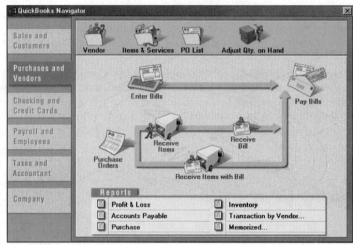

Figure 13-6: The Purchases and Vendors tab helps you keep track of what you owe.

Here's how you use some important items on this part of the QuickBooks Navigator:

- ✔ Use the Enter Bills item to track non-inventory items, such as services you buy from a vendor. Your electric bill would fit under this item.

- ✔ When you send an order to a vendor, use the Purchase Orders item to keep track of your outstanding orders. That way, you always know what's on order, and you won't accidentally place another order.

- ✔ It doesn't matter whether your vendors send their bills with their merchandise or later. Just make certain you don't enter a packing list as an invoice — otherwise, you may end up paying before it's necessary.

- ✔ When paying bills, you may want to sort the bills by the discount date rather than the due date. If your vendors give you a discount for paying early, it may be worthwhile to take the discount. For example, if someone offers a 2 percent discount for paying in 10 days, or net pricing if you pay in 30 days, you're getting 2 percent of the invoice amount for paying 20 days early. That's more than your banker will give you!

- ✔ If you have a stock item whose quantity you need to change (for example, because you discarded stock that spoiled), use the Adjust Qty. on Hand item (at the top of the screen). QuickBooks keeps track of your adjustments so that you can take a loss for the spoiled merchandise.

Paying by check or online

It's more fun to receive checks than to send them. But when it's time to pay your bills, QuickBooks can at least save you from having to write checks.

You don't *have* to let QuickBooks print your checks. QuickBooks is perfectly happy to keep track of your old-fashioned hand-written checks, too. But you'll be doing double the work by doing checks manually rather than completely within QuickBooks. In both cases, you must enter the details into the QuickBooks check register, but if QuickBooks prints your checks, you're finished after the checks are entered.

You use the Checking and Credit Cards tab to handle your payments in QuickBooks. If you've ever written a check, looked at your bank statement, or paid a credit card bill, you're going to find the items on this tab familiar. When you select an item, QuickBooks displays a blank check or a statement like those from your bank.

Not all banks offer online banking, and those that do often charge differently for different services, such as check-free bill payments. In addition, some banks require you to use proprietary software rather than something such as QuickBooks. It's a good idea to check with several banks to see how their online banking services compare before choosing one for your small business. If you're forced to use the bank's software rather than QuickBooks, you may have difficulty updating your QuickBooks records and may have to manually enter all your checks and deposits.

If you use a credit card to pay some business expenses, it's worth the trouble to open an account strictly for business use so that you don't have to separate expenses. Also, you can probably deduct the interest as a business expense if you use the account only for business.

Doing the payroll and taxes

If you have employees, you know what a hassle payroll and taxes can be. Again, QuickBooks can help.

QuickBooks does payroll for only the United States and a few of its possessions. Differences in tax laws make it impossible for QuickBooks to provide payroll functions for Canada and other countries.

You use the Payroll and Employees tab of QuickBooks Navigator to handle most payroll and tax functions. QuickBooks automatically figures the payroll taxes, social security taxes, and other taxes when you create a paycheck.

Tax tables frequently change, and as an employer it's your responsibility to use current tax tables. You can subscribe to the QuickBooks tax table update service to make certain you're always using the current versions. Select Help➪About Tax Table to see which tax table you're using and for information on subscribing.

Creating a paycheck is similar to everything else you do in QuickBooks. After you click on the Create Paychecks item, you select the correct employee, fill in the number of hours worked, and print the check. For new employees, you must supply more information, such as their hourly rate, but QuickBooks then remembers the information for the next payday.

If you want to make sure others can't create paychecks, set up a password. Here's how you set up QuickBooks to use passwords:

1. **Choose File⇨Passwords.**

   The Passwords dialog box appears, which you use to set all passwords.

2. **Click on the top Set Password button — the one under Owner Password.**

3. **In the New Password text box, type the password.**

4. **Press Tab to move to the Confirm Password text box.**

5. **In the Confirm Password text box, type the same password.**

   You need to set the Owner password before you can set any other passwords. You also need the owner password to make any changes in the other passwords, and to access the complete functions of QuickBooks.

6. **Click on OK to close the Set Owner Password dialog box.**

7. **Click on the second Set Password button — the one under Payroll Password.**

   Create a Payroll password to enable someone to access payroll functions as well as new transactions.

8. **In the New Password text box, type the password.**

9. **Press Tab to move to the Confirm Password text box.**

10. **In the Confirm Password text box, type the same password.**

11. **Click on OK to close the Set Payroll Password dialog box.**

12. **Click on the third Set Password button — the one under Data Entry Password.**

    This password allows someone to create new transactions, but prevents him or her from getting into the payroll functions.

13. **In the New Password text box, type the password.**

14. **Press Tab to move to the Confirm Password text box.**

15. **In the Confirm Password text box, type the same password.**

16. **Click on OK to close the Set Data Entry Password dialog box.**

17. **Click on OK.**

If you create passwords, keep a written record in a secure location. Don't forget to change passwords when someone leaves your company or when people move to different jobs. Guard the Owner password carefully — it provides complete access to all QuickBooks functions!

Maintaining What You Have

Even though QuickBooks does a lot for you automatically, you need to manage some tasks yourself. These remaining tasks are sort of thrown together on the Company tab of QuickBooks Navigator, as shown in Figure 13-7.

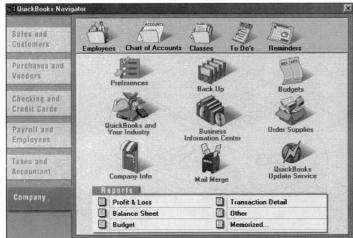

Figure 13-7: This is where you find all sorts of miscellaneous items for keeping your business on an even keel.

You can figure out most of the items on the Company tab. Here are a few you'll find important:

- ✓ QuickBooks automatically saves your work as you make entries, but there's always a chance your company file could be corrupted due to a hardware or power failure. Use the Back Up item to make sure you always have a backup of your company file.

- ✓ Tax law changes or program bugs can make it necessary to update QuickBooks from time to time. Use the QuickBooks Update Service to make certain your copy of QuickBooks has all the latest revisions.

- ✓ Use the Preferences item to change the way QuickBooks looks and works. For example, if you decide to begin charging interest on late payments, you can use the Preferences dialog box to set up the terms.

✔ If you decide to send a mailing to current customers, vendors, or employees, use the Mail Merge item to create a file of their names and addresses.

✔ To find additional tips on how to use QuickBooks for your specific type of business, click on the QuickBooks and Your Industry item. You'll find lots of information to help you get the most out of QuickBooks.

Chapter 14

Tracking Time and Keeping Your Agreements Legal

In This Chapter

▶ Keeping yourself on schedule

▶ Keeping track of your contacts

▶ Making sure your agreements are legal

*A*s a businessperson, you can't afford to waste time, which means you need to be organized. You also can't afford misunderstandings, so any contracts or agreements you create should be legal, easily understood, and well written.

This chapter shows you two different types of software. *PIMs,* or Personal Information Managers, help you maintain your schedule and keep track of contacts. Legal assistance software helps you quickly create contracts so that you don't have to seek legal advice. Both types of programs help you make better use of your time so that you can get down to business.

Tracking Your Time

Have you ever forgotten an important date or nearly missed an appointment because time got away from you? If so, you'll appreciate having your computer remind you when it's time to do something.

You have many options for tracking your schedule with your computer. You can find a PIM in each of the major office suites, you can buy a stand-alone PIM such as Sidekick 98, or you can try out several shareware PIMs on the *Small Business Computing For Dummies* CD-ROM. The issue isn't finding a good PIM; it's finding the right one for you.

In this section, I show you how to manage your calendar in Microsoft Outlook. If you decide to use a different PIM, you'll see that it has similar features.

Put it on your calendar

Executives in big companies have it easy — their office assistant handles their calendar and is responsible for making sure they don't miss important meetings. If you forget an appointment, however, you have only yourself to blame. If that missed meeting was with a potential customer or an investor, being absentminded could be costly.

No PIM can alert you to scheduled events unless it is running. If you turn off your computer when you're not using it, or if you forget to run your PIM, you can't expect it to tell you when you need to be somewhere.

Here's how you can use the Calendar folder in Outlook to schedule your appointments:

1. **Open Microsoft Outlook.**

   If you want Outlook to start automatically whenever you start your system, add Outlook to the Start Up folder.

   You may want to get *Small Business Windows 95 For Dummies,* by Steve Nelson (published by IDG Books Worldwide, Inc.) if you don't know how to add things to folders.

2. **In the Outlook bar at the left edge of the Outlook window, click on the Calendar icon.**

   If you don't see the Calendar icon, click on the Outlook button. The Calendar icon doesn't appear when either the Mail or Other button has been clicked.

   The Outlook Calendar folder appears, as shown in Figure 14-1.

3. **Click on a date in the monthly calendar display to see the schedule for that date.**

   You can choose different months by clicking on the arrows above the monthly calendars. Today's date is outlined with a little box, and dates with scheduled events are in bold.

4. **To add an event, click on a time slot and begin typing.**

   For more options when setting up an appointment, double-click on a time slot or an appointment to display a dialog box like the one shown in Figure 14-2.

5. **Click on Save.**

6. **Click on Close to close the dialog box.**

Outlook automatically saves your calendar — and your appointments are saved.

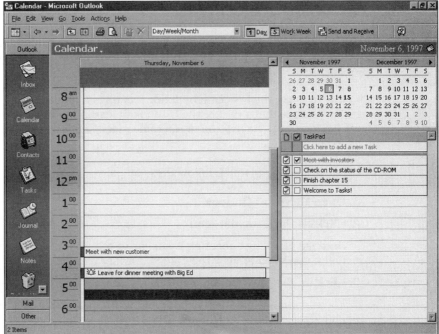

Figure 14-1:
Use the
Outlook
Calendar
folder to
keep track
of your
appointments
and you
won't have
an excuse
for being
late!

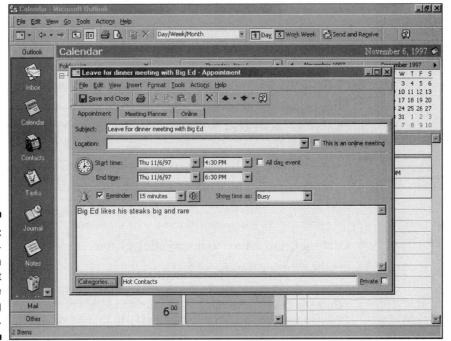

Figure 14-2:
Double-
click on an
appointment
for more
scheduling
options.

Planning a meeting

If you've ever tried to schedule a meeting, you know how difficult it can be to get everyone together at the right time. If the time is okay for Joyce, it may not fit Al's schedule.

One way to make the task of scheduling meetings a bit easier is to use the meeting planner that's part of the Outlook Calendar folder. People in the meeting don't even have to be in the same place because you can also set up online meetings!

To use the meeting planner, follow these steps:

1. **Open Microsoft Outlook.**

2. **Click on the Calendar icon.**

   Because planning a meeting is similar to scheduling any other appointment, you need to view the Calendar folder to schedule a meeting.

3. **Click on the date for the meeting.**

   You can choose a date in a different month by clicking on the arrows above the monthly calendars. When you click on the meeting date, Outlook displays the current schedule for that date.

4. **Double-click on the time slot for the beginning of the meeting.**

5. **Click on the Meeting Planner tab.**

   Initially, the Meeting Planner tab shows the meeting scheduled with one attendee — you — as shown in Figure 14-3. You'll add attendees and adjust the schedule to complete the meeting plan.

6. **Click on the text box that says Type Attendee Name Here.**

7. **Click on Invite Others to display your address book.**

8. **Choose the attendees from the address book and then click on one of the following:**

   - Required (for those people who must be at the meeting)

   - Optional (for people who you'd like to attend, but whose attendance isn't absolutely required)

   - Resources (to schedule a room or equipment)

9. **Click on OK to return to the meeting planner.**

10. **Set the meeting times.**

    You can drag the vertical bars that frame the meeting time, or you can select times in the Meeting start time and Meeting end time boxes. You can also use the AutoPick button to try to find a time when everyone can attend.

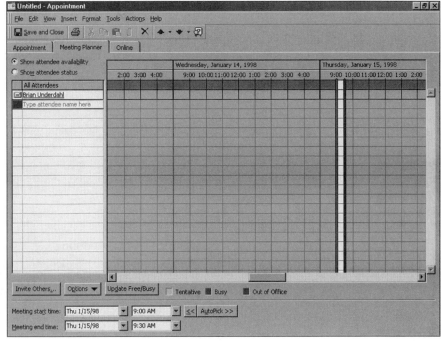

Figure 14-3:
Use the
Meeting
Planner tab
to set up
your
meeting
schedules.

11. Click on the Appointment tab.

12. In the Subject box, type a short description.

Outlook automatically places the attendee list in the To box. You must add a subject so that the attendees will know you want to schedule a meeting. You may also want to fill in the Location box.

13. Click on Send to send out the meeting invitations.

14. Choose Save and Close.

As you receive responses to the meeting invitations, you'll want to reopen the meeting planner to record those responses. Outlook can automatically include the response from people who are also using Outlook and reply to your e-mailed invitation. Figure 14-4 shows the Meeting Planner tab after the responses have been recorded, and the Show Attendee Status option is selected.

Don't forget to do it!

Setting a schedule for everything is difficult. Some tasks are a better fit on a to-do list — they can be handled when you have the time. For those sorts of tasks, you use the Outlook Tasks folder.

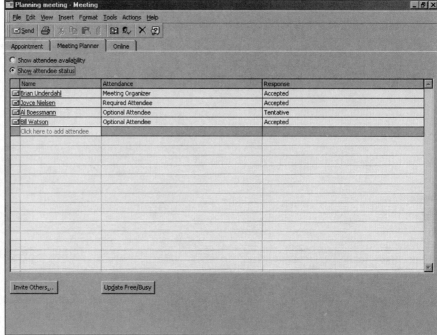

Figure 14-4:
Planning a
meeting is a
lot easier
when you
have
Outlook
to help
with the
schedule.

The Outlook Calendar view includes a small look at the *task list* — a list of things you have to do. If you want to manage your to-do list, though, click on the Tasks icon in the Outlook bar. You'll have a lot more room for your task list and will be better able to take advantage of special task list features, such as viewing additional fields that can make the list more useful.

There's one tricky part to using the task list. To add a new task, you don't click on an empty space below the list of tasks. Instead, you click on the task list header where you see Click here to add a new Task, and then begin typing. When you press Enter, your new task is added to the task list.

Following are some more things you'll want to know about using the task list:

✔ To edit a task, double-click on it in the list.

✔ To set a due date, click on the Due Date column and then click on the down arrow and select a date.

✔ To add new fields to the list, right-click on the task list column headings (Subject, Due Date, and so on) and select Field Chooser from the pop-up menu. Figure 14-5 shows the Field Chooser. Point to the field you want to add, hold down the left mouse button, and drag the field to where you want it to appear in the column headings. Release the mouse button to drop the new field right there.

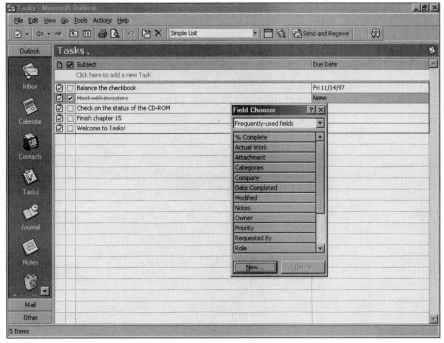

Figure 14-5:
Use the
Field
Chooser to
add new
fields to
your task
list.

✔ To move a task up or down in the list, point to the clipboard icon in the left column of the list, and drag the task up or down to where you want it to appear.

✔ To mark a task as completed, click on the check box in the second column. If you goof up, just click again.

Keeping an international schedule

If you do business internationally, it can be pretty difficult to keep track of time zones. That's okay if you do all your business by regular mail or even e-mail, but if you ever need to make international phone calls, you'd better know what the time is for the person you're calling.

Sidekick 98 offers all the standard features you'll find in most other PIMs, plus an unusual feature that makes this program important to small businesspeople who keep an international business schedule. That feature is the EarthTime display, shown in Figure 14-6.

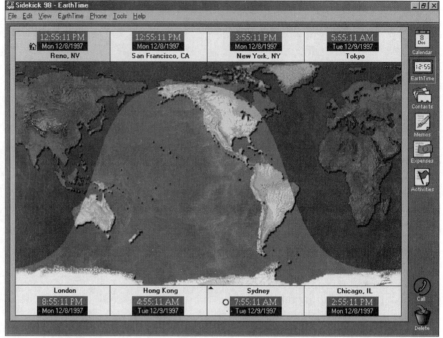

Figure 14-6:
The
Sidekick 98
EarthTime
display can
help you
manage an
international
business
schedule.

If you do business in specific locations around the world, you can modify the EarthTime display to show the facts for those specific locations. All you need to do to select a different city is to right-click on one of the city panels in the display, choose Select a Different City, and make your choice.

Sidekick 98 also includes information about the selected cities. You can view population statistics, information about the time zone, and a few more facts such as local sunrise and sunset times.

Keeping Your Contacts

It's hard to keep track of all the people you meet as you do business. Besides customers, you probably have vendors, representatives, people you call when you need a bit of assistance, and lots of others. You could keep your contact list the old-fashioned way — by writing down all the names, addresses, phones numbers, e-mail addresses, Web sites, and so on in a little black book. That may work for a while, but it will start to get messy and out of control in no time.

You can dig your way out of the contact hole by using your PIM to keep track of your contacts. In Outlook, you use the Contacts folder, which you open by clicking on the Contacts icon in the Outlook bar.

You may be surprised the first time you open the Contacts folder — especially if you've been using your system for some time and have added people to your address book. Instead of all the contacts you may expect to see, you'll probably find only yourself and a welcome message. To quickly fill your contacts folder, choose File⇨Import and Export to bring in the information from your existing address book. If you have addresses in other programs, be sure to check and see whether Outlook knows how to import those addresses, too.

Figure 14-7 shows the Contacts folder after a number of contacts have been added.

Here are some tips to using the Contacts folder:

✔ To add a new contact to your list, choose File⇨New⇨Contact. This enables you to create a contact record for this person.

✔ To change someone's information, double-click on his or her listing in the Contacts folder.

✔ To keep a record of your conversations with someone, open the person's record and click on the Journal tab. You'll be able to keep a running tab of all your conversations, along with the date and time of the conversation.

Figure 14-7:
Manage your business contacts by using the Outlook Contacts folder.

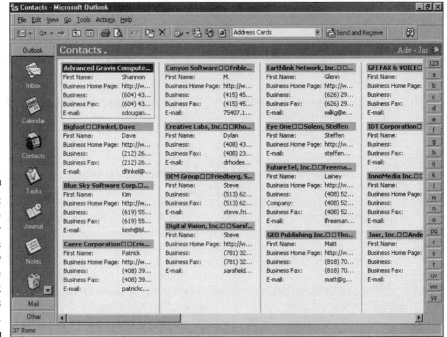

✔ To quickly move to the beginning of the listings for a particular letter in the alphabet, click on the letter in the bar at the right side of the Contacts folder.

✔ To view more contact records at one time, drag the separator bars between the columns of address cards to the left. You can also drag the bar to the right to view more details on each card.

✔ You can change the way listings are displayed by clicking on the View list box (that's the box that normally says Address Cards) and choosing a different view.

Creating Some Fine Print

How would you like a gold mine? Whenever you need spare cash, you reach into the opening of the mine, bring out some nuggets, and sell them. Imagine, though, that you had access not to gold but to another product people needed and were willing to pay big bucks for — no matter that the product was a piece of paper with some standard *boilerplate* text spit out by your word processor. You'd like to keep that easy money rolling in, wouldn't you?

Now shift gears for a minute and think how you'd feel if you realized that someone was charging you lots of dough for those pieces of paper with standardized text. You'd like to find a way to save some of that money, wouldn't you?

Most contracts and agreements your lawyer draws up are boilerplate text with a few tweaks here and there to justify the high cost. Face it — standard contracts and agreements are a lawyer's gravy train. You pay a lot for your lawyer to print essentially the same contract he or she has already sold to a hundred other people.

Why not cut out the middleman and create your own legally binding contracts and agreements? With the right software to help, you can save a bundle in legal fees — especially on contracts you use more than once.

No software can completely substitute for the legal expertise of a good lawyer. Rather than use contract and agreement software to replace your lawyer, use the software to create a contract and ask your lawyer to give it a quick going over. You'll still save a lot in legal fees, and if you reuse the same contract, you'll save even more.

Two of the best small business contract packages are Quicken Business Law Partner and Jian Agreement Builder. You can find out more about these two at http://www.intuit.com and http://www.jianusa.com.

Figure 14-8 shows a typical agreement your small business may need: a sales representative agreement. In this case, the agreement is one of the documents you'll find in the Jian Agreement Builder package.

Jian Agreement Builder is a bit different than most software you may be accustomed to. What you need isn't some fancy package that makes you learn a new way of working simply so you can write a contract. Rather, what you need is a set of ready-made contracts and clear instructions on how to adapt them for your use. Jian Agreement Builder accomplishes that by installing a set of more than 100 legal agreement document templates you can use in your regular word processor. Each document includes lots of information explaining just how to fill in the blanks.

After you install the Jian Agreement Builder contract and agreement files, you may want to change all of the files so that their read-only file attribute is set. This prevents you from accidentally changing any of the originals. If you're not quite sure how to change file attributes, you may want to get *Small Business Windows 95 For Dummies,* by Steve Nelson (published by IDG Books Worldwide, Inc.).

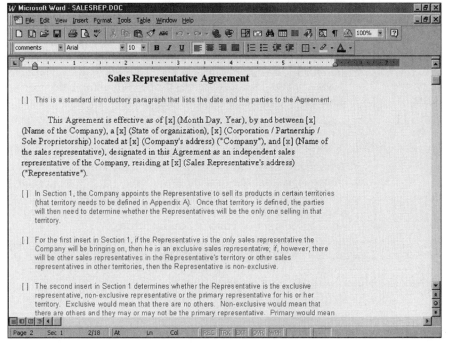

Figure 14-8:
Create your
own
standard
contracts
and
agreements
with Jian
Agreement
Builder.

To use the contracts and agreements in Jian Agreement Builder (after you install the contracts and agreements, of course), follow these steps:

1. **Open your word processor.**

   Because Jian Agreement Builder works with the word processor you already have, you don't need to learn a new program to use Jian Agreement Builder.

2. **Choose File⇨Open.**

3. **Choose the folder where Jian Agreement Builder is installed.**

4. **Open the document file you want to use.**

   The Jian Agreement Builder user's manual lists the filenames for each type of contract or agreement. You'll also want to refer to the user's manual to find out any special considerations for using the various contracts and agreements.

5. **Choose File⇨Save As and enter a new name for the document.**

   You'll want to create a new, more descriptive name for any of the contracts or agreements you use. Be sure you don't use the original Jian Agreement Builder filename when you save a document you've modified.

6. **Go through the document, replacing the text as necessary.**

   The contract and agreement templates include comments to assist you in filling in the correct information to replace the variables shown in brackets. You'll want to delete those comments before printing the final document.

7. **Save your completed document.**

8. **Print the document.**

   You may want to have your attorney look over any contracts or agreements — at least the first time you use a particular document. If your attorney has no objections or if you incorporate any suggestions in future documents, you probably won't have to worry about using the same agreement or contract in the future.

Lawyers may not like the fact that you've found out the secret of their gravy train, but why should you care? Pay your lawyer to do some real work — not just to give you copies of boilerplate documents!

Chapter 15

Putting Your Business on the Internet

In This Chapter

▶ Discovering what a Web site can do for your small business

▶ Creating a Web site

▶ Getting fancy with your Web site

▶ Staying secure on the Internet

*W*ith all the hype and stories about the Internet these days, it seems as though you can't do business without being on the Web. If your small business is ready to branch out and find more customers, your own Web site may be a good way to go.

Lots of people would be happy to take your money and build you a Web site. But you can create a basic Web site yourself much easier and faster than you may imagine. Why not give it a try and see what it's all about? You can always hire one of those computer geeks later if you want to.

Why You May Want a Web Site

How can you reach thousands of potential customers who are specifically looking for your products or services? You could spend lots of cash on advertisements, send out mailings, or even make phone calls all day and you'd still miss most of them. Or you could create a Web site and let them find you.

The Internet and the Web

Most of the time, people talk about the Internet and the Web (more correctly, the World Wide Web) as if they meant the same thing. That's because the Web is a part of the Internet. In fact, most people use only the Web because they experience the Internet through *Web browsers*, programs such as Internet Explorer and Netscape Navigator. Although technically the Internet and the Web don't mean the same thing, you can get away with using the terms interchangeably.

Estimates show that more than 100 million people around the world are connected to the Internet, and that number is growing daily. There probably are also millions of Web sites; no one knows for certain because it's impossible to keep up with the constant changes on the Internet.

If you build a Web site, how can anyone find you among all those millions of places to go? The answer is simple. A number of companies provide Web search services — indexes to what's out there. If your Web site mentions your company's custom-made Halloween masks, people who are searching for "Halloween" on the Web will probably find you.

A Web site makes it possible for you to reach people you couldn't possibly reach any other way. If you build an interesting enough Web site for your business, don't be surprised to hear from people all around the world. After your business is on the Web, you're no longer confined to your local area — the world is your marketplace!

HTML Doesn't Mean "How to Make Lunch"

If you've ever been on the Internet, you know that it can be a colorful and graphical place. If you're going to create a Web site for your business, you'll want to make certain your site looks good, too. People leave boring-looking Web sites as fast as possible.

The Web is colorful and graphical because of *HTML* (HyperText Markup Language). All Web sites are programmed using HTML, but fortunately, you don't need to worry about that. The programs you use to create Web sites create the HTML code for you.

Building a Web site

A *Web site* is made up of one or more pages, depending on your needs. *Pages* are simply the individual documents that make up a Web site. When a Web site has more than one page, the pages are *linked,* which means that they're connected, so you can go from one to another easily. You may want to start with a single page Web site and add pages later after you've had a chance to play around with creating Web pages. It's not difficult to create extra pages, but why complicate your life any more than necessary?

You can't discover everything about creating fancy Web sites in a few pages of a book, of course. But this overview can give you a taste of what it takes to design Web pages.

FrontPage Express is a Web page design tool that you get free with Internet Explorer 4. FrontPage Express is a slightly smaller version of FrontPage, a full-featured Web site design tool you can buy from Microsoft. FrontPage Express is missing a few FrontPage features, but you can always upgrade to FrontPage later if you prefer.

Follow these steps to create a Web page with FrontPage Express:

1. **Open FrontPage Express.**

   FrontPage Express is in the Internet Explorer folder. Don't worry if FrontPage Express looks like an empty page, as in Figure 15-1. You'll have a good-looking Web page in no time.

2. **Select File➪New.**

   The New Page dialog box appears, as shown in Figure 15-2. This is where you choose the type of Web page you want to create.

3. **Select Personal Home Page Wizard.**

   This wizard does a lot of the basic work of creating a Web site automatically.

4. **Click on OK.**

   The Personal Home Page Wizard dialog box appears, as shown in Figure 15-3. You choose the basic elements of your home page in this dialog box.

5. **Make sure that you check each element you want on your Web page.**

   You'll probably want Current Projects and Contact Information on your Web site, but you may not want any of the other items. If you're not sure about an item, add it to the page and decide later. It's easy to remove things you don't want, but it's not as easy to add something later.

Figure 15-1:
The
FrontPage
Express
screen
starts out
empty, but
you'll
change that
in just a few
minutes.

Figure 15-2:
FrontPage
Express has
several
templates
and wizards
to help you
create your
Web page.

6. **Click on Next.**

7. **Type a filename (Page URL) and page title for your Web page.**

You may want to use your company's name for the page title, as shown
in Figure 15-4. In most instances, you can leave the Page URL entry
alone — the default value is generally acceptable.

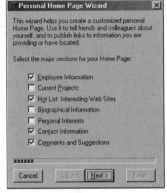

Figure 15-3:
FrontPage
Express has
a number of
sections it
can quickly
add to your
Web page.

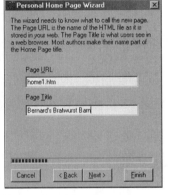

Figure 15-4:
The Page
Title
appears at
the top of
your
completed
Web page.

8. Continue to create the rest of your Web page.

You need to enter several pieces of information on a number of different pages. What you need to include depends on the elements you selected for your Web page. For example, if you decided to include the current projects section on your Web page, FrontPage Express asks you to enter the names of some current projects and how you'd like them to appear, as shown in Figure 15-5.

9. When you answer all the questions, click on Finish to create the Web page.

Figure 15-6 shows a Web page created in FrontPage Express.

10. Select File⇨Save As and click on the As File button.

Click on Save to save the page as a file on your hard disk. If you forget to click on the As File button, FrontPage Express tries to save your Web page on the Internet.

Figure 15-5:
The
Personal
Home Page
Wizard
requests
information
for each of
the elements
you choose
to include
on your
Web page.

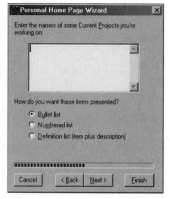

You can change the text in your Web page by simply selecting the old text and typing your new text. You can edit items by right-clicking on them and selecting the appropriate options. For example, to change the e-mail address so someone can send you a message, right-click on the underlined link `me@mycompany.com` and choose Hyperlink Properties to display the Edit Hyperlink dialog box, shown in Figure 15-7. (*Hyperlinks* are just connections to other Web pages or e-mail addresses.)

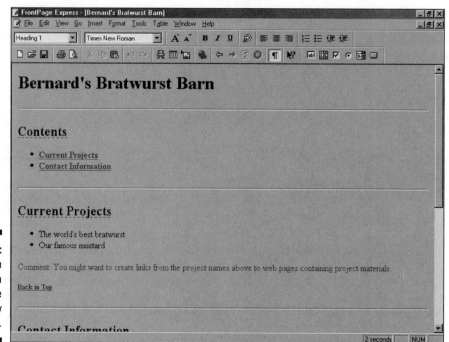

Figure 15-6:
You can
create a
Web page
in a few
minutes.

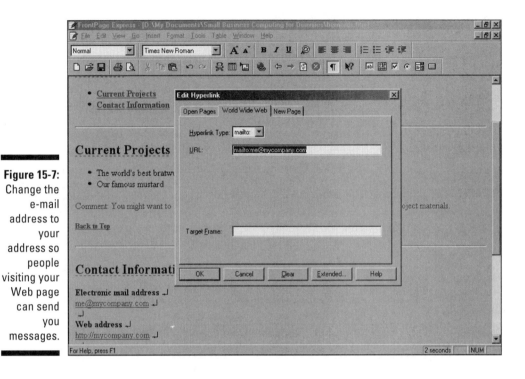

Figure 15-7:
Change the
e-mail
address to
your
address so
people
visiting your
Web page
can send
you
messages.

If you want to add images, sound, or other items, choose options from the Insert menu. You can also make quite a few changes to the appearance of the Web page by using the options on the Format menu. For example, you can add a background image that displays behind everything else on the page.

It's often better to create relatively small Web pages — at least as the top page of a Web site — and link to your more complex pages. That way, people who visit your Web site won't have to endure long delays while your entire Web site loads. You can get some idea how long your Web page should normally take to load over a 28.8 modem by watching the seconds indicator near the lower-right edge of the FrontPage Express screen. If your main page takes more than about 20 seconds to load, you're probably asking for trouble.

Using the Web Publishing Wizard

After you create your Web pages, you're ready to publish them on the Internet using the Web Publishing Wizard. You need to know where to send your files as well as any passwords necessary for access to the Web server. If you don't have this information, ask your Internet Service Provider (ISP).

Follow these steps to publish your Web pages using the Web Publishing Wizard:

1. Open the Web Publishing Wizard.

The Web Publishing Wizard is in the Internet Explorer folder.

2. Click on Next to begin using the Web Publishing Wizard.

3. Type the name of the file or folder for your Web page.

If your Web site includes multiple pages, make sure you select the folder containing the entire set of pages. If your site is contained in several folders, make sure the Include Subfolders check box is checked. Include any graphics files or other items you've included on your Web pages, too. Figure 15-8 shows the Web Publishing Wizard after the filename for the Web page was entered.

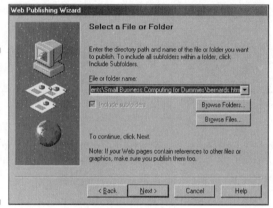

Figure 15-8:
Use the
Web
Publishing
Wizard to
place your
Web pages
on the Web
server.

4. Click on Next to continue.

5. Click on New to add a new Web server.

6. Type a descriptive name for the Web server.

7. Click on Next to continue.

8. Choose Automatically Select Service Provider.

If your ISP is shown in the list, you can select your ISP instead.

9. Click on Next to continue.

10. Type the URL (address) for your Web site.

Your ISP must provide this information, which is the Web address for your Web site. Figure 15-9 shows an example of this type of address.

Figure 15-9:
The URL is the address people will use to find your Web page.

11. **Click on Next to continue.**

12. **Enter your user name and password.**

    You may need a special user name and password to publish Web pages. Check with your ISP if you can't upload your pages using your normal user name and password.

13. **Click on OK to finish.**

    The Web Publishing Wizard dials your ISP and transmits your Web pages. Depending on your ISP, you may have to enter another password or some additional information to complete the process.

After you publish your Web pages, you can update them using FrontPage Express. If your site isn't up-to-date, fewer people will want to visit it again.

Tools for building a Web site

FrontPage Express is one of the many tools you can use to help build your Web site. FrontPage Express is one of the simpler tools around and it's free, so it's a reasonable place to start. Later, you may want to try other Web site building tools.

It couldn't be easier to try some other Web site building tools — trial versions of LiquidFX, WebForms, WebMania, Banner*Show, CGI*Star Pro, Guestbook*Star, and Site*Sleuth are included on the *Small Business Computing For Dummies* CD-ROM. You can try any or all of these for free. If you want to continue to use a particular tool after trying it out, you'll need to register it and pay a small fee.

You can also create Web pages using your favorite office suite programs. The trick is to save your document as an HTML file. In most programs, HTML is an option on the File⇨Save As menu.

Corel Office programs use a special add-in called Barista to help them create Web pages that look more like the original document. In Quattro Pro 8, for example, you can use the File⇨Send To⇨Corel Barista command to create a Web page that looks just like a spreadsheet page, including any charts or fancy formatting you've used. Barista is very interesting because most Web pages you can create using your favorite office software suite programs don't look very much like the original document — especially if you've created anything fancy.

Bells and Whistles and Java

If your Web site doesn't reach out and grab people, they're likely to move on to someplace more interesting. One way to make a good impression is to add graphics, a moving banner, or sound to your Web site, or even a special background image that appears behind the text.

Before you get too fancy, though, consider the following:

✔ The quickest way to get people to leave your Web site before they've even finished loading the first page is to have a site that loads too slowly. And the number one way to make Web pages slow to load is to add a lot of fancy stuff such as graphics, banners, and so on.

✔ Test your Web page by having someone else try to load it. Ask the tester to report any problems, such as images that don't appear where they should, as soon as possible.

✔ Not everyone will have all the software components necessary to view video or hear audio bits you've added to your Web pages. You may want to include a link to a Web site where those components can be downloaded.

✔ If you're going to include pictures, keep them small. You can always include a link to a larger version of the picture for people who are really interested in the photos.

✔ A lot of fancy Web site additions use a programming language called Java. Fortunately, you don't have to learn Java to add fancy stuff to your Web site. Many of the tools you can use to spice up your Web pages create the Java programming for you.

The Internet has lots of ready-to-use add-ons for your Web pages, as well as tools, so that you can create your own fancy stuff. Here are two places to visit to begin your search: `http://www.sco.com/SkunkWare/rr/java.html` and `http://cws.internet.com/32webimg.html` (shown in Figure 15-10).

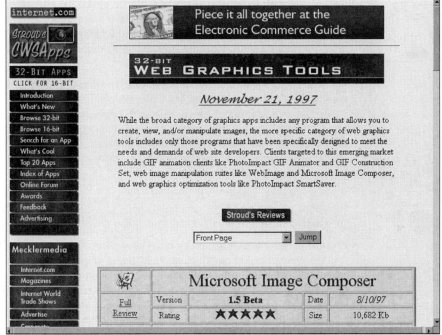

Figure 15-10:
You can find
all sorts of
add-ons for
your Web
pages at
sites like
this one.

Don't Lose Your Key

When you put your business on the Internet, you're opening your door to the entire world. Although that opens up a lot of great opportunities, it also presents some major security risks. You should make sure that you aren't taking any unnecessary chances.

You've probably heard about computer viruses that can circulate on the Internet, but you have to consider other dangers when you're doing business on the Internet. Following are some Internet security issues that can affect your small business:

✔ If you will be taking orders over the Internet, you need a secure way to accept and verify online payments. You can find out a lot about secure online payment systems at: http://ganges.cs.tcd.ie/mepeirce/Project/oninternet.html. You can also visit the Visa credit card company online at http://www.visa.com/cgi-bin/vee/fb/main.html?2+0.

✔ Secure electronic transactions use digital certificates to identify both the buyer and the seller. *Digital certificates* are an electronically encoded means of insuring that people are who they say they are. If you're going to accept online orders, you need a digital merchant certificate to establish a secure Web site.

✔ A lot of people are uncomfortable using their credit cards to buy things over the Internet, no matter how secure you insist your site is. If possible, you may want to include a toll-free phone number for potential customers to use instead of sending their credit card numbers over the Internet. Unfortunately, toll-free numbers won't help your international customers, or those people who want to place an order when your office is closed.

✔ If possible, don't host your Web site on your own computers. It's far better to place your Web site on your ISP's system because it keeps people from breaking into your computer through the Internet.

✔ If you run your small business from your home, use a post office box or a mailing service rather than your home address on your Web site. This is especially true if you sell small, expensive items such as jewelry, because you don't want thieves to know where to find easy pickings.

Chapter 16

Playing the Software Upgrade Game

. . . .

In This Chapter

▶ Finding out when upgrades are necessary

▶ Saving time and money by upgrading

▶ Moving to a different brand

▶ Uncovering the hidden costs of upgrades

▶ Finding out about the latest versions online

. . . .

Sometimes it seems as if software manufacturers make most of their money selling upgrades. Should you upgrade, stay with what you have, or switch to a competing product?

Some upgrades include important improvements that can save you a great deal of money — and hidden traps waiting to bring your business to a standstill. Before you decide whether to upgrade, you need to know all the facts. This chapter tells you how to determine whether software upgrades make sense for your small business.

When Is an Upgrade Necessary?

Most products are intended to last for a long time. No one expects you to upgrade to the newest toaster or the latest TV just because the manufacturers have released slick new models. Automobile manufacturers come out with new models every year, but that doesn't mean you have to upgrade your car each time a new model appears. So why do software manufacturers expect you to upgrade as soon as they release a new version?

Here's what you need to know to help you decide whether that upgrade is necessary:

- ✔ Software manufacturers generally give top priority to providing support for current software versions. If you lag behind by one or two versions, it's harder to get support from the manufacturer.

- ✔ Software revisions often include unannounced bug fixes. New versions may correct problems the manufacturer never admitted existed in the old version.

- ✔ Most software manufacturers try to keep menus, icons, and shortcuts as consistent as possible between revisions. The fewer of these types of changes they make, the easier it is to move to the new version.

- ✔ Some new software versions are only a way to boost a company's revenues. Unfortunately, you probably won't know if the new version has important new revisions or is just a new name for an old package until you install the new version. After you've installed it, you probably can't return it.

- ✔ Operating system revisions fall into quite a different category than application program revisions. You often need the newest operating system if you want to buy new programs or hardware.

- ✔ Don't fall for the old program-number shell game. Just because one program is labeled with a higher version number than a competing product doesn't mean that it's newer or has more features. Software manufacturers sometimes skip whole version numbers to try to make their software appear to be more advanced than a competitor's product.

- ✔ New program versions often have bugs that weren't caught in pre-release testing. Unless you absolutely must have the latest software, you may want to wait a month or so to see whether the manufacturer releases a "revised" new version.

Fortunately, most software upgrades aren't expensive. If you have several PCs in your office, you may want to designate one as a new software testing station. You can try out the software for a month or so before deciding whether to upgrade the rest of your systems.

Licenses and upgrades

Some people think they can buy one copy of a software upgrade and use it on all of their computers. This is generally a violation of your software license and is certainly a poor way to run a business. You wouldn't want your customers to pay for one item but take ten, would you? Be sure to check your software license, and don't install more copies than you've paid for!

Give Me Your Money or Your Time

Remember, you don't want to be "penny wise and pound foolish." Sometimes that saying applies to those who decide against software upgrades because what they have works okay and is good enough for them. If you've ever said something similar, you may want to reconsider your attitude.

Although it's true that some software upgrades aren't worth the money, many upgrades are worthwhile. Here are some factors to consider:

- ✔ Upgrades may save you time if the new version does something the old version couldn't do. For example, if a newer version can save files directly to the Internet, you may be able to update your company's Web site much faster than if you need to use a separate Web page editor.

- ✔ Newer versions may include bug fixes so that the program won't crash as often. If you find yourself restarting your computer several times a day because a program stopped responding, you may be able to save that lost time by going to a newer version.

- ✔ Upgrades often include incentives that make the cost more reasonable. Some versions of Microsoft Office, for example, include a mouse in the box. If you're using an old or off-brand mouse, the included mouse effectively cuts $60 off your upgrade cost.

- ✔ Many of the newest software versions include wizards or coaches to help you do things. These can cut down your learning time, and if you have employees, wizards can cut down the time you need to spend training them, too.

- ✔ Read the fine print regarding any upgrade rebates. These often require you to send in the *original* sales receipt, which may be difficult if you bought more than one item with a rebate at the same time. Check this out before you leave the store and ask to have each item rung up as a separate sale if necessary.

- ✔ Newer software versions may mean changes in the document file format. If you need to share files between systems or with someone else outside your business, try to get everyone to use the same software versions.

- ✔ Newer versions often include zippy new features that are lost if you try to save a file in an old format.

Jumping Ship

Don't tell the software manufacturers I told you this, but if it's time for an upgrade, it may be time to consider moving to a competing product. Just because your computer came with brand X doesn't mean you can't try brand Y.

The software industry is one of the most competitive businesses in the world. Software companies look at the millions of people who use their competitor's product as the great unwashed masses just waiting to jump to something better. They also like to think of their own customers as loyal believers who wouldn't dream of trying out a competing product.

Should you consider moving to a different brand of software? Maybe, but keep several facts in mind:

- ✔ If you've created a lot of documents in one brand of software, you can probably convert them to another brand just by opening them and saving them in the new software.

- ✔ Unfortunately, not all conversions are quite as good as you might like. This may be especially true in the area of formatting; converted documents may not look quite the same in the new software.

- ✔ Most software manufacturers are happy to offer special upgrade deals to people who convert from a competing brand. One neat thing you may not realize is that upgrading to a competing brand leaves you with fully licensed copies of both pieces of software. If you upgrade to the same brand you had, the license is usually transferred to the newer version, and you're not legally permitted to use the old version anymore.

- ✔ Because Microsoft sells more software than anyone else, Microsoft's competitors often offer more features at a better price. For example, Quattro Pro has many more built-in functions and can open and save files in many more file formats than Excel.

- ✔ Cutting-edge technology may be available only in a different brand. Voice dictation technology, for example, is included with Lotus SmartSuite but not with Microsoft Office or Corel WordPerfect.

- ✔ Before you jump ship to a different brand, remember that it's pretty unlikely that you'll be able to use any macros or other programming from a competing product. If you depend on custom-designed templates, you may be out of luck unless you want to go to the effort to convert them to the new format.

- ✔ Moving to a different brand may be just the incentive you need to throw out old, inefficient ways of doing things and set up newer, more efficient programs.

You Didn't Ask about That!

In the computer industry, what they don't bother to tell you is often more important than what they do tell you. Of course, no one is going to advertise all the faults and problems in their latest and greatest product — that's a job for their competitors!

Upgrading your software can result in plenty of hidden costs. Here are some possible hidden upgrade costs you should be aware of before you jump in with both feet:

✔ Newer software versions may require hardware upgrades. Look at the "System Requirements" section of the box to see whether you need to upgrade your memory or add a new hard disk to install the newer software.

✔ You may have to upgrade your operating system, too. Software manufacturers generally support the newest operating systems and ignore older versions. Upgrading to a new operating system may mean more hardware, too!

✔ Thought your macro programs and templates were safe just because you're thinking of upgrading to the same brand of software? Think again. Manufacturers often upgrade the macro or programming language, too, and that may leave you out in the cold.

✔ It's usually not possible to keep all the menus the same in newer program versions. And in some cases, the menus are so different that you spend hours learning new ways to accomplish old tasks.

✔ If the document file format is changed in the newer version, you may need to take special steps to save your work in the old format so that you can share files with people who haven't upgraded yet. Don't worry that you'll forget; you will, and the person who can't open your file will let you know.

✔ If you have an employee who uses your computer, you may find him or her wasting quite a bit of time trying out the new features in the new version. It's hard to criticize someone who's trying to learn new things, but this can be a hidden cost.

Software upgrades may solve all sorts of nagging problems, or they may cause several new ones. The new features may be the best thing since sliced bread, or pure fluff.

Everything You Could Want to Know

How can you determine whether you have the latest version of your office software suite? How can you find out what new features are included in competing office suites? The answer is to look online by visiting the office software suite home pages on the Web.

When you visit these Web sites, remember that you won't find objective viewpoints. No software manufacturer will tell you that its software may be lacking compared to the competition. But if you take the time to sift through the information on all these sites, you'll come away with a clearer understanding of how the latest versions compare. You may even decide you're happy with what you have.

Figure 16-1 shows the Microsoft Office Web site, which is at `http://www.microsoft.com/office/default.htm`. Here you're certain to find the latest news about the Microsoft Office family.

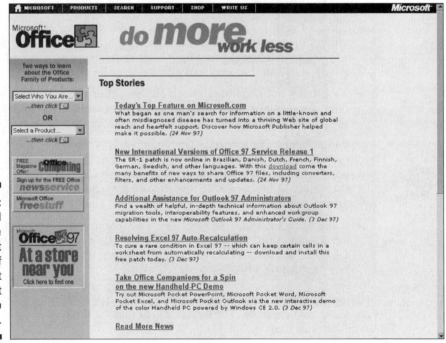

Figure 16-1:
Find out all about the latest version of Microsoft Office at this Web site.

To learn more about Lotus SmartSuite, visit `http://www.lotus.com/ home.nsf/tabs/sswin`, as shown in Figure 16-2. At this site, you may be tempted to try out SmartSuite even if you already use one of the other office software suites. The Lotus SmartSuite Web site often offers a try-before-you-buy deal so that you can sample the latest version of SmartSuite for free.

Corel makes office software for many different types of computers and operating systems. The Corel WordPerfect Suite home page, `http:// www.corel.com/products/wordperfect/`, is shown in Figure 16-3. To find out about the latest versions for your PC, choose the appropriate product and click on Go!

To see whether there are any upgrades you can download for your current software, look for a link labeled *support* or *downloads.* You may be able to download some important improvements or bug fixes for free.

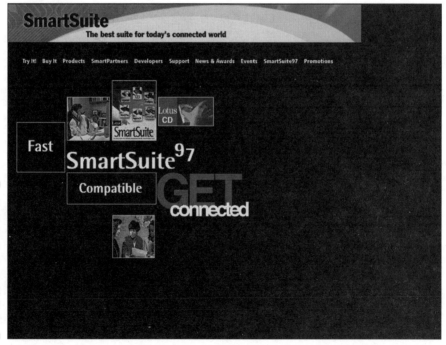

Figure 16-2:
The Lotus SmartSuite Web site gives you a chance to try out SmartSuite for free.

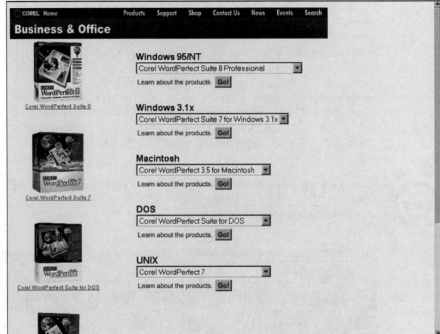

Figure 16-3:
The Corel
WordPerfect
Web site
leads to
several
different
pages —
choose the
one for your
system.

Part V
Correcting Problems

The 5th Wave   By Rich Tennant

Y'KNOW, I DON'T MIND LIVING IN A COMPUTERIZED 'SMART HOUSE,' BUT I DO MIND BEING CALLED AN IDIOT BY THE TOASTER.

In this part . . .

Have you ever noticed that problems never happen at a convenient time? They're a lot more likely to pop up when you're down to the wire and don't have the time to deal with them. Well, Part V shows you how to get your computer problems solved quickly — before they can cause even worse problems for your small business.

Believe it or not, you can probably deal with most computer problems yourself. When you know the basics and a follow a few simple steps, you can have your computer back up and running — most of the time.

Sometimes, though, it's best to know when to get outside help. When you need to wave the white flag, you can still save money or time by resolving the problem more quickly. All it takes is a little organization, the right information, and knowing how to get to the right support person.

Chapter 17

Do-It-Yourself Troubleshooting

· ·

In This Chapter

▶ Gathering the right information

▶ Preparing for the inevitable

▶ Diagnosing the problem

▶ Solving common problems

▶ Knowing when to give up

· ·

*I*t would be nice if everything always worked the way it should, but in the the real world, that just doesn't happen. When you're dealing with computers — possibly the most complex tools used by your small business — it's no wonder that you'll encounter problems at times.

Believe it or not, you can probably fix most computer problems yourself in just a few minutes. This chapter shows you how to take a logical approach to solving the most common computer-related problems. It also tells you how to determine when problems are too much for you to handle on your own, because sometimes the best course is to throw in the towel and get someone else involved.

The most important thing to remember is that you shouldn't wait for problems to strike before getting prepared. After you have a serious problem, you may be out of luck. With a little preparation, though, you may be able to get your system back up and running in no time. It's your call — you can take a few minutes to get ready now or have a panic attack later.

I Know It's Here Somewhere, Officer

Imagine for a moment that you're driving your car to a meeting with an important potential customer. You're in an area of the country you've never visited, and you didn't have a chance to get a map. The customer gave you verbal directions telling you to turn right, turn left, and turn right — but assumed that you already knew that your first turn was the first right turn onto a gravel road, your left turn was the first left after you crossed a bridge, and the final right turn was supposed to be onto the first paved driveway. You can imagine how lost you'd be without those details.

Finding out the details

You need to collect some basic system information *before* problems strike. Collecting this information isn't difficult and takes only a few minutes.

It's a good idea to keep a system information folder for each of your computers. Whenever you add new programs, you can include the new information in the same folder. That way, everything is in one place if you need to call for help.

Your computer has the tools it needs to report on itself. Which tools it has depends on which operating system is installed. Figure 17-1 shows the Windows 98 Microsoft System Information utility.

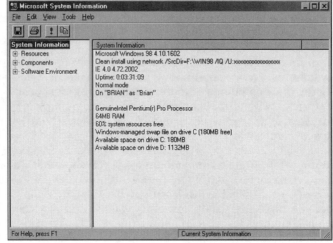

Figure 17-1:
Your computer has tools like this to report on itself.

Here are some tips on finding your system information tools:

- ✔ If you're using Windows 98, you can find the Microsoft System Information utility by choosing Programs➪Accessories➪System Tools, or by clicking on Help➪About in any Microsoft Office program.

- ✔ If you're using Windows 95, look for the Microsoft System Diagnostics (MSD) tool in the Windows folder.

✔ If you're using Windows NT, look for the Administrative Tools folder on the Start menu.

✔ If you use a Mac, look in the Apple menu.

If you decide to print a copy of the information from the Microsoft System Information utility, be sure your printer has lots of paper. The full printout may run over 70 pages!

Getting Ready before Problems Hit

Quick, what's the absolute worst time to find out you can't start your computer because there's a problem with your hard disk? That's simple: when you don't have a *boot disk* (a disk containing all the files necessary for starting your computer).

A computer can have trouble accessing a hard disk for many reasons. Something may be physically wrong with the hard disk, or a power glitch may have caused a random error in one of the files needed to start the system. You could even have a computer virus — although if you're careful about what you put in your computer, you shouldn't have to worry about that quite as much as some people think. Regardless of the reason for the problem, you'll experience that moment of panic when you see an error message and your computer stops responding.

The disk you need goes under several different names, depending on which operating system is running on your computer. It may be called a boot disk, a startup disk, an emergency boot disk, or something similar.

Following are the steps for creating a startup disk in Windows 98. The process is generally similar for other operating systems as well. (Windows NT is a special case, but you can always use the Setup disks that came with Windows NT to start a Windows NT system.)

1. **Click on the Start button.**

2. **Choose Settings⇨Control Panel.**

   The Control Panel is the place where you can adjust a wide variety of system settings.

3. **Click on the Add/Remove Programs icon.**

   The Add/Remove Programs Properties dialog box appears. It has one tab for installing or removing programs, one for changing how much of Windows is loaded, and the magic tab for creating your startup disk. Figure 17-2 shows the Startup Disk tab of the Add/Remove Programs Properties dialog box.

4. **Make sure your Windows 98 disc is in the CD-ROM drive, place a blank floppy disk in drive A, and click on Create Disk.**

   Anything on the floppy disk will be erased in the process of creating a startup disk.

5. **After the startup disk has been created, click on OK to close the dialog box.**

Be sure to test your startup disk after you create it:

1. **Leave the startup disk in drive A.**

2. **Choose Start⇨Shut Down from the Start menu.**

Figure 17-2:
Use the
Startup Disk
tab to
create a
disk that
will save
your sanity
when your
system
won't start.

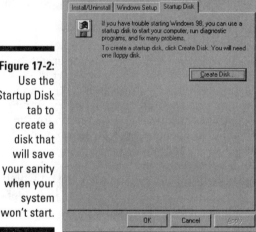

The importance of boot disks

Most of the time, your computer starts by loading the operating system from your hard disk. If anything prevents your computer from finding the operating system files on the hard disk, your only hope of being able to recover your work is to be able to start your PC from a disk. The *boot disk* you need for this must be capable of loading everything necessary to access all the important parts of your system. In most cases, this means it must have any programs or drivers needed to see the files on your hard disk and on CD-ROMs. If your hard disk is using disk compression, for example, the boot disk must contain the disk compression software.

3. Select the Restart option.

When your computer restarts, you'll see a pretty blank screen with just A:\> and a blinking cursor.

4. Make sure you can access your hard disk by typing C: and pressing Enter.

The prompt should change to C:\>.

5. Type D: and press Enter.

Use the correct letter if your CD-ROM drive isn't drive D. If you're lucky, the prompt should change to D:\>, and you don't need to do anything else except store your startup disk where you'll be sure to find it when you need it.

If you can't access your hard disk or your CD-ROM drive, it's probably because you need special drivers to use those drives. This is usually the case if your system uses a SCSI CD-ROM drive. You need to copy those drivers probably from your hard disk, and add the commands to load the drivers to CONFIG.SYS and AUTOEXEC.BAT. If you don't know how to edit these two files, ask someone to help. You'll need to include the MSCDEX command in AUTOEXEC.BAT, and the CD-ROM driver command in CONFIG.SYS. If you can't find the correct drivers (and the commands to load those drivers) on your hard disk, you'll have to dig a little deeper. You may find the drivers on the disks that came with your system, or you may have to contact tech support to locate the correct drivers.

You may also want to get a copy of *Small Business Windows 95 For Dummies* by Steve Nelson (published by IDG Books Worldwide, Inc.) to find out more about copying files to disk.

Using the Troubleshooters

You're not the first person to have problems with a computer. In fact, many of the problems you may encounter have probably happened quite a few times before. For these common problems, you can usually follow a specific set of steps to correct the problem.

The different Windows versions have a number of troubleshooting tools that can help you with a little do-it-yourself troubleshooting. Figure 17-3 shows the Windows 98 troubleshooters. Figure 17-4 shows the Windows 95 troubleshooters.

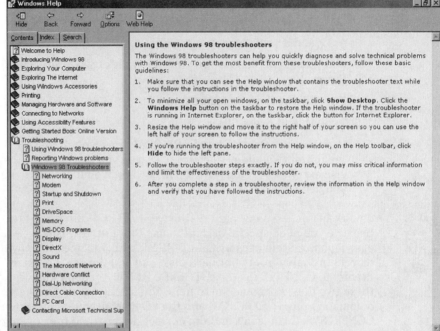

Figure 17-3:
The
Windows 98
trouble-
shooters
can help
you solve
many
common
problems.

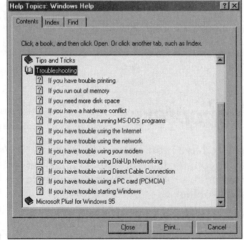

Figure 17-4:
Windows 95
includes
trouble-
shooters,
too.

To use the Windows troubleshooters, follow these general steps:

1. **Click on the Start button.**

2. **Choose Help.**

3. Click on Troubleshooting to open the troubleshooters section.

In Windows 95, double-click to open a help topic.

4. Choose the troubleshooter that applies to your problem.

5. Follow the steps listed in the troubleshooter.

While you're using the Windows troubleshooters, you'll be instructed to use a number of dialog boxes, try different settings, and possibly even restart your system. For most common problems, the troubleshooters should help you solve your problems in just a few minutes.

Don't Worry — It Happens All the Time

Very few computer-related problems are serious. Unless you actively do something to make a problem worse, you probably won't even lose any of your work. You may even discover that it just takes a few minutes to get everything back to normal.

You may encounter a number of common problems while working with your computer. Here are some ways you can probably solve many problems quickly:

✔ Can you repeat the error? If so, does the error appear if you try to do the same thing a different way? For example, if documents don't print the way you expect when you click on the Print button, try using the File⇨Print command. You may see something that's set incorrectly in the Print dialog box.

✔ Are you sure the system isn't working the way it should? You may have changed an option that changed the way a program functions. Try looking through all the program options to see whether a setting is related to the thing you want to do.

✔ Have you tried restarting your computer? Believe it or not, just restarting the computer solves the majority of problems. Just make sure you shut down the system using the Shut Down command — not by turning off the power or by pressing the reset button!

✔ Did the problem start after you installed a new program? If so, try reinstalling the program that isn't working correctly. You can also try uninstalling the new program, but that probably won't help. The reasons for this are a little complex, but it basically comes down to the way Windows programs share pieces called *DLLs*. The new program may have replaced an important DLL used by the first program (the program that quit working). By reinstalling the program that quit working, you may once again install the correct copy of the DLL.

✔ Very few problems are so severe that an entire program doesn't work. Try to narrow the problem down to the precise command or function that isn't working.

✔ If a newly installed program isn't working, have you checked the system requirements for the program? It's possible that you don't have the right equipment or even the right operating system.

✔ If your printer stops working, check to make sure that there's plenty of paper in the paper tray and that the printer is online (if you're not sure, turn the printer off and back on). Also push in both ends of the cable a bit tighter.

✔ If you can't delete or move a file, make sure you close the program that created the file. Sometimes, just closing the document itself isn't enough — you need to close the program to release the file.

✔ If you can't save a file on a disk, check the write-protect tab. The little slide at one corner of the disk has to close the square opening so that light can't shine through. Sometimes those little sliders aren't snapped totally closed.

✔ It's easy to lose files, especially if you didn't pay close attention to where the file was saved. If you saved the file, it's there someplace. Try the Find⇨Files or Folders command on the Start menu. Be sure to start the search at C:\, and make certain the Include Subfolders check box is selected.

✔ If you were interrupted in the middle of creating an e-mail message and then can't find the unsent message, look in the Drafts folder. Not all e-mail programs have a Drafts folder, but if yours does, be sure to look there before you give up.

✔ If your system seems to be a lot slower than normal, try closing all your programs and restarting the computer, especially if you've opened and closed a lot of documents during the current session.

Throwing in the Towel

Knowing when to give up and turn the problem over to someone else may be the most important problem-solving skill you can have. Ask someone to help before you turn a little problem into a big one! Chapter 18 gives you more information on what you need to do to get some outside help.

But how can you tell when a problem is too big for you to handle? Well, following are some telltale signs that you need help getting your computer back in working condition:

✔ If the system won't start at all or refuses to recognize your hard disk, you need help. Don't even think about trying to boot the computer with some old boot disk from an old version of DOS — unless you really want to make a mess of things!

✔ If your computer constantly locks up and won't respond to the keyboard or the mouse, you have a serious problem that you probably can't fix yourself.

✔ If you get a message saying that the compressed volume file is corrupted, your disk compression software has a serious problem. If that file is destroyed or inaccessible, all your files will be lost — you need help right now! Don't mess around trying to fix it; if you don't know what you're doing, you'll make an even bigger mess.

✔ If little mushrooms start growing in the spaces between the keys on your keyboard, you need help, too. But you also need to learn to keep your workspace a bit neater or move to a dryer climate!

Chapter 18

Getting Help

● ●

In This Chapter

▶ Collecting information before you get help

▶ Dealing with tech support

▶ Getting someone to accept responsibility

▶ Hiring help

● ●

Sometimes even the most experienced PC users must give up and ask someone else to help solve a problem. At some point, you may need some help, too. No matter how hard you try, you just won't be able to handle every sticky situation yourself.

Unfortunately, getting outside help can be expensive, whether it's paying someone to come in and fix a problem, paying for long-distance calls to an overloaded tech support line, or simply suffering the wasted time while you're waiting for answers. But your problems can be solved more quickly and less expensively by doing your homework before you make your call.

Get the Straight Scoop

The first step in solving problems is making sure you have all the necessary information. The clues to effective problem solving are usually buried somewhere — you just have to find them.

Suppose you were walking down the street and a stranger came up and asked you, "How do I get to my uncle's house?" You'd probably respond with a question of your own, such as, "Where does your uncle live?" But imagine that the stranger didn't know the uncle's address. You'd have a hard time helping, wouldn't you? You may be able to look up the uncle's address if you asked his name, but suppose the stranger forgot to tell you a bit more information, such as that the uncle lived in a different town?

Tech support people often find themselves trying to give help to people who don't give all the important information up front. They find themselves pulling out the facts one piece at a time. If you've forgotten to tell the tech support person all the details and facts, you're making it a lot harder for him or her to give you the right answers, and you're wasting a lot of your time and money.

Get your facts together

So, what information is important? Some information is always useful, and other information may end up being really important depending on the circumstances. For example, if your car stops running, it's important to know whether gas is in the tank, but the color of the car doesn't mean too much. If you have an accident and your fender needs repainting, however, the color is important.

You can save time and money by getting prepared before you call for help. You save time because you already have the information the tech support person needs, and you save money because you won't be getting incorrect answers based on incomplete information.

Here's some of the basic information you should have before you call for help. You may not need all this information every time, but it won't hurt to be ready:

- ✔ The type of computer you're using. Be sure you know the brand, the type of processor, and the amount of memory it contains.

- ✔ Your computer's operating system. If you've applied any service packs or updates, write that down, too.

- ✔ The name, version, and serial number of your programs. You can usually find this information by clicking on Help⇨About. The serial number may be called the *product ID* or something similar.

- ✔ If you have a network, you should know the type of network as well as the brand and model of the network adapter.

- ✔ The type of modem in your computer, what communications port it uses, and the IRQ setting.

Get ready ahead of time

Much of the basic information you need to gather won't change too often. You can save a lot of time by creating a master information sheet for your computer and then updating it when things change. Create your information sheet as a word-processing document to make updates easier. Print a copy and tape it inside your computer's case — that way, you'll have the information available even if your system is completely dead.

✔ The brand and model of your printer. (If the tech support person wants to know about your printer drivers, he or she can tell you how to find that information.)

✔ The brand and model of any other bits and pieces, such as sound cards, CD-ROM drives, and video adapters.

✔ The tech support person may also ask your name, phone number, and e-mail address. Why not include this on the information sheet, too, just to help you stay organized?

Describing the problem

Why are people so poor at giving all the details needed to solve problems? Mostly because they don't understand what's important. How many times have you thought a detail was too minor to mention, but on later reflection you realized that the minor detail was the key to the whole solution?

Problems are often a paradox. If you knew what was causing the problem, you might be able to correct it yourself without outside help. But when you don't know what's causing the problem, it's hard to find the solution. That's why you need to gather all the facts and describe the problem as completely as possible. Some detail you may dismiss as insignificant may be just what's needed to find the answer.

Here are some things to consider when you're trying to give an accurate problem description:

✔ If you've been using a program for some time without problems, and then it quits working, what has changed? And no, the correct answer isn't "nothing." Did you install new hardware or software since you last used the program? Has someone come in and "fixed up" your computer for you?

✔ Has your system given you any warnings about missing files, or has it mentioned that a file appeared to be no longer in use? A lot of programs share files, and if you uninstall a program, you may accidentally remove one of those shared files. If you see a message about files that appear to be no longer in use, it's usually safest to let them stay where they are.

✔ Can you repeat the error, or was it a one-time occurrence? It's usually best to ignore one-time occurrences — how will you know if the problem was solved, anyway? Besides, if you can't repeat the error, what are you worrying about?

✔ What were you doing just before the problem popped up? Exactly what steps led up to the error, and did you try to make the same thing happen again? Make a numbered list of the steps so that the tech support person can try the same sequence. If you can't duplicate the error, there's a good chance that someone else can't figure out what's wrong.

✔ When a problem occurs, the absolute, number one, don't-leave-home-without-it piece of information you must have is the exact error message. It's not good enough to say that "there was some error message that said the program couldn't do something." If you've ever been guilty of this, you're hereby sentenced to being blindfolded and sent out to cross the busiest street in town on your own, at night, wearing dark clothes. Error messages may seem cryptic, but they often contain important information. (Maybe *cryptic* isn't strong enough, but you get the idea!)

✔ What changes have you made recently? You might think you didn't do anything, and suddenly this problem just jumped out at you. However, you've probably changed something, haven't you?

✔ Have you added any new hardware or software to your system?

I Love That Music on Hold

Calling the tech support line at some computer companies is no fun. First, you have to find the tech support phone number, which is usually buried someplace near the back of the owner's manual (good luck finding *that* when you need it!) just after the bold headline reading "Before you call." Then you have to wade through 16 levels of voice-mail — and good luck if you make a mistake. Finally, you end up on hold listening to someone's idea of musical torture.

You can, however, do a few things to make the ordeal a little less painful:

✔ Avoid calling on a Monday. Tech support lines tend to be busiest on Monday and second-busiest on Friday.

✔ Many people call as soon as they get in the office in the morning. You may want to wait for mid-morning, when call volumes and wait times are generally reduced.

✔ Write down the sequence of numbers you have to enter to get through a voice-mail system. That way, you'll be able to get back in a lot more quickly if you get disconnected. For example, if you have to enter a 2 and then a 3 and then a 1, write down the phone number followed by a comma and then 2, 3, 1.

✔ If a vendor offers an instant-response pay-per-call number, consider
   that option — especially if the vendor guarantees to correct a problem
   for a single, set fee. After all, can you really afford to spend an hour on
   hold waiting to talk to someone?

 ✔ If you have to wait on hold, use a speaker phone and press the mute
   button while you're waiting. You'll be able to work on other things
   while you're on hold, and pressing the mute button ensures that you'll
   hear when the tech support person answers.

 ✔ If your vendor offers 24-hour tech support, try calling during non-
   business hours. You'd be amazed how quickly you can get through
   at 4 a.m!

 ✔ When you do get to talk to a real, live person, try to explain the problem as well as you can. Then tell the person all the steps you've taken
   to try to solve the problem. Tech support people often assume they're
   talking to people who don't even know where the power switch is
   located. By letting them know upfront what you've already tried, you
   may be able to eliminate a lot of needless repetition.

 ✔ Don't forget to write down the name and extension of the tech support
   person! If you have to call back for more help, you'll need to know who
   you talked with the first time.

 ✔ If possible, keep the tech support person online while you work
   through the problem. That way, you'll be able to go on to another idea
   immediately if the first suggestion doesn't solve the problem.

 ✔ If the tech support person says you need a new version of a software
   driver, ask if the driver can be e-mailed to you rather than your having
   to try to find it on the company's Web site.

Let's Play Hot Potato

Do you remember the game "hot potato?" A ball or some other object is
designated as a hot potato, and the idea is to get rid of the hot potato as
quickly as possible by tossing it to the next person. Whoever is holding the
hot potato when the music ends is the loser.

If you thought hot potato was just a children's game, though, you haven't
spent much time trying to resolve computer problems. Computer hardware
and software companies play this game and do their best to make sure the
end user — that's you — ends up with the hot potato.

Here's how the game works:

1. You buy a computer.

2. Computers are supposed to be able to do lots of different things, so you buy and install some new software.

3. The computer has all this room inside for expansion, and besides, your new software needs some extra hardware, so you buy and install some new hardware.

4. You want to do still more with this fancy piece of equipment, so you repeat Steps 2 and 3 a few more times.

5. All of a sudden, something doesn't work right, so you call the tech support number for the product that isn't working.

6. The tech support person asks you a few dumb questions, has you remove all the extra pieces you added in Steps 2, 3, and 4, and your system starts working again — as long as *only* the item you called about is installed.

7. But you really want to use all those other things you bought, so you add back the things the tech support person had you remove.

8. You reboot your system dozens of times in the process, and finally get to the point where *almost* everything is working. Now you decide to call tech support for the new item that isn't working right.

9. You guessed it: The tech support person has you remove other things and reconfigure your system until *that vendor's* product is working.

Now you're stuck in an endless loop repeating Steps 7–9 until some miracle happens or you finally give up and throw your computer into the nearest dumpster. What can you do when no one accepts responsibility?

You have several options for getting yourself out of this mess. Here are some things you may want to try:

✔ Try reinstalling everything one at a time — not just the new items you've added. Sometimes a hardware or software installation can improperly replace an important file, so reinstalling the software that stopped working may be all that's needed. You may win the lottery next week, too.

✔ Return the product that isn't working. If the store won't take it back, ask your credit card company to withhold payment.

✔ You may be able to create multiple system configurations, with different system components disabled in each configuration. In Windows 95 and Windows 98, you can do this in the Device Manager by double-clicking on an item and choosing the Disable in This Configuration option. You'll have to choose different configurations to use the conflicting products, but this solution may be workable as a last resort.

✔ If you're desperate, get a true computer expert to help you back up all your files, reformat your hard drive, and reinstall your hardware and software. This can be hazardous to the health of your data — make sure whoever does this *really* knows what he or she is doing!

✔ If nothing you try works, try the hardware or software on another computer. You may have to settle for using two computers to do the job one should do, but if it does the job, why waste more time? For example, if your scanner and your printer refuse to work when they're both connected to the same computer, putting the two on different computers on your network may be a reasonable solution.

To disable a device, follow these steps:

1. Right-click on the My Computer icon on your desktop.

2. Choose Properties.

3. Click on the Device Manager tab.

Figure 18-1 shows the Device Manager tab.

4. Double-click on the device you want to disable.

The properties dialog box for the selected device appears. For an example, see Figure 18-2.

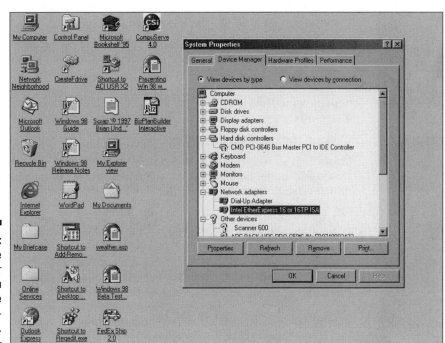

Figure 18-1: The Device Manager enables you to create multiple configurations.

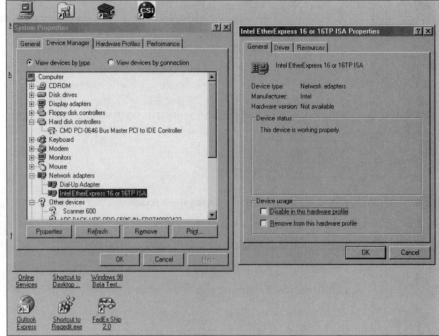

Figure 18-2:
Use the
Properties
dialog box
to control
the settings
for system
devices.

5. Click on the Disable in This Hardware Profile check box.

Items that are disabled in a hardware profile can remain in your PC, but
they won't function while they're disabled.

6. Click on OK.

You return to the Device Manager tab of the System Properties
dialog box.

7. Click on the Hardware Profiles tab.

Figure 18-3 shows the Hardware Profiles tab. You can use this tab to
create additional configurations with different sets of devices enabled
or disabled, thus avoiding conflicts between devices.

8. Click on Copy.

9. Type a name for the new configuration.

The new configuration has all the current settings, but any additional
changes you make are included only in the currently active configuration.

10. Click on OK to return to the System Properties dialog box.

11. Click on OK to close the dialog box.

You may need to restart your system before your changes take effect.

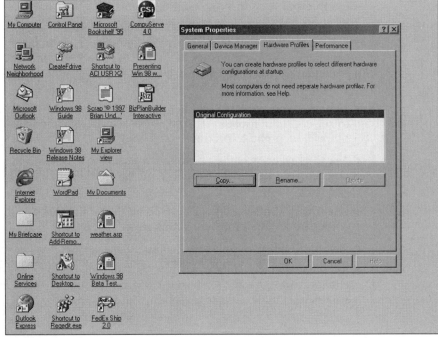

Figure 18-3:
Use the
Hardware
Profiles tab
to create
different
system con-
figurations.

Hiring a Consultant

You wouldn't hire a tree surgeon to handle a heart bypass operation, and you aren't likely to ask your plumber to fix a faulty electrical outlet. You need somebody who knows what he or she is doing — not someone who's just going to waste your time and money.

Your small business probably keeps you plenty busy without the added complication of trying to learn everything about computers, too. That's why you may find yourself in the market for a good computer consultant. But how do you find one? Isn't a consultant just someone who can't get a regular job?

Choosing the right computer consultant

The market is full of people who claim to know a lot about computers. A *few* really do know what they're talking about. Here are some tips on finding someone who can help you and avoiding the self-proclaimed experts who will just end up costing you a lot of money:

✔ Ask for references and make personal phone calls to check on those references. If this sounds like too much trouble, be ready to open your wallet and let the consultants take their pick.

✔ Interview at least three consultants. Start with the same list of questions for each and make notes during the interviews.

✔ Ask each consultant to give you a recommendation on how to solve a specific problem and justify that recommendation. Don't be snowed by someone who says you should go with a specific brand-name solution because it's better. Ask why it's better.

✔ Ask about any industry certifications the consultant holds. You'll want to see copies of those certifications — anyone who truly has a certification will be proud to produce a copy.

✔ Ask to see a copy of the consultant's business license. Someone who doesn't have a business license is probably trying to avoid other rules and regulations, too.

✔ Check with the Better Business Bureau to see whether any outstanding complaints against the consultant are in its files.

✔ Find out how much business liability insurance the consultant carries.

✔ Ask what each consultant charges. You don't necessarily want the cheapest (or the most expensive), but you should be suspicious if someone's charges are considerably different than the local average.

Establishing a consulting agreement

After you choose a computer consultant, make certain you're both talking the same language. Define what's expected so that you get what you need and don't end up spending more than you can afford.

Here are some guidelines to follow in establishing a consulting agreement:

✔ Make sure all agreements are written and signed by both parties. This applies to any amendments, too.

✔ Define what you expect the consultant to do for you, and the timetable for accomplishing the job.

✔ Specify how the consultant will be paid. You shouldn't be asked to advance large sums of money. Most reputable consultants are willing to allow customers to hold back a sizable portion of their fee until the job is satisfactorily completed.

✔ Make sure the agreement specifies which items are part of the contract and which items are separately billable (and at what rate).

✔ If the contract is for a large sum, you may want to include a clause calling for binding arbitration in the event of a dispute. Binding arbitration is generally far less expensive for everyone than engaging in a court battle.

Part VI
The Part of Tens

The 5th Wave   By Rich Tennant

SETTING UP AN INTRANET HAS REALLY HELPED OUR BUSINESS.

MUSTARD

HOT DOGS

RELISH

BUNS

In this part . . .

Do you like reading top ten lists while you're waiting in the grocery store checkout line? How about hearing TV show hosts list the top ten reasons why they like bananas? If so, you're going to love Part VI, where I include my lists of the top ten things I think will be important to your small business.

Okay, so I admit that some of the lists have a few more than ten items if you want to be really picky. I couldn't help it — consider them a bonus.

Chapter 19

Ten Ideas for Computerizing Your Small Business

*A*s a small businessperson, you need to get the most from your time and money. In this chapter, you see some ideas for doing that by making your computer work for your small business.

Make Your Computer Do the Drudge Work

Running a small business is a *lot* of work. Why are you still wasting your time doing the same things over and over again? If you haven't done the following things yet, what are you waiting for — an engraved invitation?

✔ Don't keep writing the same letter dozens or hundreds of times — save standard letters as templates and fill in the few things that change when you need to prepare another copy.

✔ Put your address book in your computer. You'll be amazed how much time you'll save once you can call up your contact list right on your computer screen!

Get Caller ID Service

If you get caller ID service from your phone company, your computer can do a lot more for you. You'll need to buy a modem that supports caller ID services, but once you do, your computer can tell you who's calling before you pick up the phone.

If you want to get fancy, you can get a program that logs all customer calls, lets you make notes about the call while you're still talking, and tells you what orders the customer has placed in the past.

The few dollars your phone company charges for caller ID will be easy to make up in the time you'll save by having the customer's records appear before you even answer the call. You can take orders a lot faster, and your customers will be impressed by the great service you provide. They'll be even more impressed by how much you remember about them.

Buy a Second Modem

You may use one phone line for voice calls and a second one to connect your computer to the outside world. Why on earth would you want to install a second modem? That's an easy one — to manage your voice calls.

Sure, you can use the old-fashioned telephone to call people and answer calls, but if you want to be efficient, why not let your computer do some of the work? If you're going to have your address book in your computer, and especially if you get caller ID service, you'll want one modem to dial your outgoing calls and to tell you who's calling. It can replace your answering machine, and you can even set up a voice-mail system if you want to annoy everyone. Your second modem will be the one your computer uses to talk to other computers.

Modems are cheaper than ever. The fanciest modem you can buy won't cost you as much as a good telephone set and answering machine.

Protect Your Power

If your business needs what's on your computer, can you depend on your computer? You can't if your computer can't depend on having power when it needs it. An uninterruptible power supply — a UPS — isn't a luxury. It's absolutely necessary.

Don't forget that Mr. Murphy knows the absolute worst time to strike. Power outages are one of the worst enemies of computers. If the lights blink out before you've saved your work, you'll lose everything since the last time you clicked on the Save button. If the power drops *while* you're saving a file, you could lose the whole file or worse. If his timing is just right, Mr. Murphy may decide to kick out your power just when your system is saving the file space information — thus scrambling lots of files, not just the one you were saving.

Make Sure They Can Find You

Businesses that are easy to find do a lot more business than companies people have to search for. That's why you'll see so many listings for AAA This or AAA That — everyone wants to be at the top of the list.

The Internet has changed the way a lot of people do business. Potential customers may be just as likely to look on the Internet as in the Yellow Pages. If your business is on the Internet, you'll want to make certain those customers can find *you*. How can you do that? Here are a few ideas:

- ✔ When you build a Web site, make sure your major products or services are mentioned on your home page so that people who use search engines can find you when they search for any of the related words.

- ✔ If you want to get fancy, have someone show you how to add the special tags to your home page to generate *hits* in search engines. You may want to check out *Small Business Internet For Dummies* by Greg Holden with Stylus Media (published by IDG Books Worldwide, Inc.) to find out more about adding the tags yourself.

- ✔ Make sure your business cards and any ads you place include both your e-mail address and your Web site address.

- ✔ Make sure your Web site includes a phone number and mailing address, too. Some people may feel comfortable locating you on the Internet, but not placing orders there.

- ✔ Offer to trade *links* with other Web sites where potential customers may be looking for your products or services.

Save Money on the Internet

Because you're going to use your phone, your computer, and the Internet anyway, why not combine the three and save lots of money? After you're on the Internet, you can go just about anywhere in the world. By using the Internet to handle your voice and fax calls, you can cut your long-distance bills down to size.

When Internet *telephony* first appeared, sound quality was poor, both parties had to have PCs, and making a connection took some planning. Today, all that has changed. A number of companies have been working to improve both the quality and ease-of-use of telephony. Now you can make cheap long-distance calls directly from one phone to another via the Internet. If you make international calls, the savings are even greater!

Here are a couple of companies you'll want to try out:

- ✔ To send faxes anywhere in the world for almost nothing, visit the CyNet, Inc. Web site at http://www.cynet-fax.com. CyNet provides a small, free box that connects between your fax machine or computer and the phone line. When you send a fax, this little box uses the Internet to send faxes for as little as five cents per minute domestically and not a whole lot more internationally. You can reach CyNet also at 800-964-2968 or 281-897-8317.

- ✔ To make cheap voice calls using the Internet, you may want to sign up with IDT at 800-225-5438 or visit http://www.net2phone.com. You'll save at least 20 percent on domestic long-distance calls, and quite a bit more on international ones. IDT has both Net2Phone, which uses your PC, and Net2Phone Direct, which allows you to call from any regular telephone.

Add More Memory

With all that money you're going to save by making your long-distance and fax calls on the Internet, go out and buy some more memory for your system. Adding memory is the cheapest way to improve your computer's performance. And if your computer is faster, you'll be happy using it for a longer time.

Add a Network

If you have more than one PC, why not connect them in a network? You'll be able to share your files more easily on a network — you won't have to do the old disk swap routine anymore. A network also lets you share printers, so you might be able to afford that fancy printer you've been wanting. After all, the cost isn't nearly as much when it's shared across several users.

Scan Rather Than Retype Documents

If you don't have a scanner, you're missing out on one of the best laborsaving peripherals you can add to your PC. Whether you opt for a small scanner that takes a sheet at a time and sits between your keyboard and your screen, or go all the way and get a flatbed scanner, you'll be amazed at what a scanner can do for you.

Here are just a few scanner facts:

- ✔ With OCR software, your scanner can turn printed copies into documents that you can edit on your PC. Unless you're a really fast typist, a scanner and OCR software will probably enter documents ten to twenty times faster than you can manage by typing.

- ✔ When you add a scanner, your fax/modem becomes the best fax machine you can imagine. Your scanner has higher resolution than any fax machine, and you can file all your faxes electronically. There's no reason to clutter up your office with a stand-alone fax machine when you have a PC and a scanner!

- ✔ You may want to take advantage of any extra-cost scanner software upgrades you're offered. Often, you can get a package deal that includes a scanner and some high-powered graphics and OCR software for less than the normal price of the software alone. It's like getting a deal on the software and having a free scanner thrown in.

Keep Those Games Out!

Whatever you do, don't fall victim to the *games trap*. That's where you let someone add a game or two to your office PC. Sure, we all need some recreation, but computer games are the worst enemies of productivity you can imagine. You may think you're immune, but those games will trap you if they get a chance!

Chapter 20

Ten Small Business Computing Things to Watch (Out) For

*O*ne of the trickiest problems in buying computers for your small business is making certain you don't lock yourself out of exciting new technologies that may be just around the corner. That's especially true if those new gizmos and gadgets turn out to be something that can save you lots of time or money. You don't want to be kicking yourself because your new computer suddenly seems like yesterday's model — you know, the one that *can't* use that new add-on you really want.

It's almost as bad to find out you've wasted your money on something that's going out of style. For example, a few years ago, you probably could have bought beta VCRs at a real bargain price, but since beta went the way of the dodo bird, that VCR wouldn't look like such a bargain today.

This chapter examines some of the technologies that may affect small business computing in the near future. You'll see some things you'll want to be prepared for and also some things to watch out for. Take these predictions with a small grain of salt, though; nothing else changes as fast as the world of high technology and computers, and what seems like a good bet today may not be so certain tomorrow.

Voice Recognition Comes of Age

Probably the easiest small business technology prediction to make is that pretty soon you'll be able to talk to your computer and have it understand what you're saying. Oh sure, you probably say a few things to your system right now, but I'm talking about being able to dictate letters or issue commands.

Voice recognition has been a favorite topic of experimenters for some time, but most of those experiments have produced something less than you or I would care to use. Sure, you *could* dictate if you wanted to pause between every word and didn't mind going back and making a lot of corrections. But you'd probably be able type a letter a whole lot faster.

In the next few years, you'll see incredible improvements in computer voice recognition. Some products are already appearing that allow you to dictate using normal speech patterns. They're still not perfect, but they're getting a whole lot better.

How can you make certain you're ready for voice recognition? Here are some tips:

- The surest way is to make certain you get a powerful enough computer. You'll need at least a 200 MHz Pentium processor, 32MB or more memory, and a couple of hundred megabytes of free disk space.

- You'll also need a good sound card and a quality microphone, but you can expect most early voice recognition software to include either a microphone or a discount offer on one.

Faster Internet Connections

The more you use the Internet, the less satisfied you'll be using a modem for your connection. Today's modems are more than a hundred times faster than what was common when PCs were first introduced into the business place, but the graphical nature of the Web almost makes them seem slower. When you're downloading a program update that's five times the size of the entire hard drive on the original IBM PC XT, it's pretty easy to get discouraged by the speed of your connection.

Several very interesting technologies for faster Internet connections are just over the horizon. Some of them are still just pipe dreams, but here are some things to watch for:

✔ ISDN is here today — if you happen to be in the right location. ISDN can be up to about four times as fast as a typical modem connection, but ISDN is a lot more expensive to use. Look for phone companies to start offering ISDN at lower rates — especially after long-distance companies start competing with local telephone companies.

✔ xDSL is almost nonexistent today, and probably won't become common until your local phone company starts losing business to your cable company.

✔ Cable modems are available in limited areas, but look like a good bet for the future. Cable modems are fast and offer pretty cheap Internet access — with one little catch. When a lot of people in an area start using cable modems, they get slow, too. Well, not slow like a modem — what is?

✔ Satellite dishes for Internet access are currently available, but they're not cheap, and you still need a modem to send files. Look for a big change in satellite technology around the turn of the century, when Bill Gates plans to put up 800 or so special satellites.

✔ Believe it or not, your electrical utility may start offering Internet access before too long. No one knows quite what to expect in this area, but there's no technological reason your standard electrical wiring couldn't also carry you to the Internet.

How can you make certain you'll be able to use faster Internet connections when they're available? These ideas may help:

✔ Be lucky enough to locate your office in an area where faster service will be available. Right now, though, no one can say for certain which areas will get faster service or when.

✔ Call your phone company, cable company, ISP, and power company and ask about plans to offer high-speed Internet connections in your area. Ask to be placed on any waiting lists — remember that service offerings will probably be based on demand.

✔ If you need to do any rewiring in your office, consider the possibility that faster Internet access may mean more cables. You may want to leave room for extra cables so you don't end up with an even bigger rat's nest.

Real-Time Internet Video Conferencing

Pretty soon, your PC will become the video phone that was so common in science fiction movies. Oh sure, you can get tiny, jerky video right now, but over the next few years, you'll see some real improvements that will make the technology really useful.

Imagine what it will be like when a customer can call you from his or her PC and you can have a face-to-face discussion. If the customer wants to see what a product looks like, you can pick it up and turn it around right in front of your screen.

A few problems are currently holding this technology back. Connections are usually too slow to make the pictures look like real people; video cameras still aren't a part of every PC; and too many incompatible methods exist for sending video across the Net.

All those problems will disappear pretty quickly, and real-time video conferencing will soon be as common as CD-ROM drives are today.

What can you do to get ready for video? Here are a few suggestions:

✔ If you're buying a new system, make certain it has at least one USB port. Not all video cameras require this, but it's likely that more will as USB ports become more common.

✔ Make certain you have the highest speed Internet connection you can get. This may be a case of the chicken and the egg, especially if you still can't get high-speed Internet access.

✔ If you're looking at video hardware and software, make certain you don't buy a proprietary system that interacts only with the same brand of equipment. Standards are slowly emerging, and right now the most universal ones seem to revolve around Microsoft NetMeeting. You may be safe if the camera and software will work with NetMeeting.

Flat-Panel Displays

You can buy big flat-panel displays today — if your pockets are deep enough! Most of us, though, are stuck with those relics of the past — monitors that look more like TVs than anything else.

Just as the typical PC monitor has grown in size and come down in price, you're soon going to see the same thing happening in flat-panel displays. Why have a 50-pound, 18-inch-deep monster on your desk when you could just as well have a 5-pound, 4-inch-thick beauty sitting there? Flat-panel displays use a lot less power, too.

How can you get ready for flat-panel displays? There's really only one thing you need to do: Save lots of money! You could easily spend as much (or more) on a flat-panel display as you would for the rest of a very high-end computer system.

NT on Every Desktop

Windows NT will soon be appearing on a desktop near you — your desktop, to be specific. Windows 98 is likely the end of the line for the current consumer line of Windows, and Apple Computer will soon be selling Windows NT on their systems — which will come with Intel processors.

Oh sure, you'll still have a few holdouts — just as we did when the IBM PC came along and some people clung to their CP/M-based computers. But the handwriting is on the wall — whether people want to read it or not.

Future versions of Windows NT will look a bit different than today's operating systems. Your computer will be smarter, and will do a lot more things for you as it learns how you work. Star Trek, here we come!

What should you do to get ready for Windows NT? Here are the basics:

- ✔ Don't even think about buying a computer that doesn't have at least a 200 MHz Pentium processor. Even faster would be better!

- ✔ Get at least 32MB of memory. Heck, at today's prices, go for 64MB or even 128MB — you'll be glad you did!

- ✔ Don't buy any type of Mac. There are rumors that future models of the Mac may run Windows NT, but those systems will likely have Intel processors, too. None of the current models will run Windows NT.

Digital Photography

The first digital cameras looked a lot like 35mm cameras on the outside, but they sure didn't produce the same kind of photos. No one would ever mistake today's typical digital camera's photos for the old-fashioned film-based photos.

Over the next few years, though, digital photography will finally come of age. Digital cameras will be easier to use, produce much higher quality photos, and become a whole lot cheaper.

Along with these changes will come another change. Far fewer people will go down to their local photo shop to get conventional prints. Expect to see people distribute photos over the Web and on electronic media such as disks and CD-ROMs. When people do want prints, they'll turn to the color printer right next to their PC.

For small businesses, the move to digital photography means you'll be able to update your Web site a lot faster, and send a customer a product photo instantly.

Make sure any digital camera you buy has removable photo storage; otherwise you'll need to download your photos to your PC as soon as you've filled the camera's memory. Try to find a camera that uses a standard type of storage card, too. You don't want a camera that uses a proprietary storage card that may be expensive and hard to find.

How can you get ready for digital photography? Here are a few tips:

✔ Make sure your PC has a Zip drive, a Jaz drive, a CD-R drive, or some other type of removable storage. Image files take lots of room, and you probably won't want to completely fill your hard disk.

✔ Although the methods of transferring images from digital cameras to computers vary quite a bit right now, you may want to make certain your PC has a USB port. It's likely that future digital cameras will use USB ports to transfer images to PCs.

Automatic Updates Using the Web

Probably the rarest beast in the world of personal computing is the software program that never has a problem that needs to be corrected. Software manufacturers spend lots of time and money correcting those problems, but until recently, there was an even bigger problem — most users never knew when updates were available.

Windows 98 is bringing a new way of supplying software updates to the table. With the click of a button, you can tell your PC to connect to the Internet and look for any updates that should be applied. After those updates are automatically downloaded and applied, your system simply continues — problems solved without any additional work on your part.

Although the Windows 98 update feature currently won't update your application programs, there's no reason to expect that won't be added soon, too. And if you don't want to even be bothered with having to click on a button, the Windows 98 Task Scheduler can eliminate that step!

How can you make certain you'll be able to get automatic updates through the Web? Here are a few basics:

✔ If your PC came with Windows 95, upgrade to Windows 98.

✔ Although it's not certain Windows NT 5 will have automatic Web updates, Windows NT 4 users should probably upgrade to Windows NT 5 when it's available. Some type of update over the Internet option will almost certainly be included in Windows NT 5.

✔ If your system doesn't have a modem or you're not connected to the Internet, it's pretty obvious that you'll need to add a modem and get connected before you can get updates.

Wireless Connections

If you hate having to deal with a rat's nest of cables, you'll love it when wireless connections become more common. Today, you can buy laptop PCs with infrared connections to keyboards, printers, and mice. Tomorrow, cables may disappear completely.

Infrared technology is the same thing that's been controlling your TV set for years. You've probably noticed some limitations — if someone stands between you and the TV, it's hard to change the channels, for example. Infrared communications between PCs and peripherals suffer from the same problems — there has to be a line-of-sight path or it just won't work.

Look for this problem to fade and wireless connections to become more popular as manufacturers start to use 900 MHz radio transmitters in place of infrared transmitters. The better cordless phones already use these frequencies, and it's only a matter of time before PCs do, too.

What should you do to get ready for more wireless connections? Here are a few considerations:

✔ Wireless connections may not work too well if a lot of electrical interference is around your PC or the wireless peripherals. If your office radio has lots of buzzing and noise even on FM stations, it may be better to stick with hard-wired connections.

✔ If you do consider the wireless option, ask to see a demonstration in *your* office before you sign the contract.

No-Show Technologies

It's hard enough figuring out what will be a success in small business computing, but it's even worse trying to figure out what probably won't be an important part of the future. Here are some guesses about things you probably won't want to spend your money on:

- ✔ Network computers running Java applications. In spite of all the hype, people want computers that do more, not less. You won't really save money buying the so-called "network computers" and you may find you need to replace them with real computers when you want to get something accomplished.

- ✔ Support for Windows 3.x programs will fade like a bad memory over the next few years. If you're still clinging to some ten-year-old program, isn't it time for a change?

- ✔ The industry standard architecture (ISA) bus will disappear from PCs around the turn of the century. Let's hope the limitations of maintaining backward compatibility with PCs from the early 1980s is flushed down the drain at the same time! Your safest bet is to make certain your PCs have as many PCI slots as possible.

- ✔ A guess about black-and-white printers is a little iffy. The world is a colorful place, and plain black printing may go the way of the daisy-wheel printer before too long. Oh sure, monochrome laser printers will still be around for several more years, but color models will come way down in price and the monochrome models will disappear just as monochrome inkjet printers essentially have.

Chapter 21

Ten Great Small Business Web Sites

*O*ut of the millions of sites on the Web, choosing the ten best small business computing sites is an impossible task. There are hundreds of great small business Web sites, and thousands of others that you'll find useful.

No matter how carefully I assembled my list of great business Web sites, I've probably left one of your favorites off the list. Sorry about that, but maybe you should consider this list to be a challenge: Why not give these sites a try and see whether you find some gems that you may otherwise have missed?

The Web sites listed in this chapter aren't in any particular order, so don't draw the conclusion that one site is better than another simply because it's listed first. All the sites in this chapter are great, and you'll find them worth a visit!

Your Small Office Web Site

Visit `http://www.smalloffice.com/` to view Your Small Office Web site. You'll find small business advice, product reviews, news that may affect your business, and even a form so you can get a free subscription to *Small Business Computing* magazine. Figure 21-1 shows an example of this Web site (but remember that it looks a bit different every time you visit).

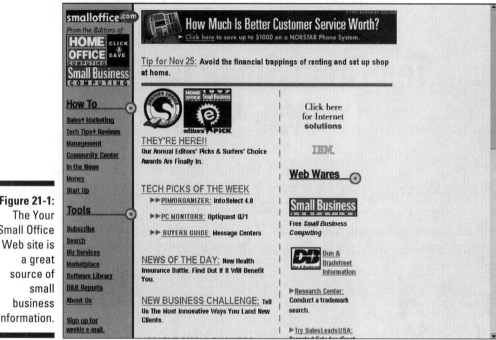

Figure 21-1:
The Your
Small Office
Web site is
a great
source of
small
business
information.

http://www.smalloffice.com/

The Microsoft Smallbiz Web Site

Whether you use Microsoft Office or one of the other office software suites, you'll find the Microsoft Smallbiz Web site at http://www.microsoft.com/ smallbiz/ another source of lots of useful information. The site pushes Microsoft products, but you'll find a lot of news and tips to keep your small business on track, too. Figure 21-2 shows an example of this Web site.

Office Suite Freebies Web Sites

This section describes three Web sites. You don't expect Microsoft to have freebies for Corel or Lotus products on its Web site, do you?

If you use one of the three major office software suites, these sites are for you. You'll find add-ons, updates, and some generally funky stuff only a programmer could come up with.

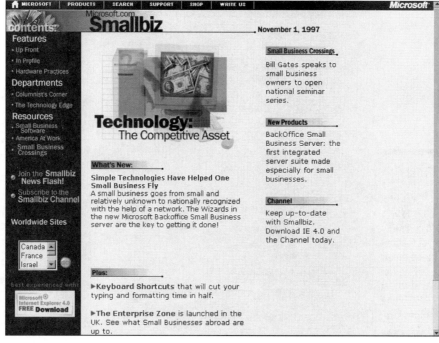

http://www.microsoft.com/smallbiz/

Figure 21-2: The Microsoft Smallbiz Web site helps you stay aware of important small business technology innovations.

The Corel Freebies Web site (see Figure 21-3) is located at http://www.corel.com/freefunfantastic/freebies/index.htm. You'll find manuals, macros, file viewers, clip art images, and all sorts of other neat Corel stuff.

The Microsoft Free Downloads Web site is located at http://www.microsoft.com/msdownload/. This site, shown in Figure 21-4, includes demos, updates, and even some beta version products you can download — if you're brave (or foolish) enough to want to try them out. This is also the place to find various Windows operating system service packs, so even if you don't use Microsoft Office, you'll want to visit this site from time to time.

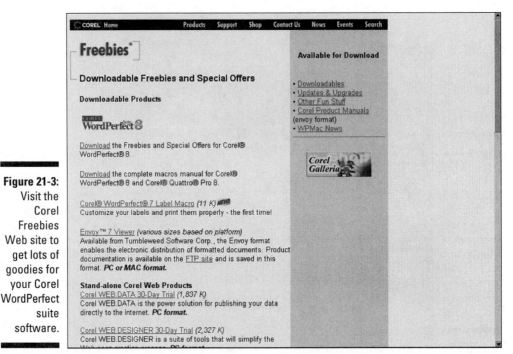

Figure 21-3:
Visit the
Corel
Freebies
Web site to
get lots of
goodies for
your Corel
WordPerfect
suite
software.

http://www.corel.com/freefunfantastic/freebies/index.htm

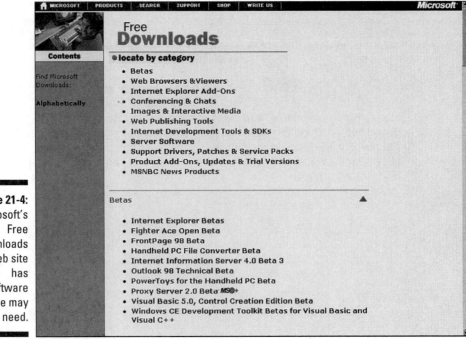

Figure 21-4:
Microsoft's
Free
Downloads
Web site
has
software
anyone may
need.

http://www.microsoft.com/msdownload/

The Lotus download site, at `http://ftp.support.lotus.com/ftp/pub/`, is a bit different than what you're probably used to seeing. It's an *ftp* site, which to you means the file descriptions will be a little cryptic, and you'll have to click on a few folders to find what you want (see Figure 21-5). Still, if you use Lotus SmartSuite, you'll want to see what's here.

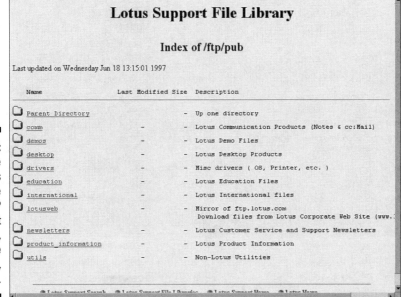

Figure 21-5: Visit the Lotus Support File Library FTP site to get updates, free software, and demos.

`http://ftp.support.lotus.com/ftp/pub/`

Web Sites for the Best Deals

Want to know where to find the best deals on that new hardware or software you need? You can shop at a lot of places on the Web, but the following two let you compare prices and terms for most of the products you may want for your small business. Check out the PC Catalog Launchpad Web site at `http://web1.pc-today.com/launchpad.html` and Computer Shopper's NetBuyer Web site at `http://client.netbuyer.com/cgi-bin/nls_ax.dll/p_index.htm`. Both sites are shown in Figures 21-6 and 21-7. It's a good idea to check both sites if you're thinking of a major purchase.

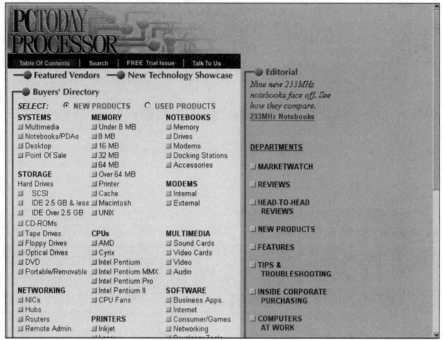

Figure 21-6:
Visit the PC
Today Web
site to find
great prices
online.

http://web1.pc-today.com/launchpad.html

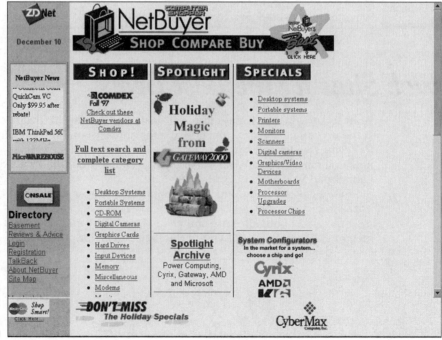

Figure 21-7:
The
Computer
Shopper
Web site is
another
place to
search for
the best
deals.

http://client.netbuyer.com/cgi-bin/nls_ax.dll/p_index.htm

Don't forget that many of the best PC manufacturers don't sell through dealers. If you want to buy a Micron PC, for example, you need to call the company directly or visit its Web site at `http://www.micronpc.com` (see Figure 21-8).

The Mother of All Small Business Web Sites

If one small business-related Web site deserves the title "The Mother of All Small Business Web Sites" it's `http://www.yahoo.com/Business_and_Economy/Small_Business_Information/`. In one place, you'll find links to so many different small business Web sites that you could spend days figuring out which ones to visit. Figure 21-9 gives you an idea of what you'll find here.

Figure 21-8: Micron's Web site gives you direct access to buying your systems right on the Web.

`http://www.micronpc.com`

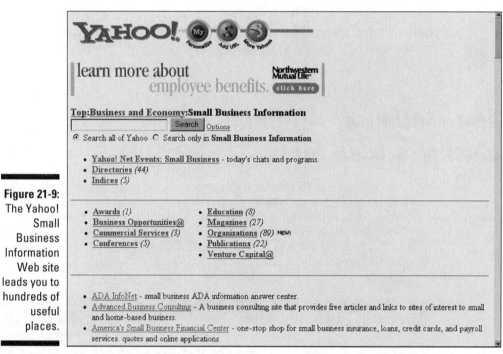

Figure 21-9:
The Yahoo!
Small
Business
Information
Web site
leads you to
hundreds of
useful
places.

Okay, so maybe I'm cheating a bit by including the Yahoo! Small Business Information Web site. But technically, it is just one site, even if it leads to hundreds of others. Hey, I told you it was impossible to choose just a few great small business Web sites.

IDG Books Worldwide

One book just can't cover everything, but if you visit http://www.idgbooks.com/ you'll find just the book you need. You'll even find a few others I've written. On this site, you'll not only find lots of great books, but also software you can download and opportunities to chat with some of the authors.

Glossary

accounting: Tracking your money, usually with a program such as QuickBooks.

accounts: The categories you use to keep track of different types of things such as income, expenses, customers, vendors, and so on.

accounts payable: The bills you need to pay.

accounts receivable: The money people owe you.

ADSL: A type of high-speed connection (generally to the Internet).

backing up: Making a copy of the important information on your computer so that disasters such as a hard disk failure won't put you out of business.

boot diskette: A diskette that has all the necessary files for starting your computer.

buses: Electrical connections to move data between your disk drives and memory, between memory and the processor, between the processor and your video adapter, and so on.

CD-R (CD-recordable): A type of CD-ROM you can record yourself if you have the appropriate drive.

CD-RW (CD-rewritable): A type of recordable CD-ROM that can be erased and reused.

clip art: Ready-made artwork (often included in office suites) that you can use to enhance your documents.

clone processors: Processors made by companies other than Intel, but designed to run the same software as Intel processors.

communications port: A hardware device that connects your computer to the outside world.

compatibility: The capability of systems to work together, such as the capability to run Windows and Windows-based programs.

credits: Items that increase your bottom line; money in the bank, you might say.

database managers: Computer programs that handle lists of related information. A database is simply a method of storing information so you can access the information in an organized fashion.

debits: Items that shrink your bottom line.

Dial-Up Networking: A part of Windows that uses your modem to dial in and connect to the Internet or to other networks.

digital cameras: Cameras that replace the film of an ordinary camera with an electronic sensor and then store the image electronically.

double-entry: Each number appears twice, once in a *debit* list and once in a *credit* list.

e-mail: Electronic mail, a method of sending messages using your computer. Most e-mail is sent via the Internet.

e-mail client: The e-mail software you use to send and receive electronic messages.

ergonomics: Products designed to work with, not against, the human body.

fields: Related types of information, such as first and last names, that you store in records in databases.

flatbed scanners: Scanners that look just like the top part of a photocopier.

GUI (Graphical User Interface): Easy-to-use replacement for the old, plain-text command line. Windows is a GUI.

HTML (HyperText Markup Language): The programming language used to create Web sites.

information managers: Software that helps you organize and keep track of information. They're also sometimes called PIMs (Personal Information Managers).

ISA (Industry Standard Architecture): The primary expansion bus on a PC.

ISDN (Integrated Services Digital Network): One of the first solutions to the problems of the speed limitations of phone lines, ISDN is a high-speed digital connection.

ISP (Internet Service Provider): The company that enables you to connect to the Internet.

letterhead: The part of a letter that identifies your business.

links: Connections between different Web pages that allow you to go from one Web page to another easily.

memory: Generally known as RAM, or random access memory. The place in your computer where your programs go to run. Memory is measured in bytes, the smallest amount of memory that can be used. Your system also has ROM, read-only memory, to control certain basic system functions, but ROM is generally not used to run programs.

modem: A special converter that changes a computer's digital signals into analog signals, and then back again at the receiving end, so your computer can talk to other computers using the telephone.

motherboard: The main circuit board in your computer.

network: A collection of connected computers that can share files and peripherals.

office suites: Bundles of the most common business application software.

passwords: Words or phrases you need to type to gain access to important files.

PCI (Peripheral Component Interconnect): An expansion bus in modern PCs that is a lot faster than the ISA bus.

peripheral: Extra component such as a monitor or a printer.

Plug and Play: A specification that allows you to add hardware to your computer without having to manually configure the system.

port: See *communications port.*

POTS (Plain Old Telephone Service): Your phone lines.

processor: The brain in the computer.

programs: Sets of instructions that tell the computer how to do simple tasks, such as add one plus one, or more complex tasks, such as dial your phone and check your e-mail.

resolution: Generally, the number of dots per inch. Often used to describe the quality levels of scanners.

scanners: A peripheral you use to get pictures into your computer.

SCSI: A type of expansion bus used to add components such as hard disks, scanners, and CD-ROM drives to your computer.

shareware: A program you can try before you decide whether or not you want to buy it.

sheet-fed scanner: A scanner that automatically scans a stack of paper one sheet at a time.

spreadsheets: The electronic equivalent of an accountant's ledger. Spreadsheets are like word processors for numbers.

tape drive: A unit that backs up data onto small cartridges holding several hundred feet of magnetic tape.

template: A basic document you can reuse.

UPS (Uninterruptible Power Supply): A battery-powered unit that protects your computer from power outages.

USB (Universal Serial Bus): Port that makes adding peripherals easier because you can just run a cable from your computer to the first USB peripheral, then run the next cable from the first peripheral to the second, and so on.

Usenet news server: A service on the Internet that enables you to view newsgroups.

Web browser: Program such as Internet Explorer or Netscape Navigator that enables you to view Web sites.

WWW (World Wide Web): The graphical part of the Internet. Also called *Web* for short.

word processors: Programs that make your computer work like a really fancy typewriter.

Zip drive: A backup device that uses a disk cartridge that holds 100MB of data.

Appendix

About the CD

• •

*T*he *Small Business Computing For Dummies* CD-ROM contains a number of useful programs I selected especially because of their value to the small businessperson. Most of these programs are trial or shareware versions, so you'll get a chance to try out the program and decide whether it suits your needs. Note, however, that shareware programs aren't free. If you decide to continue using any of these programs after the trial period, you're obligated to pay a small fee to register the program. You can use the trial versions on the CD-ROM for a specific number of days or a specific number of uses. Trial versions must also be registered if you want to use them beyond the trial period.

Registering your shareware and trial version software has many advantages. Not only do you make your use of the software legal, but in some cases, you get something extra for registering, too. And you can't really expect technical support or product upgrades unless you register.

Okay, so what are you going to find on the *Small Business Computing For Dummies* CD-ROM? Here's a quick look at a few of the programs:

- ✔ QuickBooks, a trial version of the popular small business accounting software
- ✔ DeltaCad, a shareware drafting program you can use to lay out your new office
- ✔ WinZip, the absolutely essential shareware program you need to compress files and to uncompress files you download from the Internet

System Requirements

Make sure your computer meets the minimum system requirements listed here. If your computer doesn't match most of these requirements, you may have problems using the contents of the CD.

✔ A PC with a 486 or faster processor

✔ Microsoft Windows 95 or later

✔ At least 8MB (or 16MB for best performance) of total RAM installed on your computer

✔ At least 105MB of hard drive space available to install all the software from this CD. (You'll need less space if you don't install every program.)

✔ A CD-ROM drive — double-speed (2x) or faster

✔ A sound card

✔ A monitor capable of displaying at least 256 colors or grayscale

✔ A modem with a speed of at least 14,400 bps

If you need more information on the basics, check out *PCs For Dummies,* 5th Edition, by Dan Gookin; *Windows 95 For Dummies* by Andy Rathbone; or *Windows 3.11 For Dummies,* 3rd Edition, by Andy Rathbone (all published by IDG Books Worldwide, Inc.).

Using the CD with Microsoft Windows

To install the items from the CD to your hard drive, follow these steps.

1. **Insert the CD into your computer's CD-ROM drive and close the drive door.**

2. **Click on the Start button, and then click on Run.**

3. **In the dialog box that appears, type** D:\SETUP.EXE.

   Replace *D* with the proper drive letter if your CD-ROM drive uses a different letter. (If you don't know the letter, see how your CD-ROM drive is listed under My Computer in Windows 95.)

4. **Click on OK.**

   A license agreement window appears.

5. **Read through the license agreement, nod your head, and then click on the Accept button if you want to use the CD.**

   (After you click on Accept, you'll never be bothered by the License Agreement window again.) The CD interface appears. The interface is a little program that shows you what is on the CD and coordinates installing the programs and running the demos. The interface basically lets you click on a button or two to make things happen.

6. **The first screen you see is the Welcome screen. Click anywhere on this screen to enter the interface.**

   Now you are getting to the action. This next screen lists categories for the software on the CD.

7. **To view the items within a category, just click on the category's name.**

   A list of programs in the category appears.

8. **For more information about a program, click on the program's name.**

   Be sure to read the information that appears. Sometimes a program may require you to do a few tricks on your computer first, and this screen tells you where to go for that information, if necessary.

9. **If you don't want to install the program, click on the Go Back button to return to the previous screen.**

   You can always return to the previous screen by clicking on the Go Back button. This allows you to browse the different categories and products and decide what you want to install.

10. **To install the program, click on the Install button.**

    The CD interface drops to the background while the CD begins installation of the program you chose.

11. **To install other items, repeat Steps 7–10.**

12. **When you finish installing programs, click on the Quit button to close the interface.**

    You can eject the CD now. Carefully replace it in the plastic jacket of the book for safekeeping.

To run some of the programs, you may need to keep the CD inside your CD-ROM drive. This is a Good Thing. Otherwise, the installed program would have required you to install a very large chunk of the program to your hard drive space, which would have kept you from installing other software.

What You'll Find

This section contains a summary of the software on the *Small Business Computing For Dummies* CD-ROM. If you use Windows, the CD interface helps you install software easily. (If you have no idea what I'm talking about when I say "CD interface," flip back a page or two to find the section, "Using the CD with Microsoft Windows.")

2do V1.35

Category: Productivity

This program is a PIM (Personal Information Manager) that organizes your tasks however you want. The copy on the CD-ROM is the complete version, which you can try for 30 days.

Banner*Show (32-bit)

Category: Web Page Tools

Banner*Show is a Windows application that makes it simple to generate JavaScript-based rotating banners for your Web site. With Banner*Show, you don't need to be a programmer to make your Web site look fancy.

BizPlanBuilder

Category: Office Tools

BizPlanBuilder is a program that helps you create a business plan for your business. The CD-ROM includes both a demo, so you can see how BizPlanBuilder works, and the complete program, which you can buy at a specially discounted price by calling a toll-free number and providing your credit card number to unlock the code. If you want to discover even more about BizPlanBuilder, choose Start⇨Run and type **D:\Office\BIZPLAN\Install** to see a movie about the program. (If your CD-ROM drive is not called D, be sure to substitute the correct letter.)

Campaign V2.5

Category: Web Page Tools

Campaign generates and sends personalized e-mail messages by reading data directly from a database — no need to import or export data. The program is affordable, yet effective for periodic mailings. Target a broad or narrow audience for your messages.

CGI*Star Pro

Category: Web Page Tools

CGI*Star Pro is a Windows scripting tool that can automatically generate Common Gateway Interface (CGI) scripts to e-mail the contents of HTML forms to your mailbox. With CGI*Star Pro, you can get information from people who visit your Web site.

Collage Complete V1.1 demo

Category: Accounting, Graphics, and Word Processing Tools

Collage Complete includes two handy application programs: Collage Capture, for capturing screens, and Collage Image Manager, for modifying, converting, and organizing your images.

Cuneiform OCR

Category: Accounting, Graphics, and Word Processing Tools

Cuneiform OCR is a program that converts documents you've scanned into text. Why retype the information on printed documents when your computer can do the work for you? *Note:* You must have a scanner to use OCR programs.

CyberSpell trialware

Category: Accounting, Graphics, and Word Processing Tools

CyberSpell can quickly check your documents and e-mail messages for spelling errors. A program like this helps make your documents look professional.

DeltaCad V2.4

Category: Office Tools

DeltaCad is a powerful, easy-to-learn CAD (computer-aided design) program designed to meet all your CAD needs. Why go out and spend thousands of dollars on AutoCAD, when DeltaCad will help you create precision drawings quickly and easily?

Directory Toolkit for Windows 95, NT 4.x 2.61

Category: Office Tools

Directory Toolkit allows files in two directories to be compared and synchronized. If you've ever struggled trying to manage your files, you'll find that Directory Toolkit makes the task a lot easier.

Diskeeper Lite

Category: Office Tools

Diskeeper Lite is a disk defragmenter for Windows NT 4.0. If you run Windows NT 4.0 on your systems, you need Diskeeper Lite to restore and maintain Windows NT system performance. This version is a free version you must run manually. You can upgrade to a more powerful version that can automatically maintain your disk performance.

Ecopad32 V3.50

Category: Accounting, Graphics, and Word Processing Tools

Ecopad32 for Windows is a text editor and printer application with the environment in mind. It lets you print multiple pages on one sheet by printing smaller versions of each page.

Exact 97

Category: Accounting, Graphics, and Word Processing Tools

Exact 97 1.0 is an Optical Character Recognition (OCR) application designed for Windows 95 and Windows NT 4.0 or later. With Exact 97, you can convert your printed documents into text files. This program has many advanced features, including the capability to automatically convert faxes you receive in Windows 95 into text, and the capability to retain the formatting when converting printed documents into word-processing documents. *Note:* You must have a scanner to use OCR programs.

Executive Desk V5.0

Category: Productivity Tools

Executive Desk is a complete system of contacts, schedules, to-do lists, memos, follow-ups, reminders, phone calls, and more. If you need help organizing the confusion in your life, you'll want to give Executive Desk a try.

Guestbook*Star

Category: Web Page Tools

Guestbook*Star is an all-in-one guest book creator complete with JavaScript functionality. You can use Guestbook*Star to find out who's been visiting your Web site.

Links

Category: Web Page Tools

For your convenience, I include a links page to all the Web sites that I mention in this book.

LiquidFX 3.7

Category: Web Page Tools

LiquidFX is a powerful Web site authoring package that can help you create a Web site that will get your small business noticed. LiquidFX includes many features you won't find in a simple editor such as FrontPage Express.

Mr. Burns Productivity Monitoring Package

Category: Productivity Tools

Mr. Burns Productivity Monitoring Package maintains a daily log of statistics describing the usage of the PC, including which applications have been run, how often, and for how long. You can use this program to see how your systems are being used even if you can't be in the office yourself.

Net2Phone

Category: Productivity Tools

Net2Phone enables you to make long-distance calls at a discount. When you use Net2Phone, your long-distance calls are routed over the Internet, bypassing the traditional long-distance phone lines.

PageMaster 2.03 for Windows NT

Category: Office Tools

PageMaster allows you to send pages to both numeric and alphanumeric pagers right from your computer. If you use Windows NT and need to stay in touch with your office or with outside salespeople, you'll want to try out PageMaster.

Phone Dialer V1

Category: Office Tools

Phone Dialer is a phone dialer and number database. Phone records are stored for quick access and dialing. It includes a comprehensive rate calculator and call timer. Rates are calculated by hour and minute, and settings are stored separately for each name saved in the database.

Quick View Plus trialware

Category: Office Tools

Quick View Plus is an add-on for Windows that enables you to view many different types of files without having a copy of the application that created the file. Quick View Plus is an enhanced version of the Quick View that comes with Windows.

QuickBooks & QuickBooks Pro Trial Version

Category: Accounting, Graphics, and Word Processing Tools

QuickBooks is a full-featured accounting program for your small business. This trial version can be run 25 times before you must register the program. Registering the program converts your copy into the same complete version you can buy in the store. ***Notice:*** QuickBooks is a registered trademark of Intuit Inc. *Small Business Computing For Dummies* has not been reviewed or approved by Intuit, and Intuit expressly disclaims any responsibility for its content or accuracy.

RoloDial V1

Category: Office Tools

RoloDial is three programs in one. It includes an address/phone book (with envelope printing), a phone dialer (with rate calculator and phone log), and a memo/post-it/sticky pad.

SignUp V2.0

Category: Web Page Tools

If you have a World Wide Web page with an interactive form (such as a guestbook), you probably receive data by e-mail. But storing that data in a database normally means cutting and pasting information from each e-mail message to your database. SignUp collects e-mail generated by a data-gathering Web form and distributes the information directly into your database.

Site*Sleuth

Category: Web Page Tools

Site*Sleuth is a Web site traffic reporter tool that enables you to monitor your small business Web site and learn about how it is being visited.

SmartDraw 3.11

Category: Accounting, Graphics, and Word Processing Tools

SmartDraw is a program that enables you to draw great-looking flowcharts, diagrams, and other business graphics. Its ease of use makes it particularly suitable for users who need to create professional quality drawings quickly and simply.

SomarSoft OfficeCab

Category: Office Tools

SomarSoft OfficeCab is a fast and easy-to-use document management program for Windows NT and Windows 95. If you have lots of document files, try out OfficeCab to help you keep track of the chaos.

Tax Assistant V2 for Windows 95, NT

Category: Accounting, Graphics, and Word Processing Tools

Tax Assistant is a tax record-keeping program that tracks both business and personal incomes and expenses according to 1040 methods. It totals all major tax line items, allows printing, and makes tax record keeping much easier.

The Password Thief for Windows 95

Category: Productivity Tools

The Password Thief for Windows 95 is a small application that runs hidden in the background. The program takes note of all passwords that have been entered, including user login, screen saver, and Internet access passwords.

The Surfing Spy for Windows 95

Category: Productivity Tools

The Surfing Spy is an Internet usage monitoring program for Windows 95. It is a small utility that runs hidden in the background, taking note of all the sites that have been visited using either Internet Explorer or Netscape Navigator. The name of the site, the URL, and the time and date of all visits are recorded. This demonstration version periodically displays a message notifying the user of its presence; the registered version of the program runs completely hidden from the user.

WebForms

Category: Web Page Tools

The WebForms program lets you create your own forms that you can link to your home page, allowing you to conduct surveys or collect orders for your products. The program makes doing business on the Web a snap!

WebMania

Category: Web Page Tools

WebMania is a full-featured HTML editor and forms generator that makes Web authoring easy and requires little or no HTML knowledge. WebMania has 60 programmable toolbar buttons, includes a spell checker, and allows multidocument editing.

WinZip

Category: Office Tools

WinZip is an absolutely essential program that enables you to compress files so that they require far less disk space. It enables you to also send or receive files via modem in less time. WinZip features built-in support for the following popular Internet file formats: TAR, gzip, Unix compress, UUEncode, XXencode, BinHex, and MIME.

WS_FTP LE

Category: Web Page Tools

WS_FTP LE is a popular program for transferring files to and from Web sites. With WS_FTP LE, you upload or download files easily. **_Note:_** Portions of this software are copyrighted 1991-1997 by Ipswitch.

If You Have Problems (Of the CD Kind)

I tried my best to compile programs that work on most computers with the minimum system requirements. Alas, your computer may differ, and some programs may not work properly for some reason.

The two likeliest problems are that you don't have enough memory (RAM) for the programs you want to use, or you have other programs running that are affecting installation or running of a program. If you get error messages such as `Not enough memory` or `Setup cannot continue`, try one or more of these methods and then try using the software again:

- ✔ **Turn off any anti-virus software you have on your computer.** Installers sometimes mimic virus activity and may make your computer incorrectly believe that it is being infected by a virus.

- ✔ **Close all running programs.** The more programs you're running, the less memory is available to other programs. Installers also typically update files and programs. So if you keep other programs running, installation may not work properly.

- ✔ **Have your local computer store add more RAM to your computer.** This is, admittedly, a drastic and somewhat expensive step. However, if you have a PC running Windows 95, adding more memory can really help the speed of your computer and allow more programs to run at the same time.

If you still have trouble with installing the items from the CD, please call the IDG Books Worldwide Customer Service phone number: 800-762-2974 (outside the U.S.: 317-596-5430).

Index

(continued)

(continued)

(continued)

(continued)

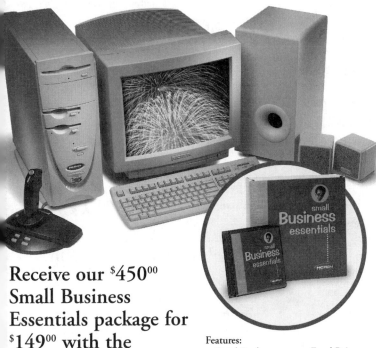

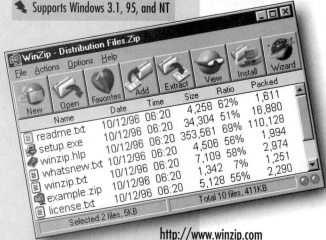

IDG Books Worldwide, Inc., End-User License Agreement

READ THIS. You should carefully read these terms and conditions before opening the software packet(s) included with this book ("Book"). This is a license agreement ("Agreement") between you and IDG Books Worldwide, Inc. ("IDGB"). By opening the accompanying software packet(s), you acknowledge that you have read and accept the following terms and conditions. If you do not agree and do not want to be bound by such terms and conditions, promptly return the Book and the unopened software packet(s) to the place you obtained them for a full refund.

1. **License Grant.** IDGB grants to you (either an individual or entity) a nonexclusive license to use one copy of the enclosed software program(s) (collectively, the "Software") solely for your own personal or business purposes on a single computer (whether a standard computer or a workstation component of a multiuser network). The Software is in use on a computer when it is loaded into temporary memory (RAM) or installed into permanent memory (hard disk, CD-ROM, or other storage device). IDGB reserves all rights not expressly granted herein.

2. **Ownership.** IDGB is the owner of all right, title, and interest, including copyright, in and to the compilation of the Software recorded on the disk(s) or CD-ROM ("Software Media"). Copyright to the individual programs recorded on the Software Media is owned by the author or other authorized copyright owner of each program. Ownership of the Software and all proprietary rights relating thereto remain with IDGB and its licensers.

3. **Restrictions on Use and Transfer.**

   (a) You may only (i) make one copy of the Software for backup or archival purposes, or (ii) transfer the Software to a single hard disk, provided that you keep the original for backup or archival purposes. You may not (i) rent or lease the Software, (ii) copy or reproduce the Software through a LAN or other network system or through any computer subscriber system or bulletin-board system, or (iii) modify, adapt, or create derivative works based on the Software.

   (b) You may not reverse engineer, decompile, or disassemble the Software. You may transfer the Software and user documentation on a permanent basis, provided that the transferee agrees to accept the terms and conditions of this Agreement and you retain no copies. If the Software is an update or has been updated, any transfer must include the most recent update and all prior versions.

4. **Restrictions on Use of Individual Programs.** You must follow the individual requirements and restrictions detailed for each individual program in the "About the CD" appendix of this Book. These limitations are also contained in the individual license agreements recorded on the Software Media. These limitations may include a requirement that after using the program for a specified period of time, the user must pay a registration fee or discontinue use. By opening the Software packet(s), you will be agreeing to abide by the licenses and restrictions for these individual programs that are detailed in the "About the CD" appendix and on the Software Media. None of the material on this Software Media or listed in this Book may ever be redistributed, in original or modified form, for commercial purposes.

5. **Limited Warranty.**

   (a) IDGB warrants that the Software and Software Media are free from defects in materials and workmanship under normal use for a period of sixty (60) days from the date of purchase of this Book. If IDGB receives notification within the warranty period of defects in materials or workmanship, IDGB will replace the defective Software Media.

   (b) **IDGB AND THE AUTHOR OF THE BOOK DISCLAIM ALL OTHER WARRANTIES, EXPRESS OR IMPLIED, INCLUDING WITHOUT LIMITATION IMPLIED WARRANTIES OF MER-CHANTABILITY AND FITNESS FOR A PARTICULAR PURPOSE, WITH RESPECT TO THE SOFTWARE, THE PROGRAMS, THE SOURCE CODE CONTAINED THEREIN, AND/OR THE TECHNIQUES DESCRIBED IN THIS BOOK. IDGB DOES NOT WARRANT THAT THE FUNCTIONS CONTAINED IN THE SOFTWARE WILL MEET YOUR REQUIREMENTS OR THAT THE OPERATION OF THE SOFTWARE WILL BE ERROR FREE.**

   (c) This limited warranty gives you specific legal rights, and you may have other rights that vary from jurisdiction to jurisdiction.

6. **Remedies.**

   (a) IDGB's entire liability and your exclusive remedy for defects in materials and workmanship shall be limited to replacement of the Software Media, which may be returned to IDGB with a copy of your receipt at the following address: Software Media Fulfillment Department, Attn.: *Small Business Computing For Dummies*, IDG Books Worldwide, Inc., 7260 Shadeland Station, Ste. 100, Indianapolis, IN 46256, or call 800-762-2974. Please allow three to four weeks for delivery. This Limited Warranty is void if failure of the Software Media has resulted from accident, abuse, or misapplication. Any replacement Software Media will be warranted for the remainder of the original warranty period or thirty (30) days, whichever is longer.

   (b) In no event shall IDGB or the author be liable for any damages whatsoever (including without limitation damages for loss of business profits, business interruption, loss of business information, or any other pecuniary loss) arising from the use of or inability to use the Book or the Software, even if IDGB has been advised of the possibility of such damages.

   (c) Because some jurisdictions do not allow the exclusion or limitation of liability for conse-quential or incidental damages, the above limitation or exclusion may not apply to you.

7. **U.S. Government Restricted Rights.** Use, duplication, or disclosure of the Software by the U.S. Government is subject to restrictions stated in paragraph (c)(1)(ii) of the Rights in Technical Data and Computer Software clause of DFARS 252.227-7013, and in subparagraphs (a) through (d) of the Commercial Computer–Restricted Rights clause at FAR 52.227-19, and in similar clauses in the NASA FAR supplement, when applicable.

8. **General.** This Agreement constitutes the entire understanding of the parties and revokes and supersedes all prior agreements, oral or written, between them and may not be modified or amended except in a writing signed by both parties hereto that specifically refers to this Agreement. This Agreement shall take precedence over any other documents that may be in conflict herewith. If any one or more provisions contained in this Agreement are held by any court or tribunal to be invalid, illegal, or otherwise unenforceable, each and every other provision shall remain in full force and effect.

Installation Instructions

● ●

*T*he *Small Business Computing For Dummies* CD-ROM contains all sorts of exciting programs. See the "About the CD" appendix for installation instructions and more details.

IDG BOOKS WORLDWIDE
BOOK REGISTRATION

We want to hear from you!

Visit **http://my2cents.dummies.com** to register this book and tell us how you liked it!

- ✔ Get entered in our monthly prize giveaway.
- ✔ Give us feedback about this book — tell us what you like best, what you like least, or maybe what you'd like to ask the author and us to change!
- ✔ Let us know any other *...For Dummies*® topics that interest you.

Your feedback helps us determine what books to publish, tells us what coverage to add as we revise our books, and lets us know whether we're meeting your needs as a *...For Dummies* reader. You're our most valuable resource, and what you have to say is important to us!

Not on the Web yet? It's easy to get started with *Dummies 101*®: *The Internet For Windows*® *95* or *The Internet For Dummies*®, 4th Edition, at local retailers everywhere.

Or let us know what you think by sending us a letter at the following address:

...For Dummies Book Registration
Dummies Press
7260 Shadeland Station, Suite 100
Indianapolis, IN 46256-3945
Fax 317-596-5498

BUSINESS AND GENERAL REFERENCE BOOK SERIES FROM IDG

COMPUTER BOOK SERIES FROM IDG